HYBRID
MODERNITIES

THE MIT PRESS   CAMBRIDGE, MASSACHUSETTS   LONDON, ENGLAND

HYBRID MODERNITIES

ARCHITECTURE AND REPRESENTATION
AT THE 1931 COLONIAL EXPOSITION, PARIS

PATRICIA A. MORTON

This book was set in Centaur by Graphic Composition, Inc., and was printed and bound in the United States of America.

Library of Congress Cataloging-in-Publication Data
Morton, P. A.
    Hybrid modernities : architecture and representation at the 1931 Colonial Exposition, Paris / Patricia A. Morton.
        p. cm.
    Includes bibliographical references and index.
    ISBN 0-262-13362-8 (alk. paper)
        1. Exposition coloniale internationale de Paris (1931)—Buildings. 2. Exhibition buildings—France—Paris—History—20th century. 3. France—Colonies—Exhibitions. I. Title.
    NA6750.P4 E956 2000
    725′.91′094436109043—dc21   99-052584

To my parents, Howard L. Morton and Gloria Isaak Morton

CONTENTS

ACKNOWLEDGMENTS

I would like to thank the institutions, friends, and family members who helped me through the long process of writing this book. Work on this project, in its earliest stages, was supported by a predoctoral fellowship from the Getty Center for the History of Art and the Humanities, 1992–1993. In particular, I thank Fran Terpak of the Getty Center Special Collections for her help finding and obtaining images of the 1931 Colonial Exposition and related subjects. I greatly benefited from my participation as resident fellow in the "French Cultural History and Theory in a Global Frame" research group at the University of California Humanities Research Institute, Irvine, California, in winter 1996. I thank the members of this group for their apt criticisms of my work. I received invaluable assistance from my colleagues and students in the Department of the History of Art at the University of California, Riverside, for which I am grateful. I owe particular thanks to my research assistants, Jenny Pizzolo, Susan Ogle, and Erin Mohr.

My friends, colleagues, and mentors gave me encouragement, advice, and time, without which I could not have finished this book in its present form and for which I give them my deepest thanks: Emily Apter, Zeynep Çelik, Annie Chu, Jean-Louis Cohen, Beatriz Colomina, Alan Colquhoun, Penelope Deutscher, Deborah Fausch, Raymond Gastil, Ann Gilkerson, Robert Gutman, Amelia Jones, Ralph Lerner, Mary McLeod, Christine Magar, Marco de Michelis, Wallis Miller, Alessandra Ponte, Chester Rapkin, Moshe Sluhovsky, Katherine Fisher Taylor, Georges

Teyssot, Stanislaus von Moos, and Gwendolyn Wright. My special thanks go to Anthony Vidler, advisor and friend extraordinaire.

At The MIT Press, I also thank Roger Conover for his confidence in this project and his patience with its author, Sandra Minkkinen, for seeing this book through production, and Jean Wilcox for her design.

Eric, Howard, and Gloria Morton, and the extended Dutton clan deserve more thanks than I can give for all their support. Last, but never least, I thank John A. Dutton for his faith, his aid, and for everything else.

HYBRID
MODERNITIES

INTRODUCTION

From May 6 to November 15, 1931, *L'Exposition coloniale internationale de Paris* welcomed the public to celebrate the accomplishments and the future of colonialism. That same year, the Dakar-Djibouti Mission left Paris for its voyage across Africa, Albert Kahn's *Archives de la Planète* ceased photographing and filming the world, and Aimé Césaire came to Paris as a student. Publicized as *Le Tour du Monde en Un Jour* (The Tour of the World in One Day), the Exposition displayed the people, material culture, industries, manufactured goods, raw materials, and arts of the global colonial empires, with the exception of the British Empire, which had staged its own exhibition a few years earlier.[1] Its French organizers, led by Maréchal Hubert Lyautey, understood this exposition as a didactic demonstration of the colonial world order, based on cooperation among the colonizing powers and the West's responsibility to continue colonization and its good works. The purpose of the Exposition, as stated by Lyautey, was to demonstrate that "colonial action, so long misunderstood, deformed, sometimes shackled, is a constructive and beneficial action."[2] Architectural critic Marcel Zahar declared that Lyautey's noble idea had been to "erect before Paris . . . the model of the colonial world, to mark the memory of explorations and conquests with rare documents and masterpieces, to present exotic treasures, to prove by diagrams and photographs the progression of the beneficial French effort." By these means, the Exposition could publicize the "good colonial news, pose the problems, resolve them, and diffuse the solutions, instruct, build, then inform."[3]

By contrast with these sober, edifying goals, the Colonial Exposition was popularly understood in the tradition of fairs and carnivals, transgressive sites where visitors could jettison their normative social roles and indulge in ordinarily taboo activity.[4] Russian philosopher and literary theorist Mikhail Bakhtin divided fairs into the official and the carnivalesque: the official event is "a consecration of inequality," whereas the carnival enacts social equality and irreverence for authority.[5] The Exposition was not intended to be a popular, carnivalesque entertainment like colonial displays at previous universal expositions or amusement parks. In the eyes of Lyautey and the French colonial elite, it explicitly was not an amusement park, but was a model city representing the actual or projected state of the colonies. Lyautey described it as a "picturesque and striking miniature" of the French empire and the activity of French colonization.[6] As opposed to the carnival and its "oriental despotism" of legerdemain, sensual perception, and optical exhibitionism, the Exposition was intended to be an exhibition of scientific, lisible rationality.[7]

In seeking to avoid the seduction of optical hedonism and the allure of the exotic, Lyautey and his colleagues set themselves a problem: how to represent the colonies and colonization accurately without recourse to the suspect images already established by intercourse between the Occident and the Orient; how to avoid exoticism and inauthenticity and still refer to the plethora of images created by colonialism, through which most Westerners understood the rest of the world. In response to this dilemma, the Exposition's organizers resorted to a mixture of established strategies to achieve visual and experiential verisimilitude, including dioramas, written panels, human displays, and recreated environments of various types and scales. The recreated environments produced, or attempted to produce, the "real" context for the people and things brought from the colonies, aided by pavilions that "authentically" reproduced indigenous architecture. In this respect, the Exposition followed the scientific model established by natural history museums and ethnographic exhibitions, such as those developed during this period by Paul Rivet and Georges-Henri Rivière at the Trocadéro museum, as well as precedents of nineteenth-century world's fairs. It corresponded to the display of real events, people, and places in French, turn-of-the-century popular culture, in which proof of authenticity was a central concern for the exhibiting institutions of the press, morgue, wax museum, diorama, and cinema.[8]

Although Lyautey aspired to create an exposition without vulgar exoticism, he could not totally exclude the picturesque imagery associated with the colonies. As writer Robert de Beauplan explained: "In order to draw visitors and hold them, it was essential to turn to all the seductions of the picturesque and the irresistible magic of art."[9] The Exposition thus generated a contrast between colonies as the Orient—the site of rampant sensuality, irrationality, and decadence—and colonies as the laboratory of Western rationality. In the official press accounts and documents, this dichotomy was obfuscated to the greatest degree possible in favor of a unified picture of colonial order.

> A gramophone sings. An airplane roars. Through a clearing, I glimpse, at the same time, the towers of Angkor, the thatch roofs of Togo, the red kasbahs of West Africa, and the circumflex, surprising, aerial accent of these Sumatra houses. All the curves of the geometry, all the surfaces, all the solids, this ingenious animal. Eupalinos will employ them to ornament these shacks. A gramophone sings; an airplane roars. Very far away the tom-tom of a Negro summons up the most ancient rhythms. I love to find in this enclosure of Vincennes the Melody of the World, and its History.[10]

André Maurois's description illustrates the basic mechanism by which the Exposition demonstrated the colonial order: through the contrast between metropolitan "civilization" and colonial "savagery." The gramophone and airplane are metonymies for France, the pinnacle of European civilization, whereas the tom-tom and native architecture represent the backward natives of the colonies. By making this dichotomy visible and legible, the Exposition was intended to provide a rationale for French colonization. The vast abyss of evolutionary difference between the "advanced" peoples of Europe and the "primitive" peoples of the colonies authorized Europe's subjugation of the "primitives" in the name of progress.

> I always concern myself ... to see that ranks and hierarchies are preserved and respected, that people and things stay in their ancient places, that the natural leaders command, and that others obey them.[11]

> The first thing which the native learns is to stay in his place.[12]

The Exposition was founded on an additional scopic principle: radical segregation of the European and native worlds. The key to maintaining colonial power was absolute visibility of its hierarchies. For the native to know his or her "place," the perceptible world had to be completely legible, separated into what belonged to the colonizers and what to the colonized. "Acknowledgment of authority depends on the immediate—unmediated—visibility of its rule of recognition as the unmistakable referent of historical necessity," according to Homi Bhabha.[13] The two realms were not two halves of a whole, but were unequal divisions of the world's population into "superior" and "inferior" peoples, with material spoils going to the conquerors. In Benedict Anderson's words, the colonial state aspired to create a "human landscape of perfect visibility" by classifying everyone and everything.[14] This system organized difference into visible and legible categories, maintained by force and manifested in skin color, language, the built environment, and culture.

Architecture served as one of the principal means for rendering visible the colonial order. The pavilions, landscaping, and lighting produced "authentic" environments for displaying the natives and artifacts brought from the colonies, thereby physically demonstrating the difference between the colonies and the *Métropole*.[15] Architecture summarized the cultures of colonial peoples in accessible images, metonymic representations of barbarity clothed in the familiar language of exoticism. The colonial segregation principle was embodied by separate architectural languages for the colonies and colonizing nations.[16] On one side of the Exposition's representational divide, pavilions that represented French civilization, such as the Cité des Informations and the Section Métropolitaine, were designed in classicizing variations on the Art Deco style. On the other side, colonial pavilions were constructed in specific "native" styles that represented indigenous cultures. The contrast of the sophisticated, urbane style of the former and the primitive styles of the latter gave evidence of Europe's civilization and the natives' savagery.

This was architecture's mission at the Exposition: to make concrete inherent differences between Europe and the colonies and to represent Europe's *mission civilisatrice*. The *mission civilisatrice* was the responsibility of the civilized white race to bring enlightenment and progress to the benighted savages of the world in the form of colonization. According to sociologist Charles Depincé, a more enlightened race with higher civilization and moral standards had an obligation to impose a rudimentary civilization and elementary moral standards on primitive races.[17] Born out of a complicated mix of republican abolitionist fervor and opportunist rhetoric, the *mission civilisatrice* served as vindication for the subjugation of colonized peoples.

The Exposition's purpose and message contained, however, an internal contradiction that troubled the neat representational division between colonized and colonizer: the colonized peoples had to be proved barbarous to justify their colonization, but the *mission civilisatrice* required that they be raised above this savagery. If the colonized peoples acquired too much civilization and became truly assimilated to France, colonization could no longer be defended, having fulfilled its mission. The ways in which architecture mediated, successfully or not, the contradiction internal to its representational mission is one subject of this book. The organizers of the Colonial Exposition employed other representational means besides architecture—painting, sculpture, cinema, advertising, journalism—to create a seemingly coherent colonial environment. My method is to look for the places where the consistency, continuity, and coherence of the separation between colonizer and colonized dissolved and revealed inherent discrepancies in the *mission civilisatrice.* I treat the Exposition as an instantiation of the intertwining of colonies and *Métropole,* rather than the radically separate worlds constructed by imperial discourse. As one of those events that illuminated the confrontation between the East and the West, the Exposition can be seen within webs of interconnections and affiliations between colonized and colonizer.

Their interconnected experience is not a part of the distant past, but is a critical element of our "pre-history," as Walter Benjamin theorized it in his *Passagen-Arbeit.*[18] Benjamin studied those things that were neglected, forgotten, and repudiated in his time—world's fairs, Parisian arcades, panoramas, barricades—as a method of delving into the subterranean assumptions and values of his present.[19] "For the materialist historian, every epoch with which he occupies himself is only a fore-history of that which really concerns him. . . . The moments in the course of history which matter most to him become moments of the present through their index as 'fore-history,' and change their character according to the catastrophic or triumphant determination of that present."[20] However imperfectly processed and acknowledged our immediate past may be, I believe it informs today's institutions and norms as surely as those of the nineteenth century animated Benjamin's era. The neglected history of colonialism, often omitted from histories of the Euro-American world, is an integral element of modernism.[21] The 1931 Colonial Exposition represents one of those moments in the prehistory of the present (our present, not Benjamin's) through which we can gain insight into modernity.

In this book, I read this moment in history—France in 1931—and the ways in which French colonialism was constructed as an opposition between *Métropole* and colony, between "civilization" and "savagery." My goal is to interpret the Exposition as our prehistory, neither losing the historical specificity of its epoch nor uncritically rehearsing the ethnocentricity of the event. I have addressed this event through a series of relatively simple questions and complex answers:

> What happened when the colonies were brought to Paris in 1931?
> Were unexpected meanings produced out of the juxtaposition of the colonies to Paris?
> How were the colonies architecturally represented?
> Was the Exposition a convincing colonial environment?
> How was meaning generated by an architecture that served the dual function of representing French colonial power while it represented the colonized societies of the empire?

To answer these questions within a critical structure, rather than within the intentions and rhetoric of the Exposition's organizers, I use a series of conceptual terms: *collection, collage, hybrid,* and *physiognomy.* Lack of an architectural language adequate to these buildings and sites forced me to seek parallels with other forms of representation and other discourses. These terms are contingent, contested analytical designations, implicated in colonial practices, and subject to interrogation. They are not equivalent or interchangeable. I use them in particular instances to illuminate the institutional systems and practices of colonialism in 1931 and to submit the Colonial Exposition to a broad, interdisciplinary inquiry. This is a dual enterprise: to provide a historical account of the Exposition through the discourse of the time and to read it through our current state of knowledge. I do not, therefore, leave these terms unquestioned, but submit them to a critique of their adequacy to the events and products of the Exposition.

The first three chapters describe the official, public, and oppositional reception of the Colonial Exposition. This was a type of collecting project, a way of bringing the disappearing, primitive world to the *Métropole* and giving it order. For the colonizing countries, the colonies appeared to form an unordered archive of history from primitive to advanced civilizations. The famous Archives de la Planète, created by industrialist Albert Kahn to document the entire world in photographs and film, represents an extreme example of the European impulse to capture and categorize the globe.[22] Postcolonial theorist Kumkum Sangari elucidated the complex intertwining of modernity, colonialism, and techniques of classification:

> Not only have the critical practices which have developed around modernism been central to the development of an assimilative bourgeois consciousness, a powerful absorptive medium for transforming colliding realities into a cosmopolitan, nomadic, and pervasive "sensibility," but the freewheeling appropriations of modernism also coincide with and are dependent on the rigorous documentation, inventory, and reclassification of "Third World" cultural products by the museum/library archive. Modernism as it exists is inconceivable without the archive, and the archive as it exists is inconceivable without the political and economic relations of colonialism.[23]

Chapter I gives an account of this archive, the Tour of the World in One Day, an itinerary through the Exposition as it might have been experienced by a visitor and as described by contemporary observers.

If the colonies were an uncatalogued archive, the Colonial Exposition was one possible *collection* of their artifacts and peoples. Chapter 2 examines it as a collection that brought people and things from the colonies to Paris and reconstituted them into a new, idealized colonial world. Collecting, far from a neutral, scientific activity, was a device for ordering and dividing the unordered world of the colonies. I use the collection model to describe the coherent, ordered domain that the Exposition's organizers sought to create on the outskirts of Paris. Every collection creates its own time—through a temporal vision that edits history on the basis of predetermined criteria—and its own space—the territory within which the collection is coherent and self-contained. This book, as a collection of quotations and historical material gleaned from the archives, occupies the space and time of the same ethnocentric, hegemonic structures that it attempts to problematize: Western history. Without claiming that these structures can be transcended, my method is to use the collection to elucidate the Exposition's meaning in 1931, both its officially sanctioned meaning and resistant interpretations. My collection includes the anticolonial protests and treatises provoked by the Exposition, mainly by natives living in France. Expatriate native workers and students planned anticolonial, anti-French demonstrations, tracts, and actions around the Exposition. The Exposition seems at first examination to have been seamless and vastly successful on its own terms; my collection indicates some of the fissures and splits in its apparently hermetic discourse. Chapter 3 documents the anticolonial protests that the Exposition generated, including mild criticisms of Léon Blum, harsher diatribes of the Surrealists and their Counter-Colonial Exposition, and tracts and demonstrations organized by expatriate natives living in France.

Chapters 4 through 7 analyze the site planning and architecture of the Exposition. In chapter 4 I explore the degree to which a "collage effect" operated by analyzing the Exposition's planning, disposition of the pavilions on the site, and history of marginality associated with the site. *Collage* is a method for producing a new entity or meaning out of the juxtaposition of otherwise unrelated things (Picasso's collages) or a way of heightening the difference between juxtaposed things by means of incongruity (Surrealist collages). James Clifford has employed the second definition to propose an "ethnographic surrealism," the practice of attacking the familiar and "provoking the irruption of otherness—the unexpected." Ethnography's practice of taking cultures out of their contexts and placing them in new epistemological or phenomenological contexts is always an act of ethnographic surrealism, but an unacknowledged one according to Clifford.[24] Similarly, the Colonial Exposition displaced people and things from the colonies and replaced them in the new context of its own precinct. The question, "What happened when the colonies came to Paris?" can be answered in terms of a possible collage effect that would have heightened the contrast between the Paris and the colonies, producing a sensation of strangeness in visitors to the Exposition. This new mode of vision might have made visitors aware of the strangeness of assembling the disparate colonies into an artificial whole, juxtaposing exotic buildings to Parisian apartment blocks, and constructing a Senegalese hut next to a Cambodian temple.

A reminiscence by ethnographer Michel Leiris provided me with a taxonomy of the Exposition site: the fortifications, the *zone non aedificandi* that ringed the fortifications, and the Bois de Vincennes. In this dreamlike description, Leiris experienced this area as "a sort of bush-country, a no-man's land that extended between where the fortifications lay and the racecourse at Auteuil, and that racecourse itself."[25] He characterized this space as one of taboo—supernatural, sexual, and sacred—and of contrast between the bourgeois city and the savage bush. The fortifications, zone, and Bois carried similar exotic associations for the residents of Paris. It was a space for marginal activities, such as ragpicking and prostitution, and marginal people like gypsies and homeless workers. Eastern Paris was also "Red Paris," home to the poorer classes of Parisians and to insurgent working-class movements. The multiplication of marginal associations on this site—classified according to the taxonomy of zone, park, and city—is the subject of chapter 4. A different kind of collage effect is at work in this writing: the layering of unresolved histories.

In chapter 5 I examine hybridity at the Exposition within the heritage of earlier exposition architecture and standards for authenticity set by

Lyautey and his colleagues. The *hybrid*, an entity created out of crossing two dissimilar entities, entered postcolonial theory as a term descriptive of cultural and racial mixing generated by colonialism. Postcolonial theorists, notably Homi Bhabha, recuperated the hybrid as a powerful subversion of colonialism's binary oppositions between colonizer and colonizd, civilization and savagery, white and colored. The historical moment of the postindependence era generated multiple identities and cultural blends that give new meanings to the old, pejorative terms "hybrid," "syncretic," and "creole." The hybrid is one of colonialism's unintended consequences, however, the product of cross-breeding between the metropolitan and the colonial. The mixture of "superior" populations with "inferior ones," which produced people neither purely French nor indigenous, was the horror of colonialist fantasies. The apprehension it produced in Europeans centered on the danger that a "superior" people might degenerate to a lower level of evolution by mixing with an "inferior" one and that its position on the racial ladder would therefore sink. In this logic, the final consequences of hybridization might be erasure and blurring of boundaries between races and dissolution of codes of difference established by colonialism.

The 1931 Colonial Exposition is one moment in which we can examine specific conditions of hybridity in a colonial context. It is my position that the hybrid is not just the product of postcolonial migrations and diasporas, but is integral to colonial contact and is, in fact, the result of colonialism's institutions and systems. Chapter 5 defines the dual "civilizing mission" assigned to architecture at the Exposition: to represent the barbarity of colonized peoples and to demonstrate the modernization brought to them by France. The relationship among the French human sciences, colonial policy, and architecture of different periods in French colonization is traced in this chapter. The hybrid pavilions of the Exposition, neither French nor native to the colonies, reflect specific shifts in French colonial policy and science in the early twentieth century. In chapter 6 I examine what I call the "architectural physiognomy" of the colonies embodied by the pavilions. Equivalent to the physiognomic science that quantified physical differences between the races, the pavilions represented cultural differences between colonies and colonizing countries. The processes through which the pavilion architects created mixed architectural vocabularies and monumentalized indigenous styles into imposing pavilions, which I compare with the composite photograph, demonstrate the degree to which these buildings reinforced racist stereotypes of the colonized peoples. The pavilions' hybrid inauthenticity, however, undermined the efficacy of the architectural physiognomy as an index of difference. Another contested instance of hybridity, the vexing problem of designing the Musée des Colonies as both a French national and a colonial monument, is the subject of chapter 7.

In this work I looked for instances of hybridity, discontinuity, impurity, and resistance to mark lapses of the colonial logic at the Exposition. The hybrid pavilions embodied the intersection of the colonized's and the colonizer's experience, the "in-between" that Bhabha identified as postcolonial space.[26] The Exposition occupied a middle region of experience where the norms, rules, and systems of French colonialism both emerged and broke down, unsustainable because of their internal contradictions. I sought this territory of ambiguity by looking at the strangeness of the Exposition. By opening up such potentialities, this work gives a preliminary rendering of the "other" side of the Exposition and its consequences for the present.

LE TOUR DU MONDE EN UN JOUR

In a single day, you will have seen all these marvels. The virgin forest will have no secret for you, the mores of the fiercest tribes will have been revealed to you, you will know how to distinguish a pagoda from a mosque, a Chinese from a Japanese, you will know your geography better than your professor, in a word you will have made the tour of the world in a single day, a short distance from the Eiffel Tower.

—Maurice Tranchant[1]

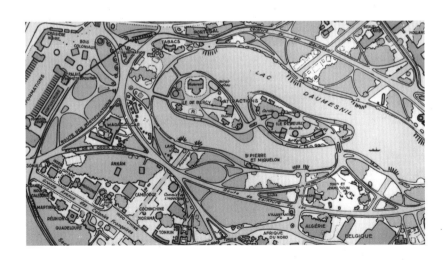

The Tour of the World in One Day took the visitor through an itinerary from the civilized splendors of Paris to the savage beasts of the zoo, with educational lessons in colonial geography and ethnography along the way (fig. I.I). The Tour usually began at the Porte d'Honneur, otherwise known as the Porte Dorée or the Porte de Picpus (fig. I. 2). The Métro station exited at the corner of the Porte d'Honneur and various bus stops were located near the entrances. Visitors in automobiles had to park in one of the garages provided around the Exposition precincts and either walk or take a bus to an entrance, of which there were twenty two.[2] From the grandiose Porte d'Honneur, visitors could enter the metropolitan pavilions grouped around the honorific Porte: Section Métropolitaine, Cité des Informations, Musée des Colonies, and various smaller pavilions (fig. I. 3). They could then make a long journey around the grounds, either by foot or by the railway that circumnavigated the Exposition, and see the assembled French and foreign colonial pavilions, the zoo, and the amusement sections.

In 1929 the Exposition's administration held a competition for the Porte d'Honneur; of the ten projects that were submitted, the jury considered none of them excellent, but it chose the project by the young architect Léon Bazin in collaboration with the sculptor Henri Navarre after suggesting numerous modifications to the original design. The approved scheme consisted of an oval lawn parterre with several fountains and a large central obelisk surrounded by twenty-two illuminated pylons.[3] On either side of the obelisk, roadways gave access to drop-offs for visitors and to Avenue Dausmenil, which was open to traffic during the Exposition. A new subway station for Métro line 8, which was extended for the Exposition, exited onto the Porte d'Honneur. To avoid motorized traffic on Avenue Dausmenil, pedestrians could take the passerelles that spanned the roadway. Ticket booths, information windows, and banks of turnstiles flanked the Porte, which opened to the two major French metropolitan pavilions: the Section Métropolitaine and the Cité des Informations. On either side of the Porte d'Honneur, a series of small pavilions was located around irregular plazas. These included the Biscuit Braun, Publicité and

1.1   Official poster (Archives d'Outre-Mer, Aix-en-Provence)

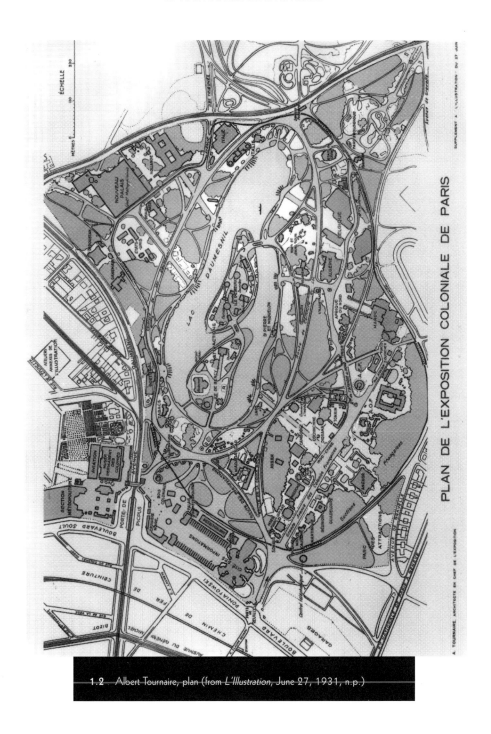

1.2 Albert Tournaire, plan (from *L'Illustration*, June 27, 1931, n.p.)

1.3 Porte d'Honneur, aerial view (from *Sud-Ouest économique* special issue, Aug. 1931, 856)

Aviation pavilions near the Section Métropolitaine, and the Croisière Noire and Bois Coloniaux pavilions in front of the Cité des Informations.[4]

The Section Métropolitaine contained 42,000 square meters of commercial exhibits that displayed goods and materials produced for export to the French colonies (fig. 1.4). Designed in a monumental Art Deco mode by Alfred Audoul, it was characterized as "a cathedral of commerce and of industry; a machine that carries an immense carriage of steel, loaded with manufactured merchandise of the first order, a delivery from the *Métropole* to the colonies."[5] Its facade featured an imposing central tower that served as a landmark throughout the grounds. Its interior consisted of one massive hall, like the Galerie des Machines at the 1889 exposition, within which individual producers erected their pavilions and displays. It was here that modernist critic Marcel Temporal found a single praiseworthy structure. For the most part, the architectural avant-garde denigrated the Expo-

1.4 Alfred Audoul, Section Métropolitaine (from Alfred Audoul, Travaux d'Architecture [Strasboug: Editions d'Architecture . . . , 1932], 6)

1.5 Albert Laprade, Museum of the Colonies, perspective by Léon Bazin (photo: Archives d'Architecture du XXe Siècle, Paris)

sition as retrograde, but Temporal singled out René Herbst's exhibition stands in the Section Métropolitaine as exemplary of the modern style.[6]

Sited next to the metropolitan section, the Musée des Colonies (fig. 1.5) was the only permanent building to remain after the Exposition's close. Its most notable feature is the sandstone bas-relief that stretches across the front facade behind an attenuated colonnade. The bas-relief by Alfred Janniot depicts "France's Contributions to the Colonies" in Beaux-Arts allegorical style. Similarly, the museum's exhibits contained historical and contemporary accounts of France's *mission civilisatrice* and her activities as a colonial power. The three rooms on the interior were lavishly decorated with murals, furnishings, metal work, lacquerwork, and fabrics by foremost designers of the day. This structure was less a colonial pavilion than a national monument to France's colonizing history.

The Cité des Informations, an Art Deco structure by Jean Bourgon and Fernand Chevalier, faced the Section Métropolitaine across the Porte d'Honneur (fig. 1.6). Lyautey conceived of the Cité as the main instru-

1.6 Jean Bourgon and Fernand Camille Chevalier, Cité des Informations (from Joseph Trillat, L'Exposition coloniale de Paris, Paris: Librarie des Arts décoratifs, [1931], n.p.)

1.7 Gabriel Veissière, Madagascar section, aerial view (from Olivier, Rapport général, vol. 5, pt. 2, 500)

ment for educating the public and as a central location for information on the colonizing countries and possibilities for investment, emigration, and importation in their colonies. As a complex consisting of a cinema, documentation center, congress halls, post office, and office of the general commissioner, the Cité promised to "give to the businessman the maximum facilities to put together projects."[7] The central dome terminated a linear garden flanked by a series of colonial information boutiques. Architectural critic Marcel Zahar criticized this central mass as a tired version of Art Deco style, "obese, heavy like a cannon ball . . . contrary to the idea of youth, rapidity, and intense life."[8]

On the next leg of the itinerary, visitors would have traveled into the Bois de Vincennes to the Madagascar section, which was marked by its immense Tour des Bucrânes (a fifty-meter tower decorated with massive cow

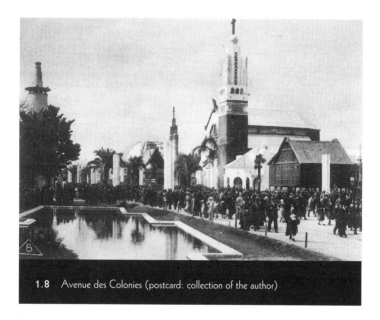

1.8   Avenue des Colonies (postcard: collection of the author)

skulls) and the monumental curved stair of the main pavilion (fig. 1.7). This was the first truly colonial pavilion that visitors encountered when following the official route. Gabriel Veissière invented the architecture out of a mix of the royal mansion in Tananarive and various cult monuments of disparate Malagasy tribes. The section formed a miniature Madagascar village, complete with recreated "fetish" steles, huts inhabited by natives, and a theater where native performers played native music and Europeanized variety acts.

From Madagascar, visitors would have proceeded to the Avenue des Colonies Françaises, location of most French colonial pavilions and one of the few monumental axes in the Exposition plan (fig. 1.8). It was also possible to enter the avenue directly from the Porte de Reuilly, one of the three main Exposition entrances. Critic Guy de Madoc described the avenue as a panoply of exotic pavilions: "The stroller finds himself in the middle of

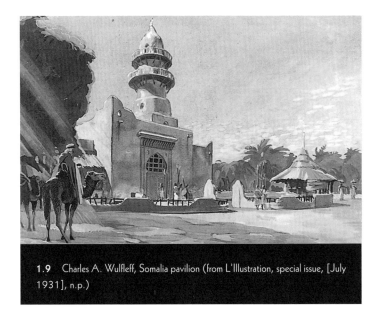

1.9   Charles A. Wulfleff, Somalia pavilion (from L'Illustration, special issue, [July 1931], n.p.)

a spacious avenue which, departing from the Reuilly gate, penetrates to the heart of the wood. At its right are the charming habitations of Martinique, Guadeloupe, and Reunion, which contrast with the rude lodgings of the fishermen of Saint-Pierre and Miquelon, the forest pavilion of Guyana, the evocative Palace of the French Indian Establishments, the shadowed houses of Tahiti, New Caledonia and their dependencies, and the pavilion of the Somali Coast."[9] There was no apparent geographical or political logic to any pavilion's placement on the avenue, with the result that the Tour du Monde could be a surrealist exercise in bizarre juxtapositions: from Somalia to French India, from New Caledonia to Martinique.

The first building on the avenue, Charles Wulfflef's Somalia pavilion, was "a mosque whose round minaret, circled with a double balcony on poles of rustic wood, [is] a little savage and strongly picturesque"[10] (fig. 1.9). The rendering in *L'Illustration* conjured the Orientalist image of an

1.10 Ernest Billecocq, Oceania pavilion (from Olivier, *Rapport général*, vol. 5, pt. 2, 822)

"Arab" on his camel in a lush jungle landscape of palm trees. This perspective, which both monumentalized the native Somali architecture and added native figures to it, is characteristic of the Exposition's scopic strategies. The natives were further evidence of the Exposition's authenticity, proof that it was no mere entertainment or exotic fantasy, but an accurate tableau of colonial life.

The Oceania section, designed by Ernest Billecocq, was a group of straw huts, one for each of the islands (fig. 1.10). The Tahitian pavilion, the main structure in this section, consisted of a "simple hut . . . with its matted walls and its roof covered with . . . boughs of screw pine specially brought from the antipodes."[11] Like most of the "huts," it was several times larger than ones found in Tahiti. The displays within the pavilions contained souvenirs of Orientalists such as Pierre Loti, whose famous novel *Rarahu* recounts the tragic love story of a French man and a Tahitian woman, and Victor Ségalen, author of the *Essai sur l'exotism.*[12] "The saber of Loti, the last palette of Gauguin, the familiar objects of Victor Ségalen" rested among pearl and coral necklaces and native costumes, with equal value as witnesses to French colonization in the South Seas.[13]

Across the avenue from the Oceania pavilions, next to Somalia, the French Indies were represented by a strange structure, an amalgam of Hindu art and architecture as conceived by architects Henri Girvès and René Sors (fig. 1.11). The French Indian possessions consisted only of the cities of Chandernagor, Yanaon, Pondichéry, Karikal, and Mahé, but they were given a prominent place in the Exposition. The pavilion was modeled after a square house with a verandah and an internal courtyard, similar to indigenous habitations on these islands. This was not an exact replica of a particular Indian building, but was an interpretation of diverse architectural traditions, according to Commissioner Ginestou.[14] Its most startling characteristic was the elephant statues at either side of the entrance, figures without any precedent in Indian art.

The pavilions of the Pacific Austral Establishments (New Caledonia, New Hebrides, and Wallis islands) evoked Melanesian residences in the form of primitive huts and grotesque fetish poles (fig. 1.12). Maurice Leenhardt extravagantly descibed their exotic allusions: "The high beehive cabin of the New Caledonian Kanaka presents a rough straw hut, it launches into the sky an arrow of pierced shells, it dresses itself savagely and proudly, its watertight wall stops curious gazes, the grimacing figures on the door frames survey intruders."[15] Gustave Saacké, Pierre Bailley, and Pierre Montenot, French architects for this section, recreated the appearance of Kanak and Maori houses out of roughly carved timbers, crudely thatched roofs, and barbarian ornaments. The troop of Kanak dancers and players, who previously performed at the Jardin d'Acclimation, were one of the section's biggest attractions. For most visitors, the Kanaka projected an image of happy, carefree natives, dancing and drumming to their

1.11 Henri Girvès and René Sors, pavilion of French Indian possessions (from Olivier, *Rapport général*, vol. 5, pt. 2, 620)

1.12 Gustave Saacké, Pierre Bailley, and Pierre Montenot, New Caledonia, New Hebrides, and Wallis Islands pavilions, perspective (from L'Illustration, special issue [July 1931], n.p.)

savage music. During the winter of 1931, however, they lived in the Bois de Boulogne, under contract to a commercial operator, in inadequate housing consisting of a leaking tent, and were badly paid and had no freedom of movement. The Ministry of the Colonies ordered an inquiry into their treatment in 1931 after receiving reports of similarly abusive and exploitative conditions at the Colonial Exposition exhibition.[16]

Several commentators noted the lack of slaves or prison laborers in the Guyanan exhibits, a conspicuous absence given Guyana's history as a penal colony (fig. 1.13). Paul Morand, the popular writer, stated that, "to come to Paris, the Guyanans have made themselves a beauty and hold out their smile of poor riches, butterflies of dark blue enamel, fine hammocks, essences common over there, here rare."[17] As devised by the architect

1.13 Oradour, Guyana pavilion (from Olivier, *Rapport général*, vol. 5, pt. 2, 868)

Oradour, the steeply pitched roof, attached verandahs, and tall entrance colonnade called forth elements of Guyanese architecture and, more generally, tropical habitations.

Across from the Guyana pavilion, buildings for Martinique, Réunion, and Guadeloupe represented France's Caribbean oldest colonial possessions (figs. 1.14, 1.15, and 1.16). These structures deviated from the Exposition's hierarchy of native architecture for colonial pavilions and Art Deco or classical styles for French metropolitan edifices. The French considered the Caribbean colonies assimilated into Greater France and therefore employed "metropolitan" styles for their pavilions: a pineapple-ornamented classicism for Martinique, an austere classical colonnade for Réunion, and a modern, streamlined pavilion for Guadeloupe. Henry-Léon Bloch's plans for the Réunion pavilion adapted the model of

1.14 Charles A. Wulfleff, Martinique pavilion (from Olivier, Rapport général, vol. 5, pt. 2, 906)

colonial residences, such as the Villa du Chaudron, "itself inspired by the eighteenth century and treated in the style of the Petit Trianon."[18]

The architectural and political integration of the Caribbean colonies into La plus grande France had a sexual equivalent at the dance hall, where Caribbean women danced the beguine and the Charleston with Frenchmen. Writer Géo Baysse celebrated these contacts in his book, *En dansant la biguine,* an homage to the women of Guadeloupe and Martinique. Baysse effused about their "natural" suppleness and rhythm and called on them to take their rightful place in French civilization. He composed a conversation between Georges, the French narrator, and Flore, his Guadeloupan interlocutor, in which Georges hypothesized the transformation she might produce in a naive Frenchman. On conversing with her, the Frenchman would be surprised to find that her language and expressions were his and that the color that she brought to their conversation captivated and

1.15 Henry-Léon Bloch, Réunion pavilion (from Olivier, Rapport général, vol. 5, pt. 2, 1006)

haunted him.[19] Baysse speculated that, many years later, the Frenchman would "recall with pleasure the memory of the little flirtation that you had on one of those lovely, unforgettable summer evenings, while dancing the beguine . . ."[20]

Although no criticism was made of the classical Réunion and Martinique pavilions, the modern Guadeloupe pavilion by Ali Tur generated an intensely negative reaction from Commissioners Lyautey and Olivier. In memos to the head of the Guadeloupe delegation, both men complained that the pavilion's lighthouse tower had a disastrous effect on the neighboring Angkor Wat palace and that it spoiled the exotic panorama along the Avenue des Colonies. The tower did not harmonize with nearby structures and should be removed, they insisted.[21] Other critics, however, viewed it as a welcome relief from the unrelieved exoticism of the Exposition's architecture. Pierre Courthion called it "among the most

1.16 Ali Tur, Guadeloupan pavilion (from Trillat)

happy specimens of living architecture ... a construction of ravishing proportions, forming with its annex an ensemble of the most happy effect."[22]

The Catholic and Protestant Missions provided an imposing counterpoint to the Guyana and Indochina pavilions on either side. The visitor first encountered the Protestant Mission by Henri Chauquet, an amalgam of rope moldings, crenellations, and towers bearing a huge cross (fig. I.17). Paul Morand considered Paul Tournon's Catholic Mission more of a success due to its subtle evocation of Asia in white and blue faience tiles and the harmonious relationship between its vaguely Arab tower and principal building[23] (fig. I.18). These pavilions contained exhibitions on Christian missionaries' good works in the colonies and provided spaces for worship. After the Exposition, the Catholic Mission pavilion was moved to a new site in Enghien and reconstructed in reinforced concrete and brick.[24]

The Indochinese pavilions, representing the union of Southeast Asian nations created by the French, formed one of the most significant sections of the Exposition. At the Indochinese section, a restaurant, press club, and commissariat offices provided culinary and propaganda services to the public and the press.[25] The key structure was a partial reconstruction of Angkor Wat on one side of the avenue, the tower of which served as another landmark in the grounds and the focal point for an entire village of Indochinese pavilions (fig. I.19): "At the extremity of a paved water course, the central mass of the temple of Angkor Wat, pride of Khmer architecture, raises its five jagged domes toward the sky. Surrounding this pompous mass, a gracious Annamite pavilion, a Cambodian pagoda, a straggling village of Laotian fishermen, and a great Tonkin village of the Delta, with its Mandarin house and its market, completes the unforgettable vision of Indochina."[26] Each of these pavilions composed a hybrid of indigenous architectural and decorative elements, which often roughly approximated actual Indochinese monuments, as interpreted by French

1.17 Henri Chauquet, Protestant Missions pavilion (from Olivier, Rapport général, vol. 5, pt. 2, 313)

1.18 Paul Tournon, Catholic Missions pavilion (from Trillat)

1.19 Charles and Gabriel Blanche, Angkor pavilion, Indochina section, Colonial Exposition, Paris, 1931, perspective (from L'Architecture 53/4, 131)

architects and colonial administrators. The plaster moldings on the Angkor Wat pavilion, for example, were produced from molds taken at the original temple in Cambodia.

The Cambodia pavilion was designed by Georges Groslier, director of the Cambodian Arts Service and a long-term resident of the colony (fig. 1.20). Students of the School of Cambodian Arts at Pnom-Penh, a colonial artisanal school, executed the carved wood portal at the entrance. The yellow, green, and blue tiles, golden horns, and multiple roofs borrowed aspects of Chinese and Indian architecture. Critic Jean Gallotti adjudged the result too flamboyant and variegated for the Parisian atmosphere, although it was authentic in Groslier's view.[27]

By contrast, the Annam buildings were austere and sober compositions, based on such local monuments such as the Royal Palace in Hue (fig. 1.21). Containing dioramas of life in Annam and the religion of its

1.20   George Groslier, Cambodian pavilion (from *Construction moderne*, Nov. 1, 1931, pl. 20)

inhabitants, the main pavilion was a reduced reproduction of the Quoc-tu-Giam, or College of the Royal Palace, designed by Craste, an architect and chief of Public Works in Annam.[28] The central Laos pavilion was a similarly uncomplicated composition, a replica of one of the oldest pagodas at Luang-Prbang, capital of Laos (fig. 1.22). Behind this pavilion, a collection of elevated huts and a pagoda formed a small village on the edge of Lac Daumesnil.

The colony of Cochichina, part of present-day Vietnam, posed a problem for the French as a "country without a particular architecture," even if it had evolved considerably under French rule.[29] Architect Paul Sabrié, who had lived in Cochichina and served as its chief of Public Works, composed a pavilion in cream-white walls, red-brown roof tiles and green ridge tiles, and small gables adorned with sculpted panels, all

1.21 Craste and Blanche, Annam pavilion (from *Construction moderne*, Nov. 1, 1931, pl. 19)

based on Chinese precedents (fig. 1.23). It contained a large interior hall where exhibitions on "its products, statistics, and the activity of the colonists" were displayed.[30]

Visitors would next reach the Tonkin section, where another southeast Asian village was located. A monumental Chinese gate enclosed the precinct and was guarded at night to "preserve the morals" of the natives housed there, according to Commissioner Guesde, head of the Indochinese section.[31] The Tonkin village consisted of a large courtyard with a water lily basin, small attached houses used as boutiques, and a principal pavilion, the *Dinh*, or communal house, where the cult of ancestors was traditionally practiced (fig. 1.24). The whole ensemble was constructed out of cream-colored stucco and roofed with brown tiles. The *Dinh* provided the backdrop for a native theater troop, brought

1.22 Charles and Gabriel Blanche, Laos pavilion (from Olivier, *Rapport général*, vol. 5, pt. 2, 718)

from Indochina to perform pseudo-authentic dragon dances and other invented entertainment.

> Next to Angkor, here is Djenné, the Songhai capital with red walls, because, from Marrakech to Tananarive, from Conakry to the Cape, all Africa is russet, from its soil to its fish and to the pearls of its seas. . . . On the walls, through the barbarously sculpted bars of the doors, the heads of Ivory Coast cattle seem like the spoils of a continent that lives under the sign of the bull.[32]

The French West African section comprised a set of red stucco structures modeled after the *tata*, or fortified palace, and Muslim mosques of the Sudan (fig. 1.25). The work of Germaine Olivier and Jacques-

1.23 Paul Sabrié, Cochichina pavilion (from Trillat)

Georges Lambert, it included a main pavilion with a tower, a mosque, a *rue Djenné* of shops, a village of huts along the lake, and a restaurant, all bristling with wood stakes, buttresses, and primitivist ornament.[33] French West Africa was another invented political entity that consisted of Dahomey (Benin), Senegal, the Sudan (including Mali), Guinea, Mauritania, Upper Volta, Niger, and the Ivory Coast. As opposed to the Indochinese quadrant, however, this section did not express each colony with its own pavilion. Instead, the various countries were lumped into the main building, with individual exhibits on French colonial activity and indigenous culture for the eight colonies. This structure was patterned after the houses and mosques of the upper Niger region, such as the famous Djenné mosque, which are constructed of stones or bricks and plastered with red mud, or *pisé,* which was approximated in Vincennes by red stucco.[34]

1.24   Paul Sabrié, Le Dinh, Tonkin Village (from *Construction moderne*, Nov. 1, 1931, pl. 71)

The neighboring pavilion for French Equatorial Africa (present-day Gabon, Chad, Congo Republic, and Central African Empire) imitated the conical houses of Oubangui-Chari, according to Orientalist writer Pierre Mille[35] (fig. 1.26). This type of "shell" dwelling is actually found in the Mousgoum villages of northern Cameroon, located between the Logone and Chari Rivers, rather than the Oubangui-Chari region of the Central African Empire. This pavilion was a strange hybrid of the Mousgoum shell and the Mangbettu houses of Zaire (then in the Belgian Congo), which have straw roofs and wattle walls decorated with yellow clay and charcoal.[36] Architect L.A. Fichet created this melange of central African architecture by mixing the Mousgoum roof and the Mangbettu walls. Pierre Courthion, an art critic, decried Fichet's design as an unhappy composition with "a cupola in the form of bananas, too fat for the

1.25 Germaine Olivier and Jacques-Georges Lambert, main pavilion, French west Africa section (from Trillat)

1.26 L. A. Fichet, French Equatorial Africa pavilion (from Sud-Ouest économique special issue, Aug. 1931, 779)

proportions of the rest of the construction." Not only were the pavilion's proportions awkward, it had none of the crude but "authentic" qualities of the adjacent West African section, and seemed too synthetic and polished to contemporary commentators.[37]

At the end of the Avenue des Colonies, the Bronze Tower of the Army terminated the vista with a symbol of the military power with which France maintained her colonial empire (fig. 1.27). This was the central building of the French army's quarter and principal monument to Les Forces d'Outre-Mer. The white and green tower was eighty-two meters high and featured four enormous bronze medallions embossed with allegorical figures from colonial history. A looming reminder of French puissance, the tower and its accompanying neoclassical colonnades and exhibit pavilion interjected a metropolitan presence into the colonial district.

1.27 Lucien Lécuyer and Emile Berthelot, Tower of Bronze, Section des Forces d'Outre-mer (Archives d'Outre-Mer, Aix-en-Provence)

1.28 Robert Fournez and Albert Laprade, main pavilion and souks, Moroccan section (from *Construction moderne*, Nov. 15, 1931, 101)

Beyond the Bronze Tower, the visitor entered the North African section where pavilions of Morocco, Algeria, and Tunisia formed a kind of Exposition Casbah. The Moroccan section was designed by Robert Fournez and Albert Laprade, both of whom had had firsthand experience with Moroccan architecture while serving Lyautey's protectorate government (fig. 1.28). The juxtaposition of the army with Morocco may have referred to Lyautey's long career as a colonial officer as as the first French governor of Morocco. Fournez and Laprade planned this section after the rambling palaces of Fez and Marrakesh, which encompass courtyards, gardens, kiosks, fountains, and walled residences. From the Places des Forces d'Outre-Mer, visitors entered the Moroccan pavilion through a monumental gate (evoking the entry gate of Bab-Mansour at Meknes) and from there traversed a labyrinth of rooms containing a library, maps, dioramas of native life, didactic exhibits, and displays of Moroccan handicrafts. Instead of evoking the poetry of ruins, the exhibits were "organized like a campaign plan, logical, synthetic," according to critic Georges Hardy.[38] The route ended in a long, narrow garden along which stretched souks. These thirty-two boutiques were manned by Moroccans who had competed for the concessions to sell indigenous artisanal goods such as carpets, embroidery, pottery, and copper work. The souks were a reconstitution of the "medieval life" that, according to the *General Report,* persisted in Morocco, but it was not intended to evoke the "oriental bazaar."[39]

By contrast, the Tunisian section was a deliberately picturesque assemblage of ruins and exotic fragments. "The Tunisian section . . . is a bouquet of local color. . . . One finds there Moorish cafes, sellers of fritters and *rahat-lokoum,* a reconstitution of the souks of the Madiva, a fort from the time of Charles-Quint, a minaret, an Arab house, and a marabou under an olive tree"[40] (fig. 1.29). The work of Victor Valensi, a French architect who practiced in Tunisia for most of his career, this section recalled the ancient and mysterious Orient in its souks and the famous courtyard houses of Sidi Bou Said in its main pavilion.[41] Although Jean Gallotti was critical of Valensi's composition as "conceived with fantasy, variety, and willful disorder," most critics praised its charm and genuinely Tunisian ambiance.[42]

Algeria, the third section grouped around the Place de l'Afrique du Nord, conjured up that colony's native past rather than its colonial present (figs. 1.30 and 1.31). France had just celebrated the centenary of its "liberation" of Algeria in 1930. As one of its oldest colonies, Algeria had been considerably altered over the previous hundred years and approached the status of a province in French legal and government systems. A portrait of Algerian architecture circa 1931 would have depicted an outpost of French culture, with Beaux-Arts monuments and Hausmannian domestic buildings.[43] Instead of this progressive vision, however, architect Charles Montaland referred to Moorish and Turkish architecture in his

1.29   Victor Valensi, Tunisian souks (from Trillat)

1.30 Charles Montaland, Algeria pavilion (from Construction moderne, July 5, 1931, 629)

1.31 Charles Montaland, Algeria pavilion, interior (from Construction moderne, July 5, 1931, pl. 159)

design, specifically the sanctuary of Sidi Abderrahmane. His first project was apparently too "French," since it was rejected and a more "colonial" design substituted in its place. The Exposition's Architecte en Chef, Albert Tournaire, called him to give the pavilion more local color in the form of a minaret and a cupola, although with references to the contemporary constructions in modern Algeria.[44] André Maurois raised doubts about the Algerian pavilion's overfamiliar quality:

> What the palace of Algeria
> Thus lacks is savageness,
> murmurs, next to me, a beautiful visitor . . .
> She is not wrong. The Moorish art, the minarets, the domes, and
>   the long mosaics of carpet designs have here taken a certain
>   European style.[45]

Like Algeria herself, both subject colony and semiprovince, this pavilion occupied an in-between cultural space that critics found sterile and dull.

France's only North American colonies, the islands of Saint-Pierre and Miquelon near Newfoundland, were represented by a fisherman's house and a lighthouse designed by Charles Lowson (fig. 1.32). Perched on the edge of Lac Daumesnil, these remnants of France's former empire contained exhibits on fishing, sea animals, and photographs of local life, all more mundane than picturesque.

The Togo and Cameroon section, however, contained an abundance of exotic imagery. Former German colonies, they became French protectorates after World War I when Britain and France divided Germany's possessions between them. After a competition in which ten teams presented projects, the jury chose the entry by architects Louis-Hippolyte Boileau and Léon Carrière, a design modeled after Bamoun and Bakileke dwellings in northern Cameroon[46] (fig. 1.33). This complex consisted of five pavilions: the main one and others devoted to the hunt, social works,

1.32 Charles Lowson, St. Pierre and Miquelon pavilion (from L'Illustration, June 27, 1931, 324)

the commissariat, and a restaurant. Like a village in Cameroon, these buildings formed an irregular enclosure. Each pavilion had a tall thatched roof, a colonnaded verandah, and ornamented walls, and housed dioramas and didactic exhibits on the two protectorates.[47]

The Belgian Congo pavilions were monumental versions of native architecture, enlarged by architect Henry Lacoste to provide a suitably grandiose expression of that colony (figs. 1.34 and 1.35). Charles D'Ydewalle described the section as "a type of Negro palace, of a kind that doubtless no Negro king has inhabited, but it passably recalls, with its domes and its palisades, certain sultanates of central Africa."[48] This

1.33 Louis-Hippolyte Boileau and Léon Carrière, Cameroon and Togo pavilions (from Construction moderne, Oct. 25, 1931, pl. 14)

1.34 Henry Lacoste, Belgian Congo pavilion (from Sud-Ouest économique, special issue, Aug. 1931, 831)

was the only foreign section among the French colonies, perhaps as a recognition of Belgian-French affinity. Ostensibly a "sensitively enlarged" paraphrase of a Congolese chief's *bomé*, the pavilion more closely resembled the Yoruba *afin* or palace of western Nigeria.[49] These complexes contain courtyard and houses linked by thatched roofed corridors that are supported by painted, carved columns similar to those in the Belgian Congo buildings.[50] Its monumental scale and the bellicose spears in the central court combined to give the Belgian section an awe-inspiring atmosphere in keeping with its reputation as the harshest of the colonial powers. Just a few years before the Exposition, André Gide had written his famous condemnation of forced labor and portage in the rubber trade and during the construction of railroads in the Belgian Congo.[51]

1.35 Henry Lacoste, Belgian Congo pavilion, interior (from Sud-Ouest économique, special issue, Aug. 1931, 833)

1.36   Albert Tournaire, Parc zoologique (from Olivier, Rapport général, vol. 5, pt. 1, 491)

After the Belgian section, pavilions for Palestine and the Protectorates of Syria and Lebanon (former German colonies) formed a grouping around a small square. They alluded to the tomb of Rachel and the Azem palace in Damascus, respectively.[52] The entrance to the zoo also faced this square (fig. I.36). The Parc zoologique was the first French "natural" zoo, modeled on Carl Hagenbeck's Tierpark near Hamburg. Instead of cages or grilled enclosures, Hagenbeck constructed open yards surrounded by deep trenches or moats that separated the animals from the visitors. The animals at Vincennes, including lions, giraffes, monkeys, and elephants, seemed to be inhabiting part of their natural habitat, although their actual sleeping quarters were hidden under artificial rocks and hills.[53] The zoo was kept in the Bois de Vincennes after the Exposition, when it was moved to a site north of the Lac Daumesnil, where it exists today.

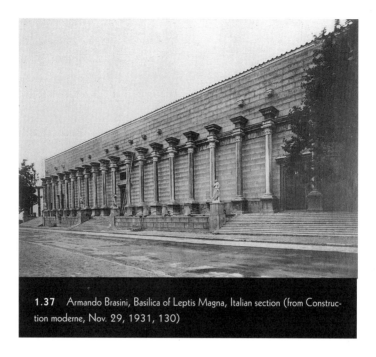

1.37   Armando Brasini, Basilica of Leptis Magna, Italian section (from Construction moderne, Nov. 29, 1931, 130)

At this point in the Tour du Monde, visitors turned north to the foreign sections where most of the other colonial powers built their pavilions. Along this route, Italy was the first among them (figs 1.37 and 1.38). The government of Mussolini and the Fascists chose to allude to their Roman imperial past, rather than the meager possessions of Italy's colonial present, by recreating the Leptis Magna Basilica of Libya and the medieval Seven Towers of Rhodes. As Jean Gallotti noted, among the barbarian huts and savage entertainments, "Rome, straight off, bars exoticism."[54] The Fascist colonial empire was of recent vintage, the product of Mussolini's invasion of Ethiopia and Libya in the 1920s, and the indigenous culture of these countries was not evoked in the pavilions. Armando Brasini, who had designed an Italian pavilion in a similar manner for the 1925 Decorative Arts Exposition, conceived the basilica as a heavy, mas-

1.38 Armando Brasini, Basilica of Leptis Magna, Italian section, interior (from *Construction moderne*, Nov. 29, 1931, cover)

1.39 P. A. J. Moojen and W. J. G. Zweedijk, first Netherlands pavilion (from *Construction moderne*, Dec. 13, 1931, pl. 42)

sive version of Roman classicism. A more modern touch was given by the Restaurant Italia by Fiorini and Prampolini in a belated "Futurist" style.

The Dutch were forced to erect two pavilions in "Hindo-Javanese" style, as the first structure burned on June 28 (figs 1.39 and 1.40). The fire, whose cause was never determined, destroyed not only the pavilion but thousands of irreplaceable art objects and native craftwork; this event prompted the Surrealists to issue their "Premier bilan de l'exposition coloniale" protesting the loss of this priceless art.[55] The Netherlands delegation quickly rebuilt a new pavilion by the same architects, P. A. J. Moojen and W. J. G. Zweedijk, and inaugurated it on August 18. According to art critic Antoine Cabaton, "The first pavilion, fruit of a slow and wise elaboration of the soil of Java itself, aspired to synthesize, in its architecture, the diverse aspects of Indian civilization in the Melanesian archipel-

1.40　Moojen and Zweedijk, second Netherlands pavilion, interior (from Nederland te Parijs, [Parijs: Oost en West, 1931], 110)

1.41 Roger-Henri Expert, Pavilion des Industries de Luxe (from Les Charpentiers de Paris à L'Exposition coloniale internationale de Vincennes [Paris: Les Charpentiers de Paris, 1931], 52)

ago. Its successor today, less ambitious in appearance and in dimensions, is inspired by ... the temples and palaces of the small island of Bali, the only point in the Dutch Indies where the beliefs and mores of Mother India are still perpetuated in our time, with fervor intact."[56] In addition to the main pavilion, The Netherlands section encompassed several Batik houses closely modeled after originals on Sumatra, a rice grange, a Sumatran house, two restaurants (Dutch and Indonesian), commissariat offices, and housing for the natives on display at this section.[57] The interior of the main pavilion contained exhibitions on Indonesian art (some objects were borrowed from the Trocadéro museum for the second pavilion), ethnography, and economic and political works in the Dutch colonies.

Two additional metropolitan pavilions were located next to The Netherlands section, the Beaux-Arts and Industries de Luxe buildings (fig. 1.41).

1.42 Charles K. Bryant, reconstruction of Mt. Vernon, and Jacques Greber, landscape, United States section (from Trillat)

Charles Halley's Beaux-Arts pavilion evoked "tropical countries," with its colonnade and formed a "suggestive ensemble" fit for tropical climates.[58] It contained works by members of the Société coloniale des artistes français and the Société des orientalistes français, the most important of such artistic groups in France, as well as unsolicited works. All works submitted were judged by a jury made up of prominent "colonial" artists and architects, including Paul Chabas, Frantz Jourdain, Paul Landowski, and Joseph Marrast.[59] The pavilion devoted to luxury goods, an Art Deco building designed by Roger-Henri Expert, created a more impressive impression by means of its prodigious cornice, tower, and entrance porch. This vast warehouse space sheltered exhibits on French luxury products, such as silk lingerie and perfume.

The United States constructed one of the strangest colonial sections: a reconstruction of Mount Vernon, a memorial of America's own colonial past (fig. 1.42). As Jean Gallotti declared: "The most modern country offers us the quite unexpected spectacle of an archeological re-constitution. The inventors of the skyscraper, the habitués of the eleva-tors of Manhattan, exhibit a white and red chalet with green shutters where Chateaubriand liked to write to the Natchez. All the regret of an absent past appears in the melancholy of these small window panes shel-tering antique furniture conscientiously fabricated after authentic mod-els."[60] On the Fourth of July, bewigged "natives" in eighteenth-century garb marched through the Mount Vernon gardens playing fife and drum and enacting a "genuine" scene from early American history. As a coun-terpoint to this Colonial American display, the Philippines, Hawaii, and Alaska had their exhibits of "brown girls, clothed in soft silks," "dancers of fire," and "bows and arrows in whale bone." Exhibits on "Indians," the Panama canal, Samoa, Puerto Rico, Guam, and the Virgin Islands ac-companied those on Lafayette, Washington, and Franklin.[61]

The decision to participate in the Exposition did not come easily to Herbert Hoover's administration, due to its reluctance to collaborate in a "colonial" event. In Puerto Rico, for example, the press agitated violently against participation as a United States colony.[62] Only after Lyautey pro-posed adding the words "pays d'outre-mer" (overseas countries) to the Ex-position's title, as used in American publicity, and to emphasize international cooperation over colonial expansion in its programs did the United States agree to come to Vincennes.[63] The Mount Vernon reconstruction was ap-parently intended to deflect criticism at home by stressing historical colo-nialism, not the country's status as a colonizing power. Even the outbuildings at Mount Vernon, which traditionally included slave quarters, were sanitized to eliminate references to the African diaspora to the New World.

Two of the less impressive pavilions, those for Hindustan and Den-mark, faced the United States section at the northern limit of the Exposi-tion grounds. The Hindustan pavilion was a late addition and consisted of a main building, which Raymond Cogniat described as a "reproduction of the mausoleum of Itimad ud Daula, constructed at Agra from 1623 to

1.43 Jules Heyman and S. Barkal, Hindustan pavilion (from L'Illustration, special issue [July 1931], n.p.)

1628 by the Empress Nur Jahan in the memory of her father," a restaurant modeled after the Kahs Mahal in Agra, and a theater[64] (fig. 1.43). The Denmark colonial empire constisted of Greenland, which was represented by an austere, modern building without exotic reference (fig. 1.44).

The last colonial section on the itinerary was Portugal, whose empire had considerably shrunk since the fifteenth- and sixteenth-century era of expeditions and conquests. This section recalled that period with three Gothic palaces and a medieval gate (fig. 1.45). Pierre Courthion disdained this style of Camo'ns and Vasco de Gama as "without character, marked by the pretentious inscription: *hic est* Portugal."[65] Despite their bland and antiquated style, these pavilions concluded the official Tour du Monde en Un Jour with an appropriately serious atmosphere.

From there, visitors might visit less exalted enterprises, such as the Parc des Attractions where carnival rides twirled and spun. Or the two

1.44   Helge Bosjsen-Moeller, Denmark pavilion (from L'Illustration, special issue [July 1931], n.p.)

Islands of Delight, Bercy and Reuilly, in Lac Daumesnil might have provided further distractions in the Thousand and One Nights quarter, with restaurants, dance halls, and other exotic entertainment. Myriad private concessions covered the Exposition's grounds, including such novelties as an aluminum pavilion, a demountable metal colonial house by Jean Prouvé, and a brasserie "Les Totems" by regionalist architect Charles Letrosne. A ride on the lake, in a native boat propelled by an African or Indochinese boatman, or a camel ride through the West African section could have equally attracted the visitor: "Lake Daumesnil—these soft waters of Asia and Africa combined—offers its embarcaderos to those who want to fish cod off Saint-Pierre and Miquelon or, in pirogues dug from the trunks of trees, to lose themselves in the foliage of the Amazon or, in rapid cruisers, to glide under the mangroves of the Antilles, under the gray cedars of the Maroni."[66] These aspects of the Colonial Exposition

1.45   Raul Lino, Portuguese section (from Olivier, *Rapport général*, 7, 356)

were more conventional and less interesting to one observer, Guy de Madoc, who complained, "I haven't seen any sensational novelties. One has already seen this almost everywhere. It is old stuff."[67]

Water and light displays by Granet and Expert provided elaborate light fixtures, colored lighting, and spectacular luminous fountains throughout the Exposition (figs. 1.46 and 1.47). The largest piece, the Théâtre d'Eau, erupted in ornate streams of water and colored light each evening. Other fountains, such as the African-themed Fontaine des Totems and the Art Deco Grand Signal, performed continuously, day and night. These displays had an old-fashioned tinge for critic Georges Charensol, who found them too reminiscent of previous expositions such as 1900 and 1925. He particularly regretted the harsh effects that the colored lights produced on the pavilions, since they caused the volumes and colors of the architecture to become invisible. He did wonder, however, if

1.46 André Granet and Roger-Henri Expert, Théâtre d'Eau (from L'Illustration, special issue [July 1931], n.p.)

1.47 André Granet and Roger-Henri Expert, Totem Fountain (from L'Illustration, special issue [July 1931], n.p.)

"the monotony of the lighting does not contribute to give the Exposition a unity which, during the day, it does not possess."[68]

Despite the Exposition's apparent heterogeneity, the French and international press depicted it as an unqualified success. One humorous account proclaimed: "We are here at 'Lyauteyville,' the magistral, picturesque, and coherent ensemble realized by our great African [Lyautey], magnificent resume of all that which old Europe has made in the Universe, rallying point for all people who love the French genius and its manifestations in the World."[69] For most visitors, the *Tour du Monde en Un Jour* seemed to be a harmonious collection of architecture, people, and artifacts from the colonies, imbued with the high degree of authenticity and sobriety appropriate to *la mission civilisatrice.*

COLLECTING THE COLONIES

THE INITIAL IDEA [FOR THE EXPOSITION] GOES BACK TO 1910. IN 1910, WE NATURALLY TURNED TOWARD EXOTICISM, THEN IN FULL NOVELTY. WE DREAMED OF RENEWING, WITH MORE BRILLIANCE AND MORE SINCERITY, THE PICTURESQUE AMBIANCE—ALTHOUGH QUITE FALSE AND SOMETIMES EXCESSIVE—OF THE SUCCESSFUL COLONIAL SECTIONS AT THE 1878, 1889, AND 1900 EXPOSITIONS. WHY NOT TRANSPORT ONCE AGAIN, IN A LARGER SETTING IN THE MIDDLE OF PARIS, THIS VISION OF THE ORIENT AND THE FAR EAST?. . .

THE ORIGINAL CONCEPTION OF AN EXPOSITION OF EXOTICISM WAS LATER ENRICHED, AMPLIFIED, AND LED TOWARD MORE ELEVATED GOALS. IT WAS NO LONGER A MATTER OF ARTIFICIALLY RECONSTITUTING AN EXOTIC AMBIANCE, WITH ARCHITECTURAL PASTICHES AND PARADES OF ACTORS, BUT OF PLACING BEFORE THE EYES OF ITS VISITORS AN IMPRESSIVE SUMMARY OF THE RESULTS OF COLONIZATION, ITS PRESENT REALITIES, ITS FUTURE.

—MARCEL OLIVIER[1]

2.1 Senegalese village, Universal Exposition, Brussels, 1897 (Resource Collections of the Getty Research Institute, Los Angeles)

The original impetus for a Parisian Colonial Exposition grew out of the popularity of the colonial section at the 1900 Paris Universal Exposition. Colonial sections had been included in all French universal exhibitions, beginning in 1878, and in most world's fairs held elsewhere (fig. 2.1). By 1900 they were extremely popular entertainments.[2] The Exposition in Paris also grew out of a long tradition of such events, including specialized fairs at Rouen in 1896, Marseilles in 1906 and 1922, Bordeaux in 1907, and Roubaix in 1911. The anthropological and architectural authenticity of these exhibits was questionable, however, and produced an amusement park atmosphere in the colonial sections (fig. 2. 2). Organizers of the 1931 Exposition were concerned with avoiding the vulgar aspects of previous exhibits, particularly their carnival ambiance, although this was the source of much of their popularity.

2.2   Andalusian dancers, Universal Exposition, Paris, 1900 (Resource Collections of the Getty Research Institute, Los Angeles)

In 1913 the municipal council of Paris and the National Assembly fixed the date for the Exposition for 1916. After this decision, a conflict arose between Paris and Marseilles: Marseilles claimed the right to host the Exposition as the colonial capital of France and as the site of the 1906 Colonial Exposition. A compromise was reached such that Marseilles would hold a national colonial exhibition in 1916 and Paris an international one in 1920. Neither event occurred on those dates because of World War I, but the National Assembly took up the issue immediately after the war (December 27, 1918).[3]

In 1919 the government voted to establish the organization necessary for an "Exposition coloniale interalliée" to be held in 1921 with participation from countries that had fought by the side of France. Since Marseilles claimed the right to the first postwar exposition, the government negotiated another agreement that scheduled that event for 1921 and the one in Paris for 1924. The national exposition took place in Marseilles in 1922, but, according to Marcel Olivier, it required seven years for the international exposition's conception to be fixed and eleven years more to realize it.[4]

Olivier's statement referred to the slowness of the Exposition's administration. The original Commissaire Général was Gabriel Angoulvant, former governor general of French Equatorial Africa, who reported to an interministerial commission of officials from a vast array of government agencies.[5] From 1920 to 1927 Angoulvant and his colleagues examined the major issues involved in staging the Exposition without resolving any of them. Angoulvant failed to find sufficient support in the government to put together a financial package, to obtain the rights to a site, or to promulgate a definitive set of regulations and goals. Budgets for 1920–1927 show that he and his staff drew salaries, but produced very little except studies of other expositions and of different sites under consideration.[6] Angoulvant became such a political liability due to his caution and lethargy that he was forced to resign so that planning could proceed.[7]

The year 1927 was the key year in the Exposition's planning. A financial arrangement was finally concluded, Maréchal Lyautey was appointed Commissaire Général, a new administration was formed, and the design for the permanent museum was approved. Maréchal Lyautey, "pacifier" of Morocco, Madagascar, and Indochina, was appointed Commissaire to eliminate the negative ambiance that Angoulvant had created. To Angoulvant's credit, important events occurred under his aegis, but the political situation was such that he could not continue in his position.[8] Lyautey asked for adjournment of the Exposition to 1931 because the Metro line was unlikely to be complete by 1929, and to avoid competition with Algeria's centennial celebrations and the colonial exposition in Anvers, Belgium, both held in 1930.[9]

In contrast with the carnival-like colonial displays at previous expositions, Lyautey intended this one to be pedagogical and authentic to

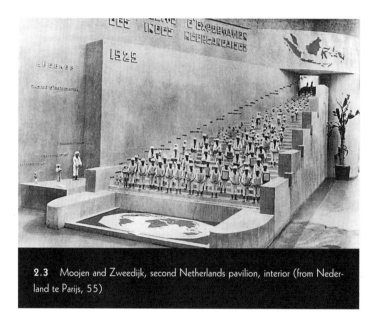

2.3 Moojen and Zweedijk, second Netherlands pavilion, interior (from Nederland te Parijs, 55)

convey the potential future as well as the current reality of colonization. He and the other directors linked French colonialism with the long history of conquest beginning with the Crusades, but they distinguished their own enlightened colonialism from the brutality of former colonization. According to their vision, a stable, pacific world had resulted from the spread of French civilization on a global scale. Lyautey and his colleagues sought to make the Exposition reflect the beneficial progress of *la mission civilisatrice* by means of scientific, authentic exhibitions, rather than vulgar, exotic entertainments (fig. 2.3).

As envisaged by Lyautey, the Exposition had two educational goals: to stimulate interest and investment in the colonies by French business, and to overcome the apathy and even hostility that the French felt toward their colonial empire. The organizers' aim of making their empire better known to the French people was accompanied by the desire to stimulate their involvement with colonial development and government. A matter of national pride was at stake, as well, and the Exposition strove to counter the image of the *casanier* (stay-at-home), lethargic French who cared nothing for their colonial holdings. Senator Léon Bérard optimistically declared the Exposition a success in that it denied the French reputation for apathy toward their empire and taught French and foreigners alike that "our nation's character does not exclude the taste for risk and adventure."[10] The Exposition had some impact on recruitment for colonial administration and on the popular imagination of the colonies, although it was limited. For a large number of French colonial officers trained in the 1930s, it influenced their choice of a career. Erik Orsenna's Prix Goncourt-winning novel, *L'Exposition coloniale*, describes how, within some French circles, it was the focus of a certain devotion to the empire.[11]

The economic realities of the Depression made the colonies more important to France than they had been before the Wall Street crash in 1929. Although the colonies were never vital to France as markets, despite the wishful thinking of many colonialists, they were essential as sources of raw materials and cheap labor. During World War I, the colonial possessions sent over half a million men to fight for France, plus thousands of workers in domestic French factories.[12] The war showed how useful the colonies could be to the *Métropole* and aroused more discussion of the ways in which they could be developed to France's benefit. When the Depression arrived in 1930, the colonies provided much-needed outlets for French goods and supplies of cheap materials, which made them a more central part of the economy. For example, the percentage of primary agricultural materials they supplied to France rose from 37.5% in 1929 to 71.2% in 1938.[13] According to General Olivier, "the more economic difficulties accumulated, the more it became obvious that, for a country like ours, colonizing is not a luxury, as we have too often repeated, but a necessity."[14] Lyautey went so far as to state that, for France the "future is overseas."[15]

Economic difficulties faced by the colonial powers were mirrored by new political problems, both in Europe and in the colonies. In response to threats of Bolshevism and anticolonial agitation, the Exposition was planned as a demonstration of solidarity among colonizing nations and a means for establishing their "communal defense" and "common plan."[16] In 1931, resistance to colonial control was increasing throughout the colonies and criticism at home was on the rise, although the latter was largely limited to the Communist party, Surrealists, and a few intellectuals such as André Gide, Albert Londres, Andrée Viollis, and André Malraux.[17] The 1924–1925 Rif War in Morocco mobilized resistance to imperialist repression among pacifists, anticolonialists, and expatriate Moroccan students and workers.[18] After the insurrection at Yen Bay in 1930, a *Comité de défense des Indochinois* was formed including Francis Jourdain, Malraux, Paul Rivet, Viollis, and Léon Werth.

In the face of this criticism, the organizers of the Exposition felt the need to justify colonialism in terms of benefits it brought to colonized peoples and the unfinished business of the *mission civilisatrice*, as exemplified by Olivier's declaration that: "We have seen [at Vincennes] that the sum of the benefits that [colonization] has distributed over the earth prevail over the sum of the evils that it has caused; we have seen, finally, that its task, if it has been fruitful, has not yet been achieved. In Africa, in Asia, there still remain uncultivated expanses and populations in lethargy. Had it only these reasons, Europe would be right to dismiss those who push it to abandon its role as guardian."[19] In addition to economic justification for colonialism, a moral imperative was at the heart of the propaganda for the Exposition. French colonization and its justificatory apparatus were based on the implicit assumption that native peoples were "retarded" or halted in the evolutionary process and unable to advance their condition toward a higher level of civilization. Although Europe had a "civilizing mission" to perform, the degree to which these backward peoples could be raised to the heights achieved by Europeans was a contested subject. Prominent colonialist Edmond du Vivier de Streel, speaking before the Musée Social in 1932, summarized France's *mission civilisatrice* in terms of a social contract between peoples. Colonization, he maintained, was more than the conquest of primitive peoples by a more evolved people. It was the occupation of their lands with the aim of realizing "material and moral progress for the double profit of the colonizers and the colonized."[20] Lyautey too believed that it brought a moral obligation on the part of colonizers toward the colonized, as well as material benefits to both. He asserted, "our arrival in the middle of retarded populations, the ones in a savage or anarchic state, the others left out of general evolution, only justifies itself if we bring to them domestic peace, social and moral progress, economic evolution."[21]

This conflation of material and moral progress within the colonial mission produced a representational mode at the Exposition that was both educational and entertaining. In addition to the "invitation to travel" contained in the Exposition's publicity, its chroniclers detected a reverse movement from the colonies to the *Métropole*, in which, "after so many centrifugal adventures, expeditions, oceanic voyages, changes of pasture, the antipodes now pay us a visit."[22] This inversion of the usual direction of travel and commerce was an important aspect of the experience of the Exposition for Europeans unused to confronting the exotic directly. Now they could see Pierre Loti's heroes and heroines, drink strange concoctions, listen to bizarre music, smell and taste unknown food, and generally immerse themselves in the exotic worlds celebrated in literature, film, art, and song (fig. 2.4).

The entertaining spectacle was intended to seduce visitors who could then be educated with didactic exhibits on French colonization's accomplishments. In contrast with the pedagogic aims of its organizers, who hoped to create greater knowledge and appreciation of the colonial empire among the French public, however, contemporary descriptions privileged the hedonistic aspects of the Exposition. Colonial expositions and colonial sections at the universal expositions had long been prime vehicles

2.4   View of the crowd outside the French West Africa section (from Sud-Ouest économique 2, no. 213, 691)

for promoting tourism and consumption of exotic products by means of a fictive colonial universe. In keeping with the fashion for imagined travel to a distant but seductive exotic realm, the 1931 Exposition was often described as if it were a substitute for an actual journey to the colonies, as if it were a distant point on the globe. Many commentators felt distant from Paris when they were in the Exposition grounds; for some of them, it was exactly like being in the colonies, whereas others recognized its hybrid character between the metropolitan and the colonial. As one author observed, "[the Colonial Exposition] is not a Colony, much less a Foreign Land, it is a strange and enchanting country."[23] Descriptions repeatedly depicted it as a hermetic entity, separate from Paris. It was likened to a city, to the whole world encapsulated in the Bois de Vincennes, and to an idealized town where a future modern world had been projected, inhabited by "whites of an olive tint," "blacks with skin of shining ebony," and "lemon Orientals." The shared element in this swarming scene was the tricolor flag, symbol of the French colonial empire's unity.[24]

THE COLONIAL EXPOSITION AS COLLECTION

In a festival atmosphere in the Bois de Vincennes, the Exposition displayed representative objects and people collected from the colonies and reconstituted them into a new colonial realm (fig. 2.5). The organizers intended it to compose a coherent, ordered domain in which every thing and every person has its proper place, a phantasmagoric microcosm of the French colonial empire. It was a *collection* of fragments, taken from their contexts and reassembled into a new whole: an ideal colonial world based on classifications of visible difference. The fragments were people and things from the colonies; the colonial world was the vision of colonization's success as seen by Marshal Lyautey and his colleagues.[25]

Thus, the Exposition served as a catalog of the colonial universe, a record of those unrecorded archives, the colonies. As a Tour of the World

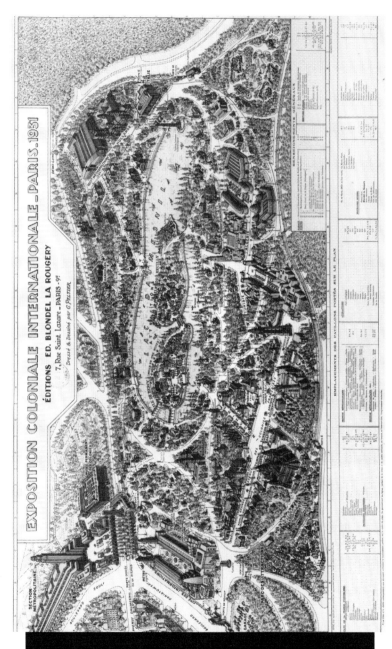

2.5 Aerial perspective (photo: Bibliothèque Nationale, Paris)

2.6 "Amusing visit to the Exposition on the back of a camel" (from Sud-Ouest économique 2, no. 213, 720)

in One Day, it was the inventory of the cultures and peoples of the world without the inconvenience and danger of global travel or "the Tropics without mosquitoes, poison snakes, or fevers," according to Paul Morand[26] (fig. 2. 6). Separated from Paris and its subversive influences and politics, the Exposition was a hermetic world constructed within its own synchronous time. Contemporary realities in the colonies, such as anticolonial riots in Indochina or production of tourist art in Senegal, were ignored in favor of a "timeless," deracinated picture of indigenous cultures and peoples carefully isolated within its precincts. The specific historical reality was eliminated. The Exposition collected and classified examples of all peoples and cultures within a schema that would keep them in their "proper" place, just as French colonial policy and practice controlled and categorized native peoples in the colonies.

Based on the classification of visible difference, the Exposition collected fictive and authentic fragments of colonial and metropolitan life and categorized them according to colonialism's hierarchies. The collection categorizes its holdings, locates them in their assigned spatial and systemic places, locates like with like, and orders the categories into relative hierarchies. The Exposition performed a similar operation on the buildings, people, and artifacts that were displayed within the hierarchies established by the *mission civilisatrice*, segregating the metropolitan from the colonial. The "author" of this collection was Lyautey, military hero and theoretician of colonization. He saw the Exposition as "the Great Book of the Colonies" in which the visitor might read the history of the *Métropole* and its exterior possessions inscribed on walls and in articulate images.[27] Within its precincts a complex regulatory system classified all themes and objects sent from the colonies, as well as metropolitan exhibits, into appropriate categories (*groupes* and *classes*) for display. For example, group I, colonial policy, encompassed class I colonial policy, class Ib principles and methods of colonization, and class Ic, results and future of colonization[28] (fig. 2.7).

Anthropology and ethnography were sources of useful information about the colonized peoples that was displayed in didactic exhibitions at the Musée des Colonies. The exhibitions were organized in the Section de Synthèse, a disparate collection of statistics, artifacts, dioramas, and artwork with little intellectual coherence. One of the principal features of this section was a study of "colonial humanity," consiting of eight statues by sculptor Fourney that depicted the "great native races that people our colonies."[29] These statues were executed from data from the Musée d'ethnographie at the Trocadéro and the Musée d'Histoire Naturelle. Next to these figures, a gallery was consecrated to displays of "colonial anthropology" organized by Dr. Georges Papillault, professor at the Ecole d'anthropologie, as a demonstration of the facts that anthropology could furnish on the "aptitudes and the value of the colonized races" and on

2.7 Exhibits, Section Métropolitaine (from Olivier, Rapport général, vol. 6, pt. 1, 172)

their relations with the *Métropole*. Vitrines contained skulls, skeletons, and photographs of racial types, accompanied by explanatory notices written by Papillault that detailed the "evolution and functional value of the human type."[30] In addition to anthropological displays, the Section du Synthèse contained exhibitions on colonial archaeology, native arts, history of French colonial conquests, modernization projects, colonial products, the Army and Navy, tourism, the merchant marine, colonial influence on French culture, transportation, missions, and colonial aquatic life.

The Colonial Exposition followed those nineteenth-century institutions that categorized and organized the world by visual criteria, such as museums, archives, libraries, the census, and world's fairs. These institutions were mechanisms for controlling the proliferation of knowledge and images by means of quantification and classification. They operated within the processes of classifying the world, which Michel Foucault described as "the ever more complete preservation of what was written, the establishment of archives, then of filing systems for them, the reorganization of libraries, the drawing up of catalogues, indexes, and inventories."[31] Like these institutions, the Exposition collected and placed persons and things in their "proper" places according to classifications of "primitive" and "civilized."

The process of collecting the colonial empires is analogous to the creation of any collection. As Susan Stewart demonstrated, the collecting enterprise is characterized by selection of representative items taken out of their contexts of origin and assembled into a constructed whole. Each component is "representative" within a new spatial context—the collection itself—that "supersedes the individual narratives that 'lie behind it.'" The new whole, the collection, is a hermetic world isolated from real time and space. Stewart defines the collection's relation to history as a freezing of time: "The collection does not displace attention to the past; rather, the past is at the service of the collection ... the past lends authenticity to the collection ... The collection replaces history with *classification*, with order beyond the realm of temporality. In the collection, time is not something to be restored to an origin; rather, all time is made simultaneous or synchronous within the collection's world."[32] It must also consist of "a set of natural or artificial objects kept temporarily or permanently out of the economic circuit, afforded special protection ... and put on display," according to Krzysztof Pomian.[33]

One of the great collecting enterprises of the twentieth century, the Dakar-Djibouti Mission began its journey across Africa just as the Exposition opened its gates. From May 1931 to February 1933, ethnographer Marcel Griaule and his team of expert and amateur ethnographers traveled through Senegal, the Sudan, the Ivory Coast, Upper Volta, Nigeria, Dahomey, Chad, Cameroon, Oubanghi-Chari, the Middle Congo, the Belgian Congo, Anglo-Egyptian Sudan, Abyssinia (Ethiopia), and the

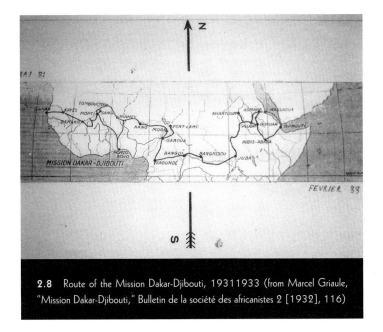

2.8 Route of the Mission Dakar-Djibouti, 1931 1933 (from Marcel Griaule, "Mission Dakar-Djibouti," Bulletin de la société des africanistes 2 [1932], 116)

French coast of Somalia[34] (fig. 2.8). The Institut de l'Ethnologie and the Musée d'Histoire Naturelle sponsored the mission along with various ministries, governmental agencies, societies, and institutes.[35] The mission used new technology, including collapsible metal boats, trucks, electric generators, film, and photographic and phonographic equipment, to perform extensive and intensive field research. One of its goals was to establish "fruitful relations between our colonies and the Museum."[36]

The objects collected and the rituals recorded by the mission were housed in the Musée d'Ethnographie du Trocadéro, later renamed the Musée de l'Homme. The mission's transcontinental voyage was primarily an object-gathering excursion that augmented the Trocadéro's rather outdated collections. The amount of material, the "booty" as Paul Rivet and Georges-Henri Rivière called it, with which the mission returned was enormous: 3,600 objects, 6,000 photographs, thousands of ethno-graphic and linguistic observations, paintings from Ethiopia, 300 amulets and manuscripts, notations on 30 languages and dialects, sound record-ings, films, and botanical specimens collected for the Natural History Museum.[37] "Each object is accompanied by a descriptive label in double, established on the model of the label in use at the Musée d'Ethnographie du Trocadéro; besides indigenous terms and information (provenance, us-age, fabrication . . .) belonging to the object considered, each label carries references to the observation cards, to the photographic collections, and, when there is occasion, to the cinematic views and sound recordings taken."[38]

The eminent ethnographer Marcel Mauss wrote a set of guidelines on collecting ethnographic objects for the mission, *Instructions sommaires pour les collecteurs d'objets ethnographiques.*[39] Missionaries, colonial administrators, and merchants along the mission's route received copies of the *Instructions* as part of a general effort to collect more artifacts for the Musée d'Ethnographie by enlisting colonial functionaries and travelers in gathering objects.[40] Mauss defined ethnography as "the sciences that study the races, civiliza-tions, and languages of the world [and] material civilization."[41] In addition to gathering objects for study, he wrote, ethnography's inquiry extended to the role that objects occupy in the life of the civilization in question. He applied ethnographic study equally to prehistoric and modern humans, which made it, therefore, of direct use to colonization:

> Ethnography. . . brings an indispensable contribution to the methods
> of colonization, in revealing the usages, beliefs, laws, and technology
> of indigenous populations to the legislator, functionary, and colonist,
> rendering possible a more fruitful and more humane collaboration
> with [the indigenous populations], and thus leading to a more ra-
> tional exploitation of natural riches.[42]

The connection between colonialism and ethnography was well established in France by 1931. The Institut d'Ethnologie de l'Université de Paris, where Mauss lectured, was founded in 1925 as an organization for research and for training specialist ethnographers and future colonial functionaries and funded with subsidies from the colonial administrations. The Dakar-Djibouti Mission collected materials with which ethnographers could construct knowledge useful to colonial officials.[43]

For Mauss, the centrality of collecting to ethnographic inquiry was established because of "the need that has always pushed men to imprint material with the trace of their activity." The ethnographic study of a civilization was possible through analysis of the objects it produces. These artifacts were better evidence than written archives because they were "authentic, autonomous objects that cannot have been fabricated for the needs of the case. . . . A collection of ethnographic objects is neither a collection of curiosities, nor a collection of works of art. The object is nothing but a *witness*, which must be envisaged in function of the information that it carries about a given civilization, and not according to its aesthetic value."[44] The "total social facts" of a culture, together with its objects, were the subject of field work and ethnography, which meant that many disparate documentary methods had to be employed in studying a culture.[45] To this end, the Dakar-Djibouti Mission exploited a panoply of technologies and procedures for collecting information and things from the colonized peoples under observation and to record their contexts and provenance.

The Colonial Exposition, by contrast, made fictions from fragments of "authentic" culture and constructed them in a new context. The use of fragments to create a new whole, a collection, is predicated on the ability to efface discrepancies among the fragments. Spatial juxtaposition of fragments also requires certain operations on the pieces for the new whole to be consistent and convincing. Fragments must be detached from their context of origin and placed in a new context: in this case, the Exposition.

These fragments could be detached only imperfectly from their political and cultural contexts in the colonies because the *Métropole* (France) itself was "contaminated" by native people, art, and images. This contamination took various forms, including Orientalist attraction for the exotic, documented in Edward Said's massive study of Orientalism, and the avant-garde's valorization of "non-rational," non-Western art and thought.[46] For several decades before the Exposition French artists and intellectuals had been fascinated by the primitive in such varied forms as American jazz, exemplified by Josephine Baker and the *Revue Nègre,* and Oceanic sculpture. During the 1920s a broader fashion for the primitive and exotic was sustained by a flood of literature, film, art, and images in the press that popularized settings, characters, and cultures from the colonies. For example, the 1921 Prix Goncourt was won by René Maran's "véritable roman nègre," *Batouala,* a novel set in Africa and told from the point of view of a native.[47] Claude MacKay's *Banjo* and Pierre Mille's *Chez les Fils de l'Ombre et du Soleil* represent the two extremes of "exotic" and "colonial" literature between the wars.[48] Films such as *L'Atlantide, Yasmina,* and *Le Bled* depicted the colonies and indigenous life according to racist standards of the day, but with increasing accuracy of detail and setting.[49] "Colonial" schools of French literature and the fine arts were officially recognized, and corresponding associations of writers and artists were established to support their work.[50] Cross-country expeditions sponsored by Citroën and Peugeot brought back images of peoples and landscapes of Africa and Asia that further intensified fascination with the colonies.

The Colonial Exposition could have exhibited this "primitivist" art except that its organizers were determined to keep it representationally separate from Parisian fashion. Cross-breeding between colonizer and colonized, so prevalent in both Paris and the colonies, had to be edited out to preserve the bipolar equation that justified colonialism. The heterotopias of both the *Métropole* and the colonies—mixtures of native and metropolitan culture and blood—had to be deleted to the greatest extent possible or the collection would not read in the desired manner. The pavilions, therefore, maintained a strict architectural hierarchy: a variant of Art Deco for the metropolitan pavilions, such as the Section Métropolitaine (fig. 2.9), and "native" styles for the pavilions of the colonies, such as the *Village Lacustre* in the West Africa section (fig. 2.10). The exteriors of these pavilions were monumental versions of "native" architectural types. The only exceptions among the official pavilions were free inventions for those colonies that had no "real" architecture of their own (such as Madagascar), the old colonies (Martinique, Guadeloupe, Réunion), which France considered assimilated to the *Métropole,* and the Musée des Colonies (Museum of the Colonies).

The Exposition classified and organized colonial objects and peoples it displayed according to principles of hierarchy and evolution, with Europe at the pinnacle and "less evolved" civilizations ranked below it. The architecture of the pavilions was the medium for bearing the "good news" of colonization and, at the same time, was the physical manifestation of this invented colonial "reality." Krzysztof Pomian theorizes the collection as a go-between between the visible world of objects and the invisible world of meaning.[51] The pavilions represented the invisible order of French colonialism made visible and concrete by the architectural expression of the colonies. Furthermore, architecture played a central role in the description and classification of cultures of the colonized races into hierarchies based on stages of evolution:

> The Colonial City . . . permits us to compare the infantile, puerile, familiar gaiety of the African populations to the cold, a little ironic, melancholy of the Oriental. She allows us to better judge the Universe.
>
> The Colonial City of Vincennes is, in pulp board, the city of tomorrow as we would like it—with necessary adaptations: Lively, active, architectural and verdant at the same time, of a large mentality where all civilizations, all tastes, all decent customs can mix and fraternize without harming themselves.[52]

2.9   Alfred Audoul, Section Métropolitaine (from Audoul, 5)

2.10 Germaine Olivier and Jacques-Georges Lambert, Village lacustre, French West Africa section (from Olivier, Rapport général, vol. 5, pt. 2, 300)

The Exposition fixed the colonies so that they could be understood as if they had remained unaltered by the changes created by colonization and were frozen at a low level of evolution. Natives brought to Paris to inhabit the pavilions wore indigenous costumes, not the European dress that was common in colonial cities. They demonstrated archaic crafts, rather than modern production techniques already in practice at home (fig. 2.11). The Exposition constructed an imaginary colonial world out of what the *colons* thought they had discovered: eternal, if backward, civilizations.

This ideal picture existed only at the Exposition, since it projected a utopia that could never be realized in the territories. Unlike the real colonies, the Exposition was populated by docile, productive natives who lived in sanitized versions of indigenous buildings and who practiced their "primitive" occupations for the delectation of the visitors. The life

2.11 A weaver from Madagascar (from Trillat)

and milieu demonstrated the beneficial results of colonization; disadvantages and atrocities were edited out, not collected.

This was, in fact, a time of escalating tensions between indigenous groups and French officials in many colonies. The *Dahir berbère* of 1930, which removed Berbers from the Islamic justice system in Morocco, was a source of considerable agitation among Muslim groups. A circle of young, French-educated Moroccans, the *Jeunes Marocains*, published a collective work, *Tempête sur le Maroc*, under the pseudonym Mouslim Barbari to protest against the *Dahir berbère*. Ferhat Abbas published *Le jeune Algérien*, which detailed the systematic abasement suffered by the Algerian people.[53] Celebrations of the centennial of the French conquest humiliated Algerians, who saw it as a repetition of their defeat. A prediction ran through the country: "The French celebrate the first centenary of French Algeria. They will not celebrate the second."[54] The *Association des Ulémas musulmans d'Algérie* (Association of Muslim Doctors of the Law of Algeria) was formed in 1931 to oppose assimilation and erosion of the power of Islamic law over Algerian life. In Yen Bay, Indochina, the February 1930 revolt of the Annamite sharpshooters, who shot their French officers, developed into riots, strikes, and marches against hunger throughout the region. In 1930, Nguyên Ai Quôc, who became Hô Chi Minh, founded the Indochinese Communist Party in Hong Kong. The vast insurrection of the Bayas in French Equatorial Africa, Cameroon, Chad, and the Congo was brutally suppressed from its inception in 1927 through 1930.[55] These tumultuous events were absent from the Exposition's collection of the French empire.

The fossilization of indigenous civilizations into "unchanging" and "timeless" cultures and societies belongs to the process of inventing traditions under colonization. As Terence Ranger indicated, invented traditions in Africa served to transform "flexible custom into hard prescription" so that behavior could be controlled by the colonial authorities.[56] Education, government, military service, and neotraditional rites were the principal tools with which the new colonial order was installed. The ideological impetus to justify Europe's domination on the basis of supposedly inherent, fixed qualities in civilizations (in other words, the need to fix the relationship between Europe and the rest of the world) inspired this search for unchanging customs. By maintaining that African societies were unchangeable, for example, Europeans could claim that colonialism was warranted for an indefinite time. Europeans' respect for rituals and customs that provided points of stability in the increasingly fragmented industrialized world was transferred to the colonies where authorities instituted order through indigenous "traditions."

Invention of traditions for colonized peoples has a parallel in the collection of objects from their cultures. Nicholas Thomas noted that artifacts from exotic cultures tend to be objectified as "expressions of a savage condition, a barbaric stage" in Western collections.[57] The collection equally affirms the primacy of Western culture by gathering exotic objects that act as "witnesses" to an earlier stage of human culture, "a common past confirming Europe's triumphant present," according to James Clifford. Western collecting follows the "salvage paradigm" in which artifacts and customs that oppose modernity, not the hybrid or historical, are "rescued" from decay or loss.[58] This model of collecting ignores the complex historical realities generated by colonization in favor of simpler systems of authenticity. In the world's fair and in the museum, according to Carol Breckenridge, the emotive, nonverbal forms of experiencing objects in the cabinet of curiosities were replaced by more disciplinary languages concerned with authenticity, connoisseurship, provenance, and patronage.[59] These forms of knowledge were equally forms of control, methods with which a usable past could be constructed out of the colonies' disordered history and present.

The 1931 Colonial Exposition was a vast catalogue of French Orientalism, exoticism, and primitivism given historical perspective and contemporary verisimilitude by the pavilions, human exhibits, and objects displayed. The messy reality of the colonies was ordered into a cohesive, pacific world. A tropical ambiance without mosquitoes, poison snakes, or alligators allowed Parisians the illusion that the colonies were benign, Edenic places. The advantage of this sanitized view was that it offered rich, exciting pictures of the colonies without any of their dirt or inconvenience. It also edited out unpleasant realities of violent conquest, forced labor and environmental spoliation. The unrelievedly positive accounts of the Exposition, the bulk of press coverage, further revised the history of French colonization and its results.

These accounts were not spontaneous expressions of support for colonialism. Subsidies given to both individual writers and newspapers and magazines explain in part the uniformly positive commentaries. Press associations, colonial journals, and numerous general interest periodicals received large sums of money for articles and special editions on the Exposition, often written from press releases and prepared copy.[60] Popular and specialized newspapers and magazines carried special editions on the Exposition with extensive written and graphic coverage. Mainstream architectural and urban journals, pamphlets, and guides produced for the Exposition, official publications, articles in political organs, and press releases all told the same laudatory story.

CHALLENGING THE EXPOSITION: THE ANTICOLONIAL OPPOSITION

No one in good faith can deny that the imperialist record, in black Africa notably, translates into spoliation, venality, plundering, brigandage, and their consequences: oppression and crime.

—Saumane[1]

Not every commentator received the Colonial Exposition with positive observations and uniform praise for its ambitions and spectacle. A few dissenting voices could be heard amidst the clamor of approbation. There were very few opposing voices, however, in part because of generous subsidies from the Exposition to the press in return for favorable articles. The Exposition's organizers displayed no doubts about the form or message of the fair and the reasons for its success. An internal document generated by Governor Olivier's office, for example, is critical only of the poor organization and inefficient bureaucracy of the Exposition, not its ideological principles.[2] Negative criticism came primarily from the Left, from Socialists and Communists in particular. A folder in the Exposition archives lists anticolonial articles in such publications as *Internationale comuniste, Pravda, Internationale syndicale rouge, Bochévik, Orient et les colonies, Communist Review,* and *Correspondence internationale.*[3]

Léon Blum criticized the Exposition for its excessively frivolous and smug atmosphere. In an article in *Le Populaire,* he noted that at the moment of the Exposition's inauguration, Annamite natives were being gunned down at May Day ceremonies. Although the history of republican colonization might contain moments of individual courage and sacrifice, Blum called on the French people to reflect what this work accomplished in cost of blood, to reflect on what it engendered in misery and revolt, that it was founded by force and maintained by force. Colonization rested on the principle of the fundamental inequality of races, a conception that the republican ideal badly accommodated and that socialism rejected, according to Blum:

> The Colonial Exposition is doubtless a beautiful spectacle, fertile in instruction and insights of all sorts. We do not object to the people of Paris, of France, of the Universe taking pleasure and profit from it. Except that we must not forget what reality hides behind this decor of art and of joy. We must not forget that everywhere conquered or subject peoples begin to reclaim their liberty. We have imposed on them our "superior" civilization; they recall against us its first

principle: their right to dispose of themselves, of the fruit of their labor, of the riches of their soil. At the Exposition, we reconstitute the marvelous stairway of Angkor and make the sacred dancers twirl, but in Indochina we shoot, or deport, or imprison. That is why we do not take part in it with enthusiasm. We would like less festivity and talk, more human intelligence and justice.[4]

This article echoed the Socialists' position on French colonialism: that it contained no inherent evils, but that it must be directed in "humanitarian" practices rather than violent suppression of colonized peoples.[5] The *Ligue des droits de l'homme* went so far as to vote a resolution favorable to "civilizing colonization" at its national congress in May 1931.[6]

The Communists were more resolutely opposed to colonial expansion and rule, beginning with Lenin's call for support of national liberation movements among colonized peoples, adopted at the Second Comintern Congress of 1920.[7] In 1928 the Sixth Comintern Congress discontinued the policy of collaboration with bourgeois groups and set a new policy of direct Communist leadership of revolutionary struggles in the colonies.[8] A *Comité d'études coloniales* was created at the 1921 Congress in Marseilles, made up of French Communists living in the colonies, and the 1922 Congress saw the organization of the *Union intercoloniale*, a group of indigenous militants living in France.[9] These groups, with various other French and indigenous Communist organizations, formed the core of the country's anticolonial resistance. *L'Humanité*, the Communist organ, published several articles on the Colonial Exposition, although most of them were short and primarily described atrocities in the colonies and developed attacks on the principle of colonization itself.[10]

THE SURREALISTS' COUNTER-EXPOSITION

Sunshine sunshine beyond the seas you angelize
the excremental beard of the governors

Sunshine of coral and of ebony

Sunshine of numbered slaves

Sunshine of nudity sunshine of opium sunshine of flagellation

Sunshine of fireworks in honor of the storming of the Bastille

above Cayenne one July 14

It is raining it is pouring on the Colonial Exposition

—Louis Aragon[11]

The Surrealists, adherents to the Communist cause, joined forces with the Communist *Ligue anti-impérialiste* to mount a counter-exposition, *La vérité aux colonies*, at the former Soviet pavilion from the 1925 Decorative Arts Exposition, which had been transformed into an exhibition hall. They also promulgated two manifestos against the Colonial Exposition: *Ne visitez pas l'Exposition Coloniale* and *Premier Bilan de L'Exposition Coloniale*. In the former, the signatories attacked the armed robbery at the heart of French colonization, the violence with which the colonial order was maintained against protesting indigenous populations, and the millions of "new slaves" forced to labor for the colonizers.[12] They named the organizers of the Exposition as those responsible for massacres in Indochina and denounced the moral justification given for colonization, reminding their readers that it was "based on a play of words insufficient to make [us] forget that there is not a week when we do not kill in the colonies."[13]

The Surrealists declared that to promulgate the "swindle" of *La Grande France*, the organizers built the pavilions of the Exposition of Vincennes: "It is to give the citizens of the *Métropole* the consciousness of proprietors, which they will need to listen without a flinch to the echo of the distant fusillades. It is to annex to the fine land of France, already stimulated before the war by a song about a bamboo cabin, a vista of minarets and pagodas."[14] They lambasted the promises of adventure and advancement held out by colonial recruitment posters, with "an easy life,

Negresses with large boobs, the non-commissioned officer very elegant in his linen suit being promenaded in a rickshaw." They also assailed the distinctions, made by the Socialist Party and the *Ligue des droits de l'homme*, between good and bad methods of colonizing as a stance complicit with colonialists in Vincennes. Their final statement was a call for rejection of the rhetoric and deeds celebrated at the Colonial Exposition: "To the discourse and the capital executions, respond by demanding the immediate evacuation of the colonies and the indictment of the generals and functionaries responsible for the massacres of Annam, Lebanon, Morocco, and Central Africa."[15]

Although this summons to anticolonial action was heeded by few French people at the time, the Surrealists' critique had resonance among indigenous workers and students living in France who formed anticolonial groups. The decolonizing movements of the 1950s and 1960s were largely underground and unknown in 1931, but the Exposition marks one of the moments when anticolonial struggles formed definite, threatening activity for the French colonial establishment. According to André Thirion, the Surrealists distributed about 5,000 copies of this tract in working-class districts, outside factories, and around the Exposition.[16]

The Surrealists wrote *Premier Bilan de l'Exposition Coloniale* after The Netherlands pavilion burned on the night of June 27, destroying with it thousands of irreplaceable indigenous objects from the Dutch Southeast Asian colonies.[17] They recognized the violence with which the Dutch acquired those objects and centered their concern on the objects' value as cultural products of colonized peoples:

> The pavilion that journalists are not ashamed to call the "Holland" pavilion indisputably contained the most precious evidence of the intellectual life of Malaysia and of Melanesia. It involved, as we know, the rarest and most ancient artistic specimens known in these regions, objects snatched by violence from those who conceived them and of

which a European government, as paradoxical as this appears, had no concern about using as advertising for its methods of colonization.[18]

Although this statement treats the native object as a metonym for the people who produced it, the Surrealists also valued these objects for their political potential. Marx and Engels, they pointed out, used Morgan's work on the Iroquois and Hawaiians in their research on the origins of the family.

Rather than placing objects in a hierarchy that elevated the white man to the top of civilization's evolution, the Surrealists inverted that order and ridiculed the vernacular objects of Western cults: "We add that if the fetishes of Insulinde have for us an indisputable scientific value and have, as a result, lost all sacred character, on the other hand the fetishes of Catholic inspiration (tableaux of Valdes Leal, sculptures of Berruguete, poor-boxes from the Bouasse-Lebel house) could never be considered from either the scientific point of view or the artistic point of view, as long as Catholicism has laws, tribunals, prisons, schools and money, and even that the diverse representations of Christ would without exception make a modest figure among tikis and totems."[19] In conclusion, Breton and his cosigners indicated a final irony: The Netherlands pavilion burned down "accidentally" along with thousands of irreplaceable indigenous objects, although this destruction was entirely consistent with the barbarity of colonialism, while another pavilion was sold for just such a purpose: "the Exposition files its first balance sheet. This balance sheet indicates a deficit that will not be wiped out with the price of the temple of Angkor, sold to a cinematographic firm—as it turns out!—to be burned."[20] For the Surrealists, the contradictions of French colonialism were obvious in this "coincidence": it showed the low value that the colonialists gave to indigenous cultures, despite the sanctimonious regrets of Reynaud, Lyautey, and others over the loss of The Netherlands pavilion. For the colonialists, they lost a symbol of Dutch colonial power, not the cultural heritage of Indonesian peoples.

On the basis of these tracts and the acuity of their criticisms, Alfred Kurella, a delegate to the Communist International, suggested to André Thirion that the Surrealists organize a counter-colonial exposition. Thirion reported that Kurella told him: "The Surrealists are practically the only ones who have demonstrated an intelligent hostility against [the Colonial Exposition] and shown their disgust through specific action."[21] Kurella proposed a counter-fair under the aegis of the *Ligue contre l'impérialisme,* an international group founded in 1927 "to coordinate the movements of national emancipation with the workers movements of all colonial and imperialist countries."[22] He offered the Surrealists money and use of the Soviet pavilion from the 1925 Decorative Arts Exposition, then located on Avenue Mathurin-Moreau and used for an occasional conference by the CGTU *(Confédération générale du travail unitaire).*[23] Apparently, the *Ligue* had tried to organize a counter-exposition in April, but failed to find a site. A document of April 16, 1931, probably from the *Service de Côntrole et d'Assistance en France des Indigènes des Colonies* (CAI), outlined the "Communist campaign against the Colonial Exposition," including efforts by the *Ligue contre l'impérialisme et pour l'indépendance des peuples* to organize it. It listed militants Herclet, Ali, Kouyaté (Secretary General of the *Ligue de défense de la race nègre*), and André Girard as its organizers and reported that although they hoped to install the counter-exposition in Montparnasse or the Latin Quarter, the hostility of patriotic students and other difficulties dissuaded them.[24]

The Counter-Colonial Exposition opened on September 20 in Melnikov's Constructivist pavilion.[25] Thirion delegated the organization of two of its three sections to his colleagues. Louis Aragon was in charge of cultural exhibits, Georges Sadoul was responsible for proselytizing, and Thirion himself took the "ideological" part, Lenin on imperialism.[26] The ground floor housed the ideological section, with "graphics, statistics, engravings, drawings, photographs, etc. relative to the conquests, exploitation, and 'development' of the colonies by imperialism," according to

Marcel Cachin's review in *L'Humanité*.[27] Thirion hung a banner at the entrance with Lenin's slogan; "Imperialism is the last stage of capitalism," along with a letter from Henri Barbusse and a citation from Romain Rolland.[28] This section recounted the "savageries and merciless cruelties" of colonial war, forced labor, exploitation of the native, and use of military and mercenaries. It also recalled that "imperialist civilization has given the native alcohol, opium, venereal diseases, massacres, and, finally, in the last two years the most dreadful crisis causing misery and famine in all the colonies."[29] A room on the second floor followed this exposé of imperialist horrors. Here, the visitor could see photographs and statistics on life in the USSR, with facts on the realization of the Five-Year Plan, organized by the *Cercle récréatif de travailleurs du 19e*.[30]

According to Louis Aragon, the main room on the second floor contained, "an exhibit of African, Oceanic, and American sculptures, of an extent never seen in Paris, which I was able to compose thanks to the participation of the principal collectors of art from the colonized countries, including several Surrealists (André Breton, Paul Eluard, Tristan Tzara, Georges Sadoul, and myself). We obtained pieces belonging to the big dealers of Paris specializing in this domain"[31] (fig. 3.1). Aragon and Elsa Triolet brought records of Polynesian and Asian music, along with some popular songs and a rumba, to play in the exhibit.[32] Yves Tanguy designed the room, which featured Marx's axiom: "A people that oppresses another cannot be free." Paul Eluard and Aragon furnished it with the sculptures, explanatory labels, and, for contrast, "a few of the most foolish devotional ornaments from Rue Saint-Sulpice," labeled '*Fétiches européens*'" (European fetishes)[33] (fig. 3.2).

La Vérité sur les Colonies attracted only 4,226 visitors and very few collective visits by leftist organizations, with the exception of several unions and the *Union des femmes contre la guerre*.[34] Although it made relatively little impact on the Parisian public at the time, even among left-wing circles, the Counter-Colonial Exposition was an important critique of

3.1 Counter-Colonial Exposition, 1931, displays (from Le Surréalisme au Service de la Révolution [Paris: Michel Place, 1976], [40])

3.2 Counter-Colonial Exposition, 1931, displays (from Le Surréalisme au Service de la Révolution [Paris: Michel Place, 1976], [40])

colonialist attitudes toward native culture and of the opposition of "civ-ilized" to "primitive" civilizations. In *Premier Bilan*, the Surrealists satirized the missionaries who mutilated fetishes even while training natives to re-produce the features of their Christ "according to the lowest European art."[35] They acknowledged the absurdity of using one set of standards for "primitive" art and another for "Western" art. Their own fascination with non-Western culture was tied to their desire to overturn European con-ventions by means of contact with denigrated and suppressed things.

This quest for alternatives to Western civilization permeated avant-garde French culture between the wars and translated into an obsession with non-Western art forms on the one hand and with the subconscious on the other.[36] In this *négrophilie* for the primitive, non-Western cultures were not just sources of new formal motifs, but were access to a more fun-damental relationship to experience and emotion. The "too strong drink" of primitive culture that Raymond Cogniat had refused was a potent and addictive concoction for Surrealists and other intellectuals.[37] Avant-gardes preferred jazz, primitive art, and African dance and music to the stale, academic products of European civilization. According to Michel Leiris, "we've had enough of all that, which is why we would so much like to get closer to our primitive ancestry, why we have so little esteem left for anything that doesn't wipe out the succession of centuries in one stroke and put us, naked, in a more immediate and newer world."[38] Leiris saw civ-ilization itself as a deeply suspect gloss of politeness and a superficial veneer of morality that could easily shatter and reveal "our horrifying primitiveness." He declared that "civilization may be compared without too much inexactness to the thin greenish layer— the living magma and the odd detritus— that forms on the surface of calm water and sometimes solidifies into a crust, until an eddy comes to break it up."[39]

Lucien Lévy-Bruhl's writings delved into this realm of ethnography and were of great importance to the Surrealists and other intellectuals and artists interested in non-Western modes of thought.[40] Lévy-Bruhl attempted to understand the role played by myths in primitive society and to define them in terms of the "primitive mentality" that constructed them. His central assertion was that within the cosmos of primitive society, the "imaginary world" of the myth, although not logical in Western terms, had a status equal to that of the perceptible or everyday world. He interpreted the two worlds as equivalent, but the sacred or mythic world created the everyday world and is, therefore, preeminent. In the Western world view, according to Lévy-Bruhl, the mythic world is hidden in ordinary life, but primitive peoples believe there is continuous contact between material reality and the sacred mythical world.[41]

The notion that the sacred is always present, that it is behind everyday life, was one of Surrealism's central tenets.[42] Unexpected events, dreams, and trances were one set of means for accessing that other world repressed by reason and rational consciousness.[43] Aragon believed that myths could be found in seemingly rational thought processes and ordinary occurrences. As he articulated in *Paysan de Paris*, he became aware that "the distinctive nature of my thought, the distinctive nature of the evolution of my thought was a mechanism analogous in every respect to the genesis of myth. . . . It became apparent to me that man is as full of gods as a sponge plunged into the open sky."[44] Lévy-Bruhl pointed to remnants of the mythical in European folklore and fairy tales, which he believed still had an attraction and appeal to that part of us that was not conquered by rationality's claims. He asserted that modern Europeans were recalled to their prehistory when they heard a fairy tale being told, which "gives us the sensation of becoming once again like the folk of long ago (who still have their counterparts in many places even today), when men looked upon the mystical part of their experience of the world, not less, but as even more truly real than the empirical."[45] The Surrealists believed that such perception of otherness in everyday things and places marked recognition of the other as an epistemological and existential category. The "other," or more specifically, the primitive, was a window into a prerational mentality that could serve as a counter to the horrifying consequences of reason's dominance in modern life. James Clifford analyzed the avant-garde enthusiasm for *l'art nègre* as a way of conjuring up "a complete world of dreams and possibilities—passionate, rhythmic, concrete, mystical, unchained: an 'Africa'."[46] The Surrealists were, as a result, captivated by Oceanic and African art.

This primitivist mentality was instantiated in Surrealist literature as the evocation of strange, alienated emotions and the habitation of a dream world. For example, the introduction to Aragon's *Paysan de Paris* is called "Preface to a Modern Mythology," an echo of Lévy-Bruhl's *Primitive Mythology,* and is followed in the second chapter by a discourse on modern religion: "Man no longer worships the gods on their heights. . . . The spirit of religions, coming down to dwell in the dust, has abandoned the sacred places. But there are other places which flourish among mankind, places where men go calmly about their mysterious lives and in which a profound religion is very gradually taking shape. . . . It is the modern light radiating from the unusual that will rivet [the wise man's] attention."[47] Aragon and the Surrealists found the strange in places like the arcades (*passages*) where modern myths resided before they were destroyed in the name of city planning. The Passage de l'Opéra was the setting for the first section of *Paysan de Paris,* as one such repository of a threatened life; when Aragon wrote his novel, it was scheduled to be demolished to make way for Boulevard Haussmann.[48]

The Surrealists particularly valued events, forms, and places that splintered the placid surface of civilization by contrast with it or by escaping its laws. The Parc des Buttes-Chaumont, for example, was the subject of the second half of Aragon's *Paysan de Paris.* The park was an artificially constructed landscape built on garbage dumps and gypsum quarries, designed by Adolphe Alphand into a fantasy of fake rocks and grottoes. In *Paysan de Paris,* Aragon, André Breton, and Marcel Noll were trying to escape boredom when they thought of the possibility that the

Buttes-Chaumont might be open after dark: "This great oasis in a popular district, a shady zone where the prevailing atmosphere is distinctly murderous, this crazy area born in the head of an architect from the conflict between Jean-Jacques Rousseau and the economic conditions of existence in Paris, all this represented for the three strollers a test-tube of human chemistry in which the precipitates have the power of speech and eyes of a peculiar color."[49] The "conflict between Jean-Jacques Rousseau and the economic conditions of existence in Paris" points to a central role of the park: that of a civilizing as well as a civilized space. Nineteenth-century theorists of the public park believed that if, according to Rousseau, the natural state of man (his "savage" state) was less miserable and wicked than his civilized condition, perhaps contact with nature could bring the urban dweller back to a more harmonious mentality.[50] Aragon, however, found the park, or garden, to be the locus of the most infantile and regressive elements of the city inhabitant:

> Everything that is most eccentric in man, the gypsy in him, can surely be summed up in these two syllables: garden. . . . Every last remnant in adults' memory of the atmosphere of enchanted forests, every last vestige in them of belief in miracles, every breath of theirs which still inhales a perfume of fairytales reveals itself beneath the wretched, crazed disguise of these feebly invented landscapes, and exposes man and his senseless treasure-chest filled with intellectual trinkets, his superstitions, his ravings.[51]

The park, for him, was analogous to Lévy-Bruhl's fairytale. In a Rousseau-like reversal, instead of producing a more civilized being, it exposed the savage still left in the city dweller. The "feeling for nature" it produced was yet another door into the sacred reality behind the everyday.

Collage was another of the Surrealists' methods for finding hidden meaning in everyday life and ordinary objects. The Cubists developed the technique of layering found materials into compositional assemblages, and the Dadas used the method extensively, as in Kurt Schwitters' merz constructions. The *Phaidon Encyclopedia of Surrealism* defines collage as "a strange encounter with a particular emotional or dream-like, 'oneiric' effect."[52] James Clifford asserted that, as practiced by the Surrealists and in journals such as *Documents*, collage constantly places the proper arrangement of cultural symbols and artifacts in doubt through juxtaposition of disparate entities.[53] When the Surrealists juxtaposed *Fétiches européens* to indigenous art in their Counter-Colonial Exposition, they challenged the assumed superiority of Western art and culture. This comparison established an equivalence between European and African fetishes that exploded the evolutionist hierarchies on which Western aesthetics depend.

The equivalence also implied another position: that non-Western fetishes and Catholic figurines were equivalent in their *primitiveness,* in their commensurate naiveté and simplicity. The Surrealists did not make their collaged comparison between European high art and non-Western fetishes, rather, their interest concentrated on the least valorized products of both traditions. Their conflation of all "naive," "prerational," or "unconscious" art ignored the intricate meanings of primitive objects and the complex methods by which indigenous artists produced them. The native object was valuable to the Surrealists only as a counter to Western logocentrism and convention, not of value in and of itself.[54] André Breton recounted how a mask from a flea market helped Giacometti out of a compositional paralysis: "The purpose of the mask's intervention seemed to be to help Giacometti overcome his indecision in this regard. We should note that here the finding of the object strictly serves the same function as that of a dream, in that it frees the individual from paralyzing emotional scruples, comforts him."[55] The mask was a means to an artistic end. Similarly, African, Oceanic, and American objects on display at the Counter-Exposition served primarily as foils for Surrealist political slogans and for the satirized "Fétiches européens."

THE NATIVE ON DISPLAY

The noise of tambourines troubles the peace of the Negro village. Around a statue of a divinity, the fanatics dance until falling with exhaustion. The sorcerers, disappearing under their bizarre ornaments, shake their fetishes. The chief of the tribe assists these choreographic and sacred revels with his watching; and the ceremony ends with a sumptuous feast and copious libations.[56]

The native was one of the Colonial Exposition's central attractions. *Indigènes* from various colonies inhabited the pavilions, performed dances and theater pieces, demonstrated craft techniques, led tourist-laden camels around the grounds, served meals in restaurants, and sold goods in recreated markets. Their physical presence in the pavilions was a crucial accessory to the exotic simulacrum, the Exposition. However convincingly the pavilions might reproduce indigenous styles and forms, natives were essential to making a properly colonial environment in the Bois de Vincennes. Every colony, therefore, had its supplement of natives to complete its exotic atmosphere.

At the West African section, *Habbés,* "fetish dancers" from Bandiagara, Sudan, mimed the behavior of savage African beasts to the beat of the *tam-tam* (fig. 3.3). Native actors enacted the theater of Madagascar, Annam, and Dahomey for the viewing pleasure of European audiences. The Indochinese section featured Cambodian dancers who performed their "hieratic" ballets within the reconstituted Angkor Wat temple (fig. 3.4). Adventurous Parisians could dance the rumba and cha cha cha in the *bals* (dance halls) at Guadeloupe and Martinique, or hire a *pirogue* propelled by a Malagasy or Sudanese boatman across Lac Daumesnil. Kanak dancers from New Caledonia moved to the sound of their drums and chants, and merchants in the Moroccan souks sold authentic products of indigenous art (fig. 3.5). Artisans and artists from West Africa, Madagascar, and Cameroon plied their traditional crafts in front of the assembled

3.3 Les Habbés, Sudanese dancers (from M. Cloche, 60 aspects de l'Exposition coloniale [Paris: Studio Deberny Peignot, 1931], n.p.)

crowds. Musicians from Tunisia, Laos, and Indonesia played in exotic atmospheres amid recreated environments, such as the Café Tunisien. Maurice Tranchant described the fabulous crowd of natives: "Black sorcerers fabricate talismans for good luck; in the souks, Syrians rub our hands with perfumes and fragrant oils; the Japanese [sic] spread out their brilliant silks in our passage. A little Arab follows you from the start of the promenade, crying: 'You want some peanuts, Missié.' The whole of this many-colored mob carries you away toward new marvels."[57]

Natives were the necessary supplement that ensured the authenticity of the Exposition and brought a "savage" aspect to it (fig. 3.6). The manifest authenticity of the exhibited people augmented the suspect verisimilitude of the setting, a necessary condition for a thoroughly exotic experience.[58] The organizers went to lengths to prevent assimilated natives

3.4 Cambodian dancers (from *L'Illustration*, special issue [July 1931], n.p.)

from appearing in Western dress, except in carefully controlled circum-stances: in those few cases, the point of the display was the inappro-priateness of natives in such clothes, "en travesti" (fig. 3.7). The natives engaged in traditional occupations, which reinforced stereotypes of their primitive life, even though the French had installed modern technologies in the colonies. They often worked in servile roles, reproducing the colo-nial experience for the Exposition's visitors.

Not all contact between French people and natives was benign or regimented by the Exposition's peaceable propaganda. The Guadeloupe delegate to the Chamber of Deputies, Gratien Candace, complained to Lyautey that one of his compatriots, Fernand Balin, an employee at the Guadeloupe pavilion, had been beaten brutally by a French security guard at Porte 7. Candace protested the "brutalities exercised against blacks who

3.5 Kanak dancers (from Trillat)

come to visit the Exposition," including one young Senegalese man who was also beaten by a guard. Lyautey's response to Candace's letter cited "provocations" from Balin and denied that the attitude of the guards regarding blacks was prejudiced in the sense implied by Candace.[59]

Native inhabitants and performers who occupied the Madagascar compound were often the object of undesirable attentions from visitors. To protect the Malagasy citizens from "malevolent or indiscreet persons," a sentinel and a guard were placed at the entrance to the theater. According to a report by a French police captain on duty at the Exposition, visitors amused themselves by forcing native guards to light their cigarettes, or by regarding them down their noses while making grimaces, or by taking their bayonets. These antics produced incidents of minor violence, such as that on July 31, 1931, between a couple, Mr. Camo and Mrs. Rattenou, who tried to enter the Madagascar compound, and Malagasy Sergeant Ralaidaoro, who barred their way.[60]

3.6 "Contrasts," Colonial Exposition, Paris, 1931 (from Trillat)

3.7 "Jeunes Filles Malgaches en Travesti" (from Trillat)

Anthropologist Burton Benedict analyzed human exhibits as a demonstration of power, a view that applies particularly well to the Exposition, where the unity of the French colonial empire was a central theme: "The display of people is a display of power. It is a symbolic performance demonstrating power relationships, but these relationships are not necessarily real. . . . Thus the displays of conquered or colonial peoples at world's fairs present a kind of spurious unity in which people who differ vastly in cultural tradition and aspirations are made to appear as one."[61] Benedict described five categories of human displays: people as technicians, as craftsmen, as curiosities or freaks, as trophies, and as specimens or scientific objects.[62] The Exposition used several of these exhibit types, although craftsmen and performers had premier place, and there were no technicians.

These exhibits had a long history at previous French expositions, at which the display of people served different purposes and employed different techniques. For example, the 1889 Universal Exposition contained the first extensive exposition of colonized peoples in France, and showed over 400 Indochinese, Senegalese, and Tahitians in pavilions and recreated villages.[63] The most famous "colonial" exhibit was the Rue du Caire, a street from Egypt's capital recreated down to the dirt on its walls and the donkeys that traversed its streets[64] (fig. 3.8).

Zeynep Çelik and Leila Kinney analyzed the extremely popular belly dance at nineteenth-century world's fairs as a hybrid of Western and "Oriental" dance motifs.[65] Although the belly dance was prohibited at the 1931 Exposition, other types of performances had a central place in the depiction of native life, with a gloss of allegedly ethnographic accuracy adding necessary believability. In 1900, critics decried the paucity of natives at the Exposition's colonial section, the diverse exhibits of which were not fully inhabited[66] (fig. 3.9). To be effective, colonial sections had to appear to teem with *natives*, just as the colonies were imagined to swarm with natives in "real life."

3.8 Rue du Caire, Universal Exposition, Paris, 1889 (from Delort de Gleon, La rue du Caire: l'architecture arabe des Khalifes d'Egypte a l'Exposition universelle de Paris en 1889 [Paris: Plon, 1889])

3.9   Colonial section, Universal Exposition, Paris, 1900 (Resource Collections of the Getty Research Institute, Los Angeles)

Colonial expositions were prime demonstrations of the imperialist vision of the "other." They were displays of the results of colonial expansion and expression of the innate superiority of Western civilization. The physical and moral "backwardness" of the conquered peoples was exhibited to justify the conquest and to show the necessity of rescuing these people from their degeneracy. This was as true for the American displays of Indians and Negroes as for the European expositions.[67] Whereas Surrealists and other avant-garde groups were attracted to the primitive as an *escape* from Western civilization and its excessive rationality, it was exactly reason and civilization that colonialists sought to affirm in these exhibits

3.10 "Tam-Tam de Man," dancers from the Ivory Coast (from L'Illustration, special issue [July 1931], n.p.)

of people. The primitive state of the natives was proof of social Darwinism's hierarchy of cultures, which used a continuous scale of development, with Europe at its pinnacle. It was therefore important that Ivory Coast dancers at the Colonial Exposition be almost nude, to show their utter difference from civilized men and to reinforce this reading of otherness as inferiority (fig. 3.10). Contemporary cartoons caricatured the natives in stereotypical terms and emphasized racial and ethnic features that signaled degeneracy and savagery. *Le Rire's* cartoonist even depicted a spectacle that did not exist at the 1931 Exposition, since the belly dance was excluded with the rickshaw (fig. 3.11).

People who came from the colonies and appeared at the Colonial Exposition attracted action from resident anticolonial militants. Lyautey's desire to bring the lessons of colonial urbanism to Paris was

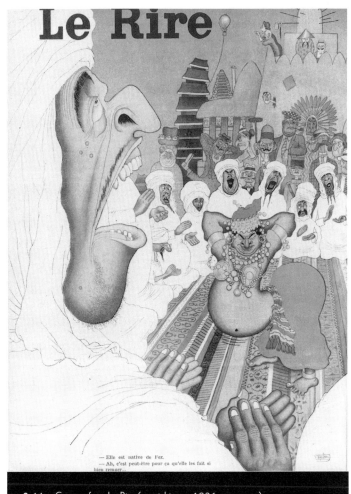

3.11 Cartoon from Le Rire (special issue, 1931, rear cover)

not matched by a concomitant wish to bring metropolitan politics to the colonies. The organizers were anxious to prevent any contamination of the Exposition from dangerous metropolitan political strains, especially Communism. Their concern focused on Soviet Russia's insidious influence and money, as well as on insurgent nationalist movements in the colonies. In his introduction to the *Rapport général,* Marcel Olivier exhorted the colonial powers to unite and fight against Bolshevism and nationalism in their colonies: "In order to combat efficiently the ferments of disorder carefully cultivated by Bolshevism and local nationalisms, a plan of joint defense is necessary."[68] Olivier's fear of Bolshevism was justified by anti-imperialist groups in Paris funded by Moscow through the French Communist Party.

The Communist Party was the principal anticolonialist organism in France throughout the 1920s and 1930s. In 1921 the French Party established a *Comité d'études coloniales* (Committee of Colonial Studies) to provide support to French militants residing in the colonies, and in 1922 it founded the *Union intercoloniale* (Intercolonial Union) for members from the colonies living in France. The Communists supported nascent nationalist movements in the colonies and agitated to ease suppression of these groups by the French government. In 1924 the *Commission coloniale* (Colonial Commission) replaced the *Comité d'études coloniales.* It was charged with coordinating the Party's contacts with nationalist organizations— the *Parti annamite de l'indépendance* (Annamite Party of Independence), *Etoile nord-africaine* (North African Star), and *Comité de défense de la race nègre* (Committee for Defense of the Black Race, also known as the *Ligue de défense de la race nègre*), in particular—and all anticolonial activities.[69] The 1924–25 Rif War in Morocco mobilized resistance to imperialist repression among pacifists, anticolonialists, and expatriate Moroccan students and workers.[70] The *Ligue anti-impérialiste* (Antiimperialist League) was another important anticolonial body in Europe and sponsored, as we have seen, antiimperialist agitation within the *Métropole.*

The Communists's *Union intercoloniale* consisted of Indochinese, Réunionese, Antillese, Senegalese, and Malagasy representatives, joined by North Africans in 1924; it was the most important anticolonial body in France during the 1920s.[71] The Communists's ability to sponsor direct action was severely limited by its lack of funds, repression occasioned by its position against the Rif War, and its "antipatriotism."[72] Articles critical of the Colonial Exposition did appear in several anticolonial journals, including two by Saumane in *Le Cri des Nègres*, a Communist "monthly journal for Negro workers," run by Kouyat, and *La Race nègre*, another Communist organ associated with the *Ligue de défense de la race nègre*.[73] *La Dépêche Africaine*, an independent journal that espoused liberal attitudes toward blacks, covered the Exposition as a positive exhibition of black culture, although it also denounced repressive policies in the colonies.[74] The Exposition served as a unifying focus for these diverse groups and parties, prompting cooperation among anticolonialist associations.

To ward off anticolonial protests, security around the Exposition grounds was particularly tight in natives' living and working quarters. The Indochinese section was under strict surveillance because of the threat of disturbance and infiltration by Indochinese militants from the Latin Quarter. Files of the Exposition contain numerous notes from police and the CAI to Exposition officials on the activities of such agitators. For example, the commissaire of the Indochinese section received reports on meetings held by militants in preparation for their protests against the Exposition on April 19 and 25, and on the leaflets they distributed in and around the grounds.[75]

Organized antiimperialist groups went further than this. On April 12, ten Indochinese militants boarded a boat in Marseilles harbor to talk to natives who had just arrived, en route to Paris and the Exposition. The activists told the Indochinese that they were "coolies," that they didn't know their own shame, and that the French had made them into slaves.

They were told that if they went on strike and refused to obey the French, the Communists would help them. The natives' response was that they were not coolies, but artisans, and they informed a colonial official of the incident.[76] The militants made similar efforts to infiltrate the Exposition grounds to proselytize for anticolonial struggle among the indigenous performers. Police records show that the wife of Sai Van Hoa, a leader of the radical student group *Association d'Enseignement mutuel* (Association for Mutual Education), obtained a place at the Indochinese restaurant coat check and was fired because she could have introduced anticolonial propaganda into the Exposition. The same restaurant employed a cook known to have expressed Communist opinions and anti-French sentiments, for which he too was fired.[77] A note from the prefecture of the police and CAI to Lyautey stated that certain members of the *Etoile nord-africaine* made contact with North African musicians at the Exposition.[78]

Various groups in southern France and Paris distributed pamphlets that agitated for demonstrations against the Exposition. The *Ligue de défense de la race nègre, Ligue contre l'impérialisme,* Communist party, and Surrealists produced tracts that they posted around Paris and smuggled onto the grounds. One such leaflet declared: "Colonialism is profitable for the capitalists, but it costs the life of hundreds of thousands of French and indigenous workers and peasants!" The same CAI report included a series of cartoons with captions in *quoc ngu* (a transliteration of Vietnamese into Latin characters) that depicted the horrors of French repression in Indochina (fig. 3.12), as well as translations of tracts in French and *quoc ngu* that called for demonstrations against the Exposition.[79] One tract,

3.12   Opposite: Anticolonial cartoon in quoc ngu, [1931] (Archives d'Outre-Mer, Aix-en-Provence)

distributed in Toulouse, stated, "The colonial sharks want to try to show that colonization is a benefit for the colonial peoples and a good deal for that which it calls France . . . The Exposition is organized at the moment when, in all the colonies of the world, a wind of revolution blows. . . . Down with the Colonial Exposition! Down with assassin Imperialism!"[80] These leaflets and tracts came from Annamite militants in Toulouse, Marseilles, and Paris who coordinated their activities with the help of the *Ligue anti-impérialiste.* The CAI further reported an April 25 meeting among "two Indochinese, one Japanese, one Korean and one Negro" to recruit members for the *Ligue,* to form action committees for each colony, and to make connections with anticolonial groups in Marseilles, Bordeaux, Toulouse, Montpelier, and Le Havre. Their aim was to protest against "all the curiosities bordering on barbarity, such as the exhibitions of cannibals in cages, negresses 'à plateau' (with extended lips) and rickshaws, and to protest the appearance of Annamite and indigenous leaders who were 'valets of imperialist colonialism.'"[81] Another poster, produced by the *Ligue de défense de la race nègre,* proclaimed: "Women shot in Cameroon, telegram of August 3, 1931." It recounted how women seeking the reduction or elimination of their taxes were imprisoned or shot by French authorities. These posters were affixed to the walls of a school near the Exposition.[82]

The most significant of the anti-Exposition tracts was *Le Véritable Guide de l'Exposition Coloniale: L'Œuvre civilisatrice de la France magnifiée en quelques pages* (The Real Guide to the Colonial Exposition: The Civilizing Work of France Celebrated in a Few Pages).[83] It contained sections on French colonization and repression of dissent in Guyana, Madagascar, Guadeloupe, Equatorial Africa, North Africa, and Indochina. For each colony, the Guide enumerated specific instances of exploitation of natives: deplorable conditions on sugar cane plantations in Guadeloupe, forced labor on the Brazzaville-Atlantic railroad, forced sales of land in Algeria and Tunisia, and poorly paid coolies in Indochinese rice fields. The Guide

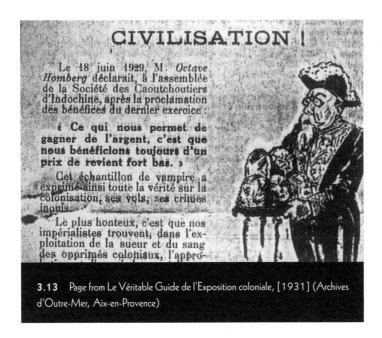

3.13 Page from Le Véritable Guide de l'Exposition coloniale, [1931] (Archives d'Outre-Mer, Aix-en-Provence)

detailed the violent repression visited by the French on those who revolted or protested against these conditions, including bombing villages in Indochina and lengthy prison sentences and deportations in Syria, Algeria, and Madagascar. These atrocities were illustrated by line drawings that depicted some of the consequences of French policy and French villains, such as Governor Pasquier holding a tray of bloody heads (fig. 3.13). The Guide called on French workers to view the repressed natives as allies and brothers and to circulate copies of this "too-short account of French colonialism." According to the CAI, Exposition guards found several of these brochures in the Tunisian restaurant and the Pavillon des Forces d'Outre-Mer in June 1931.[84]

These activities, however negligible they were, drew considerable attention from Exposition authorities. To the degree possible, the "wind of revolution" blowing in the colonies was resolutely excluded from the Colonial Exposition. The relatively democratic political atmosphere of Paris was in clear opposition to authoritarian practices of colonialism, as was implicitly recognized by Olivier in his introduction. He referred to the "latent conflict between colonizers and colonized peoples," but attributed it to the unfinished business of colonization rather than to a fundamental problem with colonialism:

> Even the most unreasonable demands of the colonial peoples are based on a promise we hold out to them. We cannot evade them without betraying our ideal and conception of colonialism. But we have an obligation to set aside those immediately impossible demands or those against the good interests of the indigenous communities. The great majority of colonial peoples accept European rule, but on the condition that the Europeans transmit a positive, concerted, and rapid action in the economic and social domains.[85]

Under the justification that more good than harm had been done during five centuries of French colonialism, Olivier defended the achievements of colonialism against those who would denigrate civilization's imperatives. Metropolitan lassitude and liberal attitudes toward cultures and peoples less civilized than the French disgusted Olivier, Lyautey, and their colleagues: "One part of the European elite has resigned itself to defeat, by snobbism, fatigue, by distaste for a civilization that was their own, but of which they wanted to retain only the gross material aspects."[86]

Natives on display at the Exposition had to be protected from the corrupting, defeatist influences of Leiris and his Surrealist kind, and the coherence of the colonial vision presented at Vincennes had to be kept intact and unchallenged. Not only were natives to be sheltered from contaminating ideas, metropolitan visitors had to be given the most optimistic and appealing picture of the colonies possible to encourage investment and tourism in French possessions. Segregation of indigenous from metropolitan sections was necessitated by this double imperative of quarantine. The natives had, however, already been corrupted by republican promises of equality, with the result that they agitated for assimilation, self-determination, or revolution. The 1930s saw the eruption of nationalist struggles and of anticolonial, anti-Western movements, of which the protests around the Colonial Exposition were a sample.

A TAXONOMY OF MARGINALITY: THE SITE

In a new geography, the Somalia Coast is opposed to the New Hebrides, Guyana is the pendant to Oceania, making a rectilinear and logical universe.
—Paul Morand[1]

The "new geography" of the Colonial Exposition included eastern Paris, fortifications that encircled the city, and Bois de Vincennes, as well as the monumental reproductions of indigenous buildings and official French colonial architecture (fig. 4.1). This area was already made exotic in literature, film, song, and art, and its inhabitants were marginalized from life in the wealthier districts. The Exposition occupied a site redolent of romantic associations as the home of marginal people exiled from Paris proper. The fortifications and the zone were depicted as undeveloped, unregulated, mysterious, and dangerous territory, an assessment that mirrored the classic conception of the Orient as mythical, sensual, irrational, and backward: both were loci of otherness. Maréchal Lyautey himself made the analogy between the colonies and eastern Paris, the poor, left-wing part of the city, as equally in need of enlightenment and development. Just as the colonies were France's "other," so the zone was the "other" of Paris. Although it was unacknowledged, the exoticism of this locale underlay the contrived romanticism of the Exposition and produced a doubling of its marginality.

The juxtaposition of the Exposition to Paris might have produced a contrast that had a potentially surreal effect. Like a Surrealist collage, comparison of dissimilar elements—in this case, Parisian apartment buildings and native huts—might have generated a sense of strangeness by defamiliarizing both apartment blocks and huts and generating new meanings out of their contrast.[2] "The singularity of the Colonial Exposition . . . is the melange and the opposition of all styles of architecture and violent colors. The reed cabin is next to the immaculate temple of Septime Severus and the cow-blood red of Madagascar. Further on, the Cité des Informations appears, ultra-metropolitan and modern."[3] As critic Paul-Emile Cadilhac noted, the Exposition removed the visitor from the familiar Parisian landscape, as if he or she had actually left France: "In the manner of Huysmans and Des Esseintes, one has realized a considerable voyage without taking either the boat or the train."[4] The

4.1 Site plan (photo: Bibliothèque Nationale, Paris)

internal colors, smells, and sights of this colonial microcosm were given particular attention.

> Constructions spring up, to the right and to the left, rounded off in a radiant dome while the muffled roll of the tambourines backing up the piercing Arab flutes mixes the nostalgia of the old Orient with the stamping of the crowd, with the guttural cries of the merchants, with the odors of cooking drenched with oil. The crowd teems, diverse, colorful, red fezes and embroidered coats . . . while the high camels sway on their hoofs above the multitude.[5]

In the literary conventions of the day, commentators described these sensual details to transport readers into its simulated colonial environment.

The Exposition was a collage of found meanings and histories layered onto the site to create a contingent, transient construction The marginality of the colonies, located on the physical and psychic edges of France, doubled the pre-existing marginality of the site. This collage had a certain territorial logic that can be traced through the history of the site and its planning.

SELECTING THE SITE

The site included land located in the Bois de Vincennes on a section of the declassified nineteenth-century fortifications, and in the *zone non aedificandi*. The Bois de Vincennes was the "other" Parisian park, a less renowned and manicured forest than the Bois de Boulogne. The fortifications, which completely encircled Paris, consisted of massive walls and earthworks with forts periodically stationed within them, and heavily guarded gates at major points of entry into the city (fig. 4.2). The zone was a band of cleared land just outside the fortifications themselves that was theoretically kept clear of any permanent structure.[6]

During Angoulvant's tenure as commissaire, a number of sites were considered and abandoned. The first project for the 1921 agreement

4.2 Serge-Henri Moreau, "Au point du jour. Le mur murant Paris" (from André Warnod, Les Fortifs, Promenades sur les anciennes fortifications et la zone [Paris: Editions de l'Epi, 1926], n.p.)

between the city of Paris and the state provided for two sites: one at the Bois de Boulogne on the training field of the Bagatelle and the fortifications between Porte de Passy and Porte Maillot, and the other at the Bois de Vincennes next to Lake Daumesnil. The planners believed that the traditional site for Parisian expositions, the Champ de Mars, was not suitable because it was used heavily for recreation and encumbered by telegraph installations. The Ministère de l'Instruction Publique et des Beaux-Arts (one of the agencies involved in the planning) considered the Halle des Vins site on the Seine next to the Jardin des Plantes, but the surface area was too small for this type of event.[7]

The public disapproved of the proposal to use the Bagatelle because of potential damage it might do to the gardens; the Convention of 26 Juillet 1921, therefore, abandoned that site. The 1921 accord allotted two sites, one near Lac des Minimes in the Bois de Vincennes, and part of the Esplanade of the Invalides, instead of the Bagatelle. The portion in central Paris included the banks of the Seine between the Invalides Esplanade and the Trocadéro gardens, along with the Halle des Machines site on the Champs de Mars. The Vincennes section was to contain the native villages, as it had in 1900, and the presentation of products exported to the colonies.[8]

In November 1921 the Exposition ceded its rights to the Invalides location to the Exposition des Arts Décoratifs, due to the costs of infrastructure (gas, water, electricity, fences) on this site.[9] On July 11, 1923, the municipal council authorized extension of the Exposition date to 1927 instead of 1925; subsequent deliberations in December 1923 altered the site to the Bois de Vincennes alone.[10] The Minister of the Colonies decided that the settlement with the Exposition des Arts Décoratifs and opposition to expositions in the interior of Paris mitigated against using the Champs de Mars.[11] This required new arrangements with the city since public transportation from central Paris to the Bois de Vincennes was poor. The state and the city signed a new convention on March 25, 1924, specifying that the Metropolitan subway be extended from the Bastille to Porte de Charenton through Porte de Picpus and Porte Dorée.[12] Not only did the city assent to the Metro extension, they agreed to expand the Vincennes site considerably to include 210 hectares from Boulevard Poniatowski to the Joinville station in Nogent and the Jardin colonial in Nogent-sur-Marne[13] (fig. 4.3).

One of the most ambitious aspects of the organizers' intentions for this site was a Musée Permanent des Colonies projected for the site of the Ecole Militaire annexes. A Musée Social document envisaged the creation of a long *allée de verdure* to be constructed in conjunction with the museum and the Exposition. This linear park would have stretched from the Bois

4.3 Proposed site, Colonial Exposition, Bois de Vincennes, 1924 (Archives d'Outre-Mer, Aix-en-Provence)

de Boulogne, down Avenue Henri Martin to the Trocadéro, beyond it to the Champ de Mars and gardens of the Ecole Militaire, and finally down the Avenues de Saxe and de Breteuil and Boulevard Pasteur to the Gare Montparnasse. The new axis would be the Champs Elysées de la Rive Gauche. Unfortunately, the Ministry of War was resistant to relocating its annexes, which housed numerous soldiers, orderlies, and horses, to a new location further than 1800 meters from the Ministry of War (on Boulevard Saint-Germain). The cost of purchasing land in that area was too high and even the site of the "Magic City" entertainment hall on the Quai d'Orsay was too expensive to expropriate.[14]

A list of plans and other drawings made by the Exposition's architectural agency shows that several other sites were under consideration. This list includes studies for the transformation of the Ecole Militaire; use of barracks on Boulevard Jourdan (near Parc de Montsouris) and rue de Babylon; Invalides/Champ de Mars site; the 1921 Bois de Vincennes site around Lac de Minimes; Bois de Boulogne; and an unidentified site in the Paris suburb of Nanterre.[15] This panoply of sites points to the confusion that reigned in the Exposition organization regarding the most elementary aspects of planning.

The December 31, 1926, avenant to the 1924 convention made a further modification of the understanding between the city and the state[16] (fig. 4.4). This contract dramatically reduced the size of the site to 100 hectares, largely to avoid destroying too many trees in heavily wooded areas of the Bois. The long extension toward Joinville, south of the Bois, was eliminated and the city delineated more specific requirements regarding public access corridors to the Bois at the Porte de Reuilly entrance. The avenant also deferred the date of the Exposition to 1928, with the possibility of delaying it until 1929 or 1930. Soon after Lyautey became Commissaire Général in 1927, he attempted to add portions of the Bois de Vincennes and fortifications at Porte de Reuilly (fig. 4.5) to the site to enclose a continuous boundary for the Exposition and to use part of the

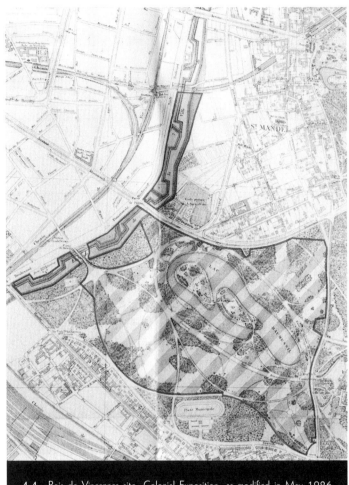

4.4 Bois de Vincennes site, Colonial Exposition, as modified in May 1926 (Archives d'Outre-Mer, Aix-en-Provence)

4.5 Additions to site on the fortifications, Colonial Exposition, 1927 (Archives d'Outre-Mer, Aix-en-Provence)

military Champ de Manœuvres for garages. The final avenant of 1930 ceded the last sections of land needed to create large entrances at various points and a consistent perimeter.[17]

The Exposition's final site plan contained separate areas for French metropolitan pavilions, French colonial pavilions, foreign sections, and amusements. On the demolished fortifications, the metropolitan buildings of the Cité des Informations, Porte d'Honneur, and Section Métropolitaine formed an Art Deco barrier between the savage delights within the Exposition and the apartments of the 12th arrondissement. After the metropolitan pavilions, reconstructions of primitive native buildings were placed along the Grande Avenue des Colonies. Farther east, the Belgian Congo and other colonial sections provided additional exotic color and form. The culmination of this excursion was the zoo, a naturalistic recreation of the African savanna complete with monkeys, lions, and elephants. The large triangle of land north of Lac Daumesnil contained other sections, primarily foreign participants: Italy, United States, Holland, Portugal and a few other metropolitan exhibits. To the extent possible within the irregular, gerrymandered site, the plan avoided any mixture of or contiguity between colonial and metropolitan sections.

THE SITE PLAN

The strange parcels produced by the myriad avenants and conventions forced awkward planning decisions on Albert Tournaire, the Exposition's architect. Tournaire was a Beaux-Arts-trained architect who had won the Grand Prix in 1888 and was a member of the Institut de France; he had extensive public and private building experience, including the extension of the Palais de Justice.[18] In early plans of the Exposition, including one by Léon Jaussely, the architect before Tournaire, the Avenue des Colonies ran from a main entrance gate at Porte de Reuilly to the Tour des Forces d'Outre-Mer. This grand axis ran from the main entrance and then at Porte de Reuilly, into the Exposition, and created a clear circulation pattern through the site. After the convention of 1927, the shift of the principle entrance to the Porte Dorée duplicated the Porte de Reuilly gate and isolated the southern Avenue des Colonies axis. The difficulty resolving these two entries and lines of circulation into a coherent plan is clearly shown on Tournaire's 1928 plan, in which the two "main" entrances compete with each other. In the 1928 plan, Tournaire attempted to create local symmetries and axes, as in the foreign sections, but little of this effort endured in the final plan (fig. 4.6).

The 1930 avenant added parcels of land along the fortifications and created a unified site, but the problem of the two parallel axes remained, exacerbated by the picturesque paths of the Bois. Tournaire used the Madagascar pavilion to build a focal point between the axes and to generate a secondary axis south of the Porte d'Honneur, but he was not successful in making a direct connection from the Porte d'Honneur to the Avenue des Colonies. The most defined sequence in the plan continued to be the axis between the Porte de Reuilly and the Forces d'Outre-Mer tower (fig. 4.7). Disjunction between axes and lack of a clear focusing element within the site made articulation of colonialism's hierarchies difficult. By comparison, the 1922 Marseilles Colonial Exposition clearly expressed the dominance of French culture and power over her colonies by placing the Grand Palais at the terminus of the Grand Allée (fig. 4.8).

The Avenue des Colonies engendered a series of bizarre juxtapositions among the various colonial pavilions. From the Cité des Informations on the left, a visitor would have passed, in sequence, Somalia and Oceania, the French Indies and New Caledonia, Guyana and Martinique, the Missions and Reunion, the Indochinese hunting and fishing pavilion, and Guadeloupe before reaching the great Angkor Wat cross axis. Marcel Zahar commented on these disjunctive relations:

> At certain points of the Exposition, one meets curious effects of contrast: thus, the central part of the Temple of Angkor-Vat, a stratified

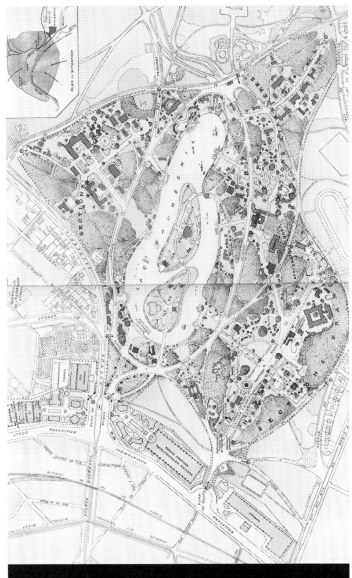

4.6 Albert Tournaire, site plan, Colonial Exposition, Paris, 1928 (from *L'Illustration*, Aug. 11, 1928, 150–151)

4.7   Avenue des Colonies (from Petit, n. p.)

block, cut like a jewel, covered all over its surface with admirable chiseled motifs, is next to a district in Djenné, a West French Africa village where huts of a summary art appear conjured from enormous
chignons of clay run through with stakes.[19]

Raymond Cogniat noted the Exposition's lack of uniform style and
attributed it to the diversity of colonized civilizations represented. He believed that the 1925 Decorative Arts Exposition had achieved a consistent
style and a unity out of the "needs and aspirations of the Europeans."
The comparison of such different civilizations at the Colonial Exposition, however, produced greater differences in style, in Cogniat's opinion:
"The complicated refinement of the Asian arts cannot be compared with
the grandeur and the simplicity ... of the arts of Equatorial Africa: one
must be able to admire Arab creations without thinking of Oceania. If, in
1925, it was correct to connect the pavilions together, at Vincennes, it is

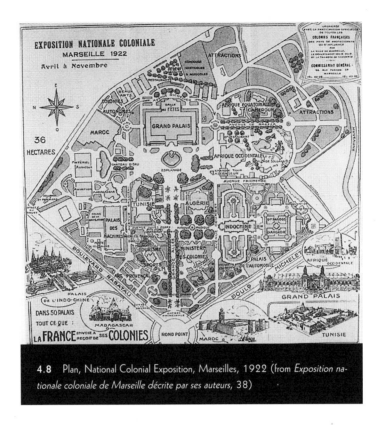

4.8 Plan, National Colonial Exposition, Marseilles, 1922 (from *Exposition nationale coloniale de Marseille décrite par ses auteurs*, 38)

necessary to isolate them."[20] The necessity of giving each colony a self-contained representation reduced each pavilion to a sign for the colony it represented, equal to every other pavilion or culture.

Contemporary accounts rarely described the relationship of the Colonial Exposition to Paris or the visitor's transition from one domain to the other. The journey from Paris to Vincennes via Metro was not recapitulated, nor was the sensation of walking from the Metro entrance into the Exposition. There were very few places within the grounds where a visitor could see the surrounding Parisian buildings. An unusual comment from one visitor noted that the Exposition's internal coherence was so complete

4.9 Colonial section, Universal Exposition, Paris, 1900 (Resource Collections of the Getty Research Institute, Los Angeles)

that leaving the precinct could produce a sense of unreality in the observer such that "one is surprised to find oneself in France."[21] By comparison with other fairs, which usually occupied the center of the city, the Colonial Exposition was isolated from Paris' urban and political life. In 1900, for example, the Moroccan pavilions sat under the Eiffel Tower in a startlingly direct contrast between Orient and Occident (fig. 4.9). Even a relatively self-contained exposition such as the 1922 Marseilles Colonial Exposition fronted directly on the Rond-Point at its main entrance.

Separation of French and native sectors in colonial cities—a central tenet of contemporary French colonialism—had its direct corollary in

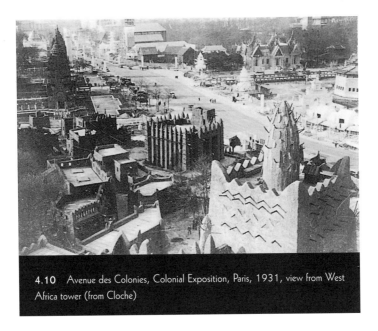

4.10 Avenue des Colonies, Colonial Exposition, Paris, 1931, view from West Africa tower (from Cloche)

the 1931 Exposition's site plan. The relationship between Paris and the Exposition was based on the strict segregation of the two territories. Vacant land where fortifications once stood formed a convenient barrier between the city and the Bois, reinforced by the Cité des Informations, Section Métropolitaine, and garages (fig. 4.10). Twentieth-century French colonial urbanism created segregated European and indigenous quarters with radically different typological characters and levels of hygienic improvement. The Congress on Urbanism in the Colonies and Tropical Countries, held at the 1931 Exposition, declared that urban plans for the colonies be organized according to "the beliefs, the mores and traditions of the races composing" the urban centers in question.[22] In a more direct statement, prominent colonialist Edmond du Vivier de Streel maintained that, in an "urban agglomeration," one must "never mix the native and the European populations," an axiom that "Lyautey had made a law."[23] The most prominent application of the segregation principle was Henri Prost's plan for Rabat, executed under Maréchal Hubert Lyautey's governorship of Morocco, which established a new European district and left intact the existing Medina.[24] The Colonial Exposition was the embodiment of this segregation principle.

Janet Abu-Lughod called this system "apartheid" because the indigenous quarters remained inferior by European standards of sanitation, light, and air.[25] The French justified their practice of constructing new European districts outside traditional cities of North Africa and Indochina by an argument for the preservation of "native cities" as the sites of cultures that, although inferior to European culture, should be respected. They invoked hygienic reasons for this segregation, but the primary rationale was separation of traditional city centers from new French districts.

The site plan also rehearsed the imperial trope of a journey backward in time, the primary theme of travel accounts.[26] The Tour of the World in One Day repeated the imperial narrative into what Anne McClintock calls "anachronistic space." This journey progressed from civilizations of Europe outward to far-flung antipodes of their empires, from advanced societies of the present to archaic, prehistoric ones. The return journey echoed the "evolutionary logic of historical progress," according to McClintock: "Geographical difference across *space* is figured as a historical difference across *time*."[27] The colonies were represented as different in both geographical location and historical time in this schema. The progression from Paris to the colonial pavilions was terminated by the zoo, the culmination of the visitor's voyage from civilization (France) to savage territories (the colonies).

TAXONOMY OF THE SITE

The site harbored the forgotten people and things of Paris, its own type of primitive life. Michel Leiris, in his description of the edges of Paris as a site of "the sacred of everyday life" gives us a model for understanding the layers of marginality that were superimposed on this site:

> As far as outdoor places are concerned, I remember two that, with time's passage and ideas since formed, seem to have been permeated for me, a religious child in other respects, with a sacred character: the sort of bush-country, a *no-man's land* that extended between where the fortifications lay and the racecourse at Auteuil, and that racecourse itself.
>
> When our mother or older sister took us for a walk either in the Bois de Boulogne or the public gardens adjoining the Paris green-houses, it often happened that we would cross this ill-defined pace. Contrasted with the bourgeois world of houses, just as the village— for those belonging to so-called savage societies—can be contrasted with the bush, which is the hazy world specific to all the mythical adventures and strange encounters that begin as soon as the duly staked-out world making up the village is left behind, this was a zone where the scarps were really haunting. We were told then, if we happened to stop and play, to beware strangers (actually, I realize now: satyrs) who might, under false pretenses, try to take us off into the bushes. A place apart, extremely taboo, an area heavily marked by the supernatural and the sacred, so different from the parks, where everything was planned, organized, raked, and where the notices forbidding you to walk on the grass, though signs of taboo, could only endow them with a sacred grown cold.[28]

In this reminiscence, Leiris identified an element of Parisian urban structure, the zone and fortifications, that connected with then popular notions of the exotic. The strangeness of bringing the colonies to Paris was matched, in his account, by the preexisting strangeness of the zone. As an ethnographer, Leiris observed the exoticism of the site and gave us an ethnographic taxonomy of Paris' margins, by means of which I will trace the coincidence of the colonies' marginality with that of the zone.

The Exposition occupied the three spaces of Leiris's taxonomy: city, zone, and park. Leiris correlated the relations between these spaces and their exotic associations in the following manner: the city was the village, the zone was the bush or no-man's land, and the park was a domesticated natural space that had lost its sacred character. He identified a set of cultural affinities that were more than personal myths. An array of writers and artists had already mystified his spatial taxonomy in their quest for the mysterious just outside ordinary life. The three territories carried their own associations of liminality onto which the Exposition was collaged, thereby doubling its marginality. Through Leiris's associations, I have constructed a taxonomy of city, zone, and park with contemporary documents to understand the ways in which "otherness" was inscribed and layered onto the Exposition site.

Paris-Village

The city as the village represents the bounded "bourgeois world of houses," the least magical of Leiris's spaces. The village is "duly staked-out" in this account: its limits are indicated, measured with markers, and under surveillance. This is the space of civilization and the order of streets and property boundaries in which every foot is allocated. The district adjoining the site was, however, less tame and bourgeois than other Parisian quarters since it housed the "savages"—working class and poor—who were associated with social barbarity and dangerous customs.

If Leiris viewed the city as the staid world of the bourgeois, eastern Paris was even duller to contemporary observers in search of tourist attractions. "The populous industrial districts in the East of Paris, with the exception of the Buttes-Chaumont and Père Lachaise, have little to offer that is of interest to the average visitor," according to one contemporary guide book.[29] Another guide contained a map entitled "Paris

Sociologique" that graphically depicted the class structure of Paris in the 1920s. It divided Paris into categories, each indicated in a different color: *Parcs et jardins, Classes riches, Classes moyennes aisées, Commerce, Quartiers ouvriers, Quartiers pauvres,* and *Quartiers misérables.* All the *Quartiers misérables* were in the eastern half of Paris, as were most of the *Quartiers pauvres,* and while the *Classes riches* were in the West. The 12th arrondissement, abutting the Bois de Vincennes, was made up of *Quartiers pauvres* and *Quartiers misérables.*[30]

The infamous *îlots insalubres,* areas with a high frequency of tuberculosis, were almost exclusively concentrated in the eastern districts. The municipal council designated the *îlots* in 1919 after a survey of buildings showed a high level of tuberculosis mortality during the previous twenty five years. They totaled 257 hectares in 17 districts, with 13 located in densely occupied parts of the peripheral arrondissements and 4 in the historic center. The population of the districts totaled 186,597 persons, housed in 4,290 buildings. Most of these *îlots* were intact in 1931 due to the slowness with which they were demolished and rebuilt.[31] In addition to slum housing, the 12th arrondissement accommodated various undesirable institutions. The town of Charenton le Pont, just to the south of the Exposition, incorporated the Maison nationale de santé, an enormous lunatic asylum founded in 1641, and the Asile national de convalescence, a large public hospital.[32] Not far away were the Entrepôts des vins along the Seine in Bercy and industrial quarters around the Place de la Nation.

The greatest danger in eastern Paris lay in its politics, in the revolutionary and subversive working-class movements that incubated with the tuberculosis bacterium, in the view of conservative observers. In 1872, Paul Leroy-Beaulieu, a well-known theorist of French colonial policy, turned his attention to the moral and sanitary conditions of Parisian slums. His formulation of French social and hygienic ills rested on the equation of poor living standards with moral turpitude: "If family life does not exist among the working classes, it is linked to the smallness and filth of the dwellings. The cabaret thus becomes a place of meeting and relaxation: one becomes there at the same time envious, greedy, revolutionary, skeptical, and finally a communist."[33] The eastern districts were famous for their denizens' discontent and their left-wing politics.[34] This culturally and politically marginal quarter had little initial appeal for the Colonial Exposition's organizers, even Lyautey who had made a showcase out of the unprepossessing material of the Moroccan city of Rabat.

In 1927, when Lyautey joined the Exposition administration, he had a strongly negative attitude toward the Vincennes site and eastern Paris. Albert Laprade, architect of the Permanent Museum and Morocco pavilions, recalled that Lyautey, in his initial interview with Laprade in January 1928, told him that only one thing interested him: *Paris,* meaning central Paris. The Vincennes site did not interest him, especially as the site for the permanent Colonial Museum.[35] Two reports prepared for Lyautey in October and December 1927 by a Mr. Bourdaire, Perpetual Secretary of the Académie des Sciences coloniales, reinforced this opinion.

Bourdaire's review of the Vincennes location was also unfavorable. He believed that there was only one reason for putting the museum at Porte Dorée: the generous hope of "affecting the popular spirit and imagination and, thus, bringing them to the colonial idea."[36] In Bourdaire's opinion, even these limited gains would be negated after the end of the Exposition when the population of the quarter would absent themselves from the museum and the Bois had reverted to a children's playground. Worse, since the museum was being located outside the intellectual, industrial, and commercial center of the city, the number of its visitors would quickly diminish. "Little by little, we will forget even its existence and it will take enormous blows on the *tam-tam* to render it alive and efficacious," he asserted.[37] A site on the fortifications in the 16th or 17th arrondissement would have been ideal, but the city and state hesitated to lose the proceeds of the sale of the land. Bourdaire proposed the Jardin d'Acclimation in the Bois de Boulogne as a possible solution. In his letter of December 9, 1927, he suggested that if it was impossible to abandon the Vincennes site, at least the museum might be located at the Jardin d'Acclimation.[38]

By contrast, Léandre Vaillat, architectural critic and columnist for the daily newspaper *Le Temps*, strongly championed the Vincennes site. In an article written in March 1928, he stated that he believed it was logical to avoid the center since it would be difficult to reconcile the classical monuments of central Paris and the exotic palaces of the Exposition. He maintained that Angkor Wat next to the Invalides would be disharmonious. The center was like a work of art, not to be touched, but the east needed new monuments because of the overdevelopment of western Paris. The Exposition could give the eastern districts transportation and other infrastructural improvements, but the most important legacy would be "the taste for colonization, which has until now been reserved for the richer or more cultivated classes." In Vaillat's view, the museum would become the Louvre of the people and Porte Dorée a magnificent entry like the Porte Dauphine to the west.[39]

Lyautey took up this optimistic line of reasoning in his public pronouncements on the Exposition. In a speech on July 23, 1928, to the Federation of French Industrialists and Traders, Lyautey answered some of the criticisms of the Vincennes site. Of the alternatives proposed, he stated, the Jardin d'Acclimation was too small and the Bois de Boulogne would be destroyed. He declared, however, that "just as when I created the port of Casablanca, we will march ahead anyway." The Exposition could have a happy influence from a social point of view and could even make the Bois de Vincennes fashionable. Better yet, it would be implanted in the downtrodden quarters of the East, thereby aiding the fight against Communism: "We have positioned ourselves in the middle of disinherited quarters, where a population lives that is scarcely accustomed to see a crowd. In that way it is interesting! The East of Paris, is it not a region . . . won by Communism? It is interesting, very interesting, extremely interesting to plant our colonial shoots amidst this popular world. . . . I am convinced that the Exposition can be a great factor of social peace in this area of Paris."[40] Despite his original dislike of the Vincennes site, Lyautey found a politically expedient discourse that justified the Exposition as an instrument of social reform.

Lyautey discovered another debate useful to his goal of establishing new colonial institutions: the call for the creation of an avenue de la Victoire in eastern Paris, projected to pass through the Porte de Vincennes to Meaux, "the gate to the battle fields of the Marne."[41] Advocates for this avenue simultaneously argued the need to celebrate France's victory in the Great War with an appropriate memorial and proselytized for the "Haussmannization" of the eastern arrondissements. The avenue de la Victoire was to be for the East what the avenue de la Grande Armée was for western Paris and was to give the east the monumental boulevard and accompanying grand edifices it had always lacked. Its proponents tied this project to the Colonial Exposition, which they believed might lead to creation of a new colonial district. According to Marius-Ary Leblond in *La Vie*, eastern Paris offered cheap land and the chance to decongest the center while simultaneously creating a Quartier colonial of the various colonial agencies then dispersed throughout Paris.[42] The Exposition was not by chance placed in the Bois de Vincennes, he declared, and, by the same logic, the Third Republic must give Paris its avenue de la Victoire and Ville coloniale.

In the same issue of *La Vie* Lyautey called for the "Haussmannization" of eastern Paris on the model of the urbanism he had encouraged in Morocco and elsewhere.[43] He wrote to Wladimir d'Ormesson, a poet and confidant, in the same terms:

As soon I applied myself to the plan of [the Exposition], Paris, and its suburbs, I was possessed with the desire to exercise myself much further than the Exposition itself, to the Haussmannization of the East of Paris, a modern and up to date Haussmannization. I have already used certain commissions to start it. But I have come into conflict with skepticism, objections, practical impossibilities! I feel the . . . absence of a directing authority and of a unity of direction. I know that I could do it if I were the boss, with Prost, Le Corbusier and several others. But there is no boss, I do not see how I could be the one and I regret it because I feel in good form and I see myself devoting my remaining years to this transformation of Paris, to this urban revolution.[44]

Lyautey saw the Exposition as a step toward the creation of other colonial institutions, such as a Maison des Colonies uniting various colonial agencies and application of his colonial experiences with urbanism to the Parisian context. Extension of the Metro to Porte Dorée and development of fortifications along the Exposition site was, for him, the potential impetus for a grand renovation of eastern Paris.

Zone-Bush

In an obituary for the obsolete fortifications, Jean-Jacques Brousson lampooned his fellow writers who went to the zone in search of titillating material:

There are those who minutely describe the exact "Fortifs" from their mahogany libraries. And there are the intrepid ones who go there as far as the *barrière* (city gate), equipped with a first class, round trip ticket for the Metro. One fall morning, they take a hundred steps on the exterior boulevards, inhale the suburban air, which seems to them charged with assassination and savagery, turn back toward the *barrières*, furnished with customs officers and cops, gulp down the cheap white wine of La Villette or Ménilmuche at a dirty bar. They return by Metro, burdened by documents, after an excursion of twenty-five

4.11 Children of the zone, c. 1935 (photo: Keystone)

minutes that must furnish them with some three hundred pages on the low life of Paris.[45]

The fortifications and zone were external to the cafés, arcades, theaters, music halls, and streets of popular Paris *intra muros.* Writers and artists who immortalized the "fortifs" and zone depicted them as the locale of picturesque settlements, occupied by people outside the economy and culture of Paris proper. The zone was the site of what was "other" to Paris, which did not physically or socially fit in the city (fig. 4.11).

In 1862 General Adolphe Thiers built the fortifications to protect the city from exterior attack, but the disastrous 1870 Prussian siege proved them obsolete.[46] After 1870, the fortifs and zone accumulated whatever was unwanted or displaced in Paris: people evicted from buildings in Haussmann's path, noxious or illegal industries such as ragpicking and tanneries, sports facilities, prostitution, gypsy encampments, and bars and cafes that escaped Parisian taxes by being outside the city limits. In its French definition, the word "zone" is synonymous with haphazard development, inferior or second-class housing, and run-down districts in general.[47] Its exoticism and marginality were celebrated in films, novels, journalistic accounts, and photographs by such notables as Eugène Atget, Colette, Apollinaire, and Blaise Cendrars, along with less famous figures such as poet Jean Ajalbert and painter Jean-Francois Raffaelli.[48]

In Leiris's taxonomy, the zone was an outdoor place permeated with a sacred character. He described this quality as "objects and places that awake in me that mixture of fear and attachment, that ambiguous attitude caused by the approach of something simultaneously attractive and dangerous, prestigious and outcast—that combination of respect, desire and terror that we take as the psychological sign of the sacred."[49] For him, the sacred evoked a world distinct from the ordinary. It did so by means of things from everyday life that allowed one to move into this other realm of the sacred, rather than through the officially sacred institutions of "religion, fatherland, morals."[50] The zone belonged to no one; it was a border between the city and the country and a place for executions. "Bush country" implies a wilder landscape farther removed from urban civilization. Conforming to a topography modeled on the principle, "The good in the center, evil on the periphery," Roger Caillois made the bush the site of the "impure forces that implement magic."[51]

The "ill-defined" zone was associated with haunting, magic, strangeness, and adventure, according to Leiris. Its very lack of definition provided the opportunity for unconventional activity since it was apart from the ordered world of houses and villages that oversees emotion and action. He found danger as well as the exotic there, personified by strangers (satyrs) who might, under false pretenses, take unsuspecting children into the bushes. The risk of violence menaced those who visited this "haunting" place where the magical, or an assassination, might happen might take place.

For this reason, the zone was a place apart, taboo, and marked by the supernatural and the sacred. For its delineation as the place of possibility and magic versus the village as the locus of reason and order, their separation was necessary, according to Leiris. At the end of his poem "Zone," Guillaume Apollinaire connected the zone with the primitivism fashionable between the wars:

> You walk toward Auteuil you want to walk home
> To sleep among your fetishes from Oceania and Guinea
> They are the Christs of another form and of another belief
> They are the inferior Christs of obscure hopes.[52]

The walk through the zone ended in sleep among another culture's totems that connect to the aspirations of the sleeper, to enigmatic or hidden desires. This mythology of the primitive entranced the avant-garde, as evinced by the extensive non-Western art collections held by Tristan Tzara, Louis Aragon, Pablo Picasso, and others.[53]

The primitivism of the zone was largely constructed out of descriptions of the people who lived and worked there, *zoniers* or *zonards*. Several types repeatedly feature in these characterizations: *chiffonier* (ragpicker), *Apache* (petty criminal or gang member), *poucier* (flea market merchant), *prostituée* (prostitute), and proprietor of a *jardin potager* (vegetable garden). These were the "other" Parisians who inhabited the "other" space of the zone. They were the lowest of the city's lower classes. During the 1920s and 1930s, according to Madeleine Fernandez, "the zonard was the scapegoat in the midst of the 'urban neo-proletariat'" in the suburbs.[54]

The history of this attitude can be traced to the nineteenth-century pathology of *les misérables*. The poorest of the poor, they represented the moral and physical degeneration of the lower classes, according to reformers of mid-nineteenth-century France.[55] Zonards, as part of the miserable classes, formed the marginalized caste of the working class. Their lives and practices were as fascinating and as exotic to Parisians as the *tam-tam* dances of west Africa, and their life in the zone was depicted as if it occurred in a distant, exotic space. In 1854, for example, Alexandre Privat-d'Anglemont described the Villa des Chiffoniers as "farther than Japan, more unknown than the interior of Africa, in a quarter where no one has passed." This city "no more resembles the other Paris than Canton resembles Copenhagen." It was the "capital of misery lost in the middle of the country of luxury." The house of one woman, who burned peat to make charcoal for footwarmers of the Salpetrière hospital, had an insupportable atmosphere, more like an oven than a house, next to which "the climate of Senegal must be an eternal spring."[56]

André Warnod's paean to the fortifications, *Les Fortifs, promenades sur les anciennes fortifications et la zone*, written as the city demolished the fortifications, was another mythical account of life in the zone. With atmospheric illustrations by Serge-Henri Moreau, his book documented the disappearing life of the zoniers (fig. 4.12). In one section, he described a part of Saint-Ouen called Le Touzet or Morocco, "as the natives have nicknamed this lugubrious passage."

> The detritus and filth invade everything, here is a pile of chicken carcasses, further a heap of old Camembert boxes, elsewhere a small mound of rags; the same filth covers the walls, the pavement of the streets, and all that lives in this empire. The humanity that swarms in the refuse seems to form a body with it. Clothed in rags, unkempt women desperately excavate the heap to separate the wood from the iron, the wool from the silk, the bone from the paper; their arms are covered with wounds badly dressed by dirty linen, their red and weeping eyes tell of the grinding dangers of this corruption . . . but what is unimaginable is the filth that covers their skin, a black filth that scars their faces, blackens their cheeks and makes their eyes and mouth appear white.[57]

4.12 "Complement de romanichels, Porte de Vincennes" by Serge-Henri Moreau (from Warnod)

The filth of "Morocco" transformed the zonards into black natives, degrading them by comparison with "white" Parisians. Warnod contrasted this swarming humanity with Madame Pompadour and her circle, who had their chateaus on that very site. The vast, flat terrain on which ragpickers sorted garbage was once the home of the Dukes of Rohan and Nevers and was the place where Louis XVIII presented Talleyrand with the preface to the constitutional charter. For Warnod, the past glories of Saint-Ouen provided evidence of the devolved and primitive state of the ragpickers, "noble savages" of the zone.

The reference to Le Touzet as Morocco was not a neutral reference to an exotic locale, but one redolent of the violence of the Rif War, still raging when Warnod wrote *Les Fortifs* in 1926.[58] The allusion pointed to zonards' backwardness and estrangement from Parisian life. It also referred to the politics of "red" Paris, which was potentially capable of erupting into revolt. In a famous passage, Warnod documented the conditions in La Cité Blanchard, another chiffonier settlement: "The houses are constructed in a hundred diverse fashions, cabins made of everything and nothing, ends of wood and ends of iron with roofs in tarpaper or in corrugated tin, a chimney pierces a roof like a jack-in-a-box. Here is a small castle surrounded by a garden and there a sunflower, a magnificent golden sun, that tops the roof of the house where the gardener sleeps."[59] Lack of substantial construction, running water, and sewers made the zone both a throwback to deleterious conditions in the Parisian *ilôts insalubres* and a parallel to primitive conditions in the colonies. As we have seen, the analogy between natives of the zone and of the colonies had occurred to Lyautey, who used it as a rationale for locating the Exposition in eastern Paris.

The final piece in Warnod's book described the destruction of small garden plots (jardins potagers) on an unnamed part of the zone. Warnod interviewed an old man who, "broken-hearted," watched the devastation of his garden. He had had a great deal of trouble making the soil yield anything, he said, but he had succeeded in the end, in raising cabbages, lettuce, and potatoes. The vegetables were not the main reason for his affection for the plot and for his desolation at not having another like it, as he explained: "For someone who has the habit of having his garden, this will be hard. It was an occupation and on Sundays we came here as a family; I had constructed a small cabin of planks, we put the beer to cool in a pail of water, we believed ourselves proprietors!"[60] As compensation for loss of the garden, the city gave the man twenty-five francs for the plants, but nothing for the land since he had occupied it illegally and had only a provisional right to its use.

The zone was the site for such lower-class occupations and upper-crust distractions of the Auteuil race course. It was the site of sports facilities such as stadiums and velodromes many of which are still located in the area. Families that had no garden plot would go to the zone for picnics and a stroll. Although the fortifs had a dangerous reputation among the bourgeoisie, it was a favorite spot for taking *nature à bon marché* ("nature on the cheap") on Sundays. As the space of refuge and leisure for poor Parisians, the zone and fortifs served as the equivalent of the countryside for those who could not afford a train ticket to the outer suburbs. "Three sous for the tramway, it's nothing!" On any given sunny Sunday, there were food stands, street musicians, strolling singers, games, balloon sellers, and some 10,000 Parisians eating, drinking, and promenading.[61]

After the fortifications became obsolete, the zone was also the site of political and legal battles over its appropriation and use. The 1919 law declassifying the fortifications as a military installation ceded the land to the city of Paris, but did not resolve the question of expropriating property held by the zoniers. As early as 1894 the zoniers had formed a union (*La Ligue de défense des zoniers de Paris*) to protect their rights under the declassification laws.[62] Although the city could, by right, demolish the fortifications, claim the land, and sell it to private developers or the municipal housing bureau, this legal statute did not stop its bitter struggle with the zoniers over compensation for their illegal constructions.[63] The difficulty lay in the military corps of engineers' practice of selling parcels of land in the zone with authorization to build temporary structures, not permanent buildings. The zoniers knew that they had no right to build such constructions, but in light of the laxity of enforcement, many of them constructed permanently (*en dur*).[64]

The city faced the problem of at least 5,000 proprietors in the zone whom it had to pay for their property. The city enacted three decrees, in 1925, 1929, and 1930, to clarify legal mechanisms for acquiring the zone from zoniers. These measures allowed proprietors and renters to stay on the zone if they conformed to surrounding communities' urban plans, although most towns had no such plans. The 1930 decree prolonged the acquisition process until 1965 and legalized constructions built before 1919. The cost of expropriations slowed the process, and after 1930 the economic crisis further impoverished the municipal budget because the land could not be sold for profit. Under the Vichy regime, the state requisitioned the zone for the city in 1940 and authorized demolition of all structures under the pretext of security and health risks (fig. 4.13). Zone residents then became renters of city property, whether or not they had built the structures. The Vichy government had largely cleared the zone by the Liberation, although some edifices survived until the 1970s.[65]

By the late 1920s the rate of land acquisition had slowed dramatically because of high costs and political considerations that made it impossible to take land in some districts. This problem affected the Colonial Exposition because the *Paris université club* (PUC) had built an illegal sports stadium near bastion 5, just south of Porte Dorée (fig. 4.14). In 1922, the city of Paris granted the PUC (the athletic branch of the *Association générale des étudiants et étudiantes de Paris*) permission to use part of the fortifications at Porte Dorée for sports fields and a temporary sports facility. The club built a permanent and very expensive (over 2 million francs) stadium in 1924, despite protests of the city administration. After the stadium was

4.13 Zone near Porte Dorée with the Musée des Colonies in the background, 1942 (Bibliothèque Historique de la Ville de Paris, Paris)

built, the club was unable to pay construction bills and fell into bankruptcy. To clear the site for the Exposition, the 1924 convention between the city and state stipulated the stadium's removal and its transfer, at the expense of the Exposition, to another part of the zone. It was not rebuilt due to difficulties finding an open plot of land that could be wrested from the zoniers. The PUC eventually evacuated the stadium in November 1929 and the city demolished it in spring 1930, after a long series of stalling maneuvers by the court-appointed administrator of the PUC, including a petition to open a dog track in the stadium.[66]

The only other obstacles on the Exposition site were some small *jardins potagers* on the fortifications north of Porte Dorée. In February 1928 the Exposition's operations administration posted signs at the gardens: "The International Colonial Exposition informs the occupants of

4.14 Aerial view of the Colonial Exposition site, c. 1928 (Archives d'Outre-Mer, Aix-en-Provence)

the gardens on the fortifications between Avenue Daumesnil and the Vincennes railway that it will soon occupy all or part of these gardens. It denies all responsibility regarding the preparatory work or plantings rendered useless by this fact."[67] The sad story of the *jardins potagers* continued at every such instance of expropriation, effacing the marginal history and culture of the zoniers in the name of progress. In its place rose the invented history of France's colonial empire as represented at the Colonial Exposition.

Park-Bois de Vincennes

The park was the ordered world where, in Leiris's ethnography, "notices forbidding you to walk on the grass, though signs of taboo, could only endow them with a sacred grown cold." The park belonged to civilization as a locale where everything was in its place, but Leiris implied that it had once contained a sacred quality marked by signs forbidding access to the grass. The zone, by contrast, contained the lively, potent taboo of supernatural places set apart and uncontrolled by modern civilization's penchant for the organized, the raked, and the planned. The park was domesticated nature. It was wholly artificial, down to its concrete rocks and mountains, but it could evoke nature as opposed to civilization. In *Paysan de Paris*, for example, Louis Aragon celebrated the wild appeal of the Buttes Chaumont as "this great oasis in a popular district, a shady zone where the prevailing atmosphere is distinctly murderous."[68]

The Bois de Vincennes had far less prestige than the Bois de Boulogne, its opposite in fashionable western Paris. According to a 1921 guide, it was "interesting only for its chateau and its forest."[69] Its origins date to the early kings of France, who hunted there. In 1162 Louis VII built a hunting lodge in Vincennes, which his son, Philippe Auguste, later enlarged at the same time that he enclosed the Bois with a fortified wall. Philip VI of Valois began the present château, to which his grandson Charles V added residential and reception rooms. Louis XI added the residential portion and

Louis XIII enlarged it. In 1560, Catherine de Medici laid the foundations of the Pavillons du Roi and de la Reine, which were finished in 1614. Under Mazarin's direction, Levau considerably altered the château. Louis XIV made further alterations to the château, but in 1668 he removed the court to Versailles and deserted Vincennes. Louis XV replanted the Bois in 1731 and converted it into a park for the use of Parisian citizens.[70]

In 1852 Emperor Napoleon III gave the Bois de Vincennes as a grand public park to the faubourg Saint-Antoine and the eastern districts of Paris to replicate what he had accomplished in the Bois de Boulogne. The same team that realized the Bois de Boulogne—Baron Haussmann, Jean-Claude-Adolphe Alphand, Gabriel Davioud, and horticulturist Barillet-Dechamps—enacted the plan for Vincennes. Haussmann declared that the park was to create, for the working classes of eastern Paris, "a promenade equivalent to that given to the rich and elegant quarters in the west of our capital."[71]

In this conversion the general area of the Bois de Vincennes was enlarged from 875 to 900 hectares by the addition of the vast plain stretching to Saint-Mandé, Charenton, and the fortifications. Alphand restored what the military left of the rectangular paths and plantings created under Louis XV and transformed the lawns and military grounds into an English park crossed by curving paths. He supplied water to the plain to create lakes and fountains with appropriate architectural embellishments (kiosks, chalets, rustic bridges, and a rotunda), and massed trees throughout the forest. He pursued these operations, funded by public money, for two years (1858–1860), when the Bois was ceded to Paris.[72]

By 1921 the Bois contained 2,308 acres of land and was the largest Parisian parks, divided by military maneuver grounds and a race course. The Jardin d'horticulture et d'arboriculture, a municipal and departmental school of horticulture, was located in the western part of the Bois, near the Porte de Picpus. The thirty-acre Lac Daumesnil had two islands—the Ile de Reuilly and the Ile de Bercy—that were connected to the bank by

suspension bridges. A cafe with a bandstand and various amusements occupied part of the Ile de Reuilly. A little Doric temple by Davioud above
a grotto stood near the bridge. On the Ile de Bercy the Pavillon des forêts
from the Exhibition of 1889 contained the Museum of Forestry.[73]

In the view of the Exposition's planners, this picturesque landscape
acted well as a public park, but the trees and lawns of the Ile de France did
not harmonize with the savage beauty of Angkor Wat or the *tata* of West
Africa. They augmented the forest with more appropriate plantings of palms
and tropical flowers in an attempt to create more exotic scenery, with particular attention to the entrances. To this end, gardeners planted 90 large palms
at the Porte d'Honneur and along the Avenue des Colonies Françaises, 1,200
agaves, cacti, Mimosa trees, orange trees, yuccas, and coconut palms[74] (fig.
4.15). Thus supplemented, the Bois de Vincennes provided a suitably ver-
dant setting for the pavilions, but its picturesque planning posed difficulties
for Tournaire. The grand axes normally part of the plans could not be effected in Alphand's version of an English landscape park. As John Dixon
Hunt notes, the "extravagant curvilinear landscape" of the Bois de Boulogne
and the Bois de Vincennes was "totally at odds with the straight lines of
Haussmann's new city avenues," as it was with the Beaux-Arts axes that Tournaire sought to insert into the plan.[75] In this sense, the Bois was consistent
with Leiris's ethnography of the margins as a picturesque realm opposed to
the rectilinear city and representative of a more taboo realm.

MARGINALITY DOUBLED

Situating the Exposition on the fortifications and Bois de Vincennes
served the city's purposes by allowing it to expropriate bastions 4, 5, 6,
and 7 and to demolish the PUC stadium and the gardens on the zone. The
improvements made at Porte Dorée, which was enlarged to 40 meters, and
the permanent Musée de Colonies created a new monumental ensemble
that embellished eastern Paris. The Metro extension to Porte de Charenton, widening of avenue Daumesnil and of boulevards Carnot,

4.15 Palms at Porte d'Honneur (from Trillat)

4.16 View of Porte Dorée, 1991 (photo: author)

Poniatowski, and Soult, and new sewer and water lines increased the value of the expropriated land on the zone and furthered the city's plans for its development. Tramway and bus service was ameliorated to the Vincennes area. Renewed paths and lawns improved the Bois.

Besides these limited improvements, however, the Exposition left few permanent traces. Lyautey never realized his grand vision for the renewal of the poor, Communist quarters of the east. Instead, the city developed the fortifications and zone as *habitations à bon marché* (HBM, middle-class housing) units of the same mediocre design as the rest of the fortifs (fig. 4.16). Le Corbusier referred to the former fortifications as *trente kilomètres de honte* ("thirty kilometers of shame") because of the indifferently designed housing.[76] The opportunity for a radical reorganization of the Porte Dorée-Porte de Charenton area or creation of a model urban renewal project in the form of a Cité Coloniale was lost, to the chagrin of Lyautey and others committed to the renovation of Paris.

In August 1931 Léandre Vaillat wrote a bitter article in *Le Temps* in which he reviewed the progress made as a result of the Exposition. He attacked the "mediocre preamble" in the renovated Avenue Daumesnil-Porte Dorée ensemble and the lack of substantial urbanistic results from this "brilliant if ephemeral manifestation of colonial propaganda."[77] Although the Exposition had made it possible to plan monumental avenues and squares for the east, Vaillat asserted that Marshall Lyautey was discouraged from attempting to reform the capital, "having measured the distance that separates modern Morocco from old Paris, or, more exactly, from a old-fashioned Paris." The complete absence of a coherent doctrine that could guide the organization of the capital confirmed his skepticism.[78]

Albert Laprade also referred to Lyautey's bitterness over his failure to translate the Exposition into a permanent colonial institution and criticized the poor planning of Porte Dorée and the Musée des Colonies. In an article in *La Cité moderne,* Laprade noted that the Exposition had offered three areas of interest to the modern city. First, it left a legacy to Paris: amelioration of the Métro, tramways, and lighting, a monumental square at the Bois de Vincennes, and the Musée des colonies. Second, it spurred interest in colonial urbanism and its accomplishments. Last, it provided a purely architectural interest in the comparison of specimens of exotic buildings.[79]

Laprade emphasized that the first possibility had not been realized because the Exposition's benefits to Paris were too few and because even Marshall Lyautey, accustomed to thinking big, had been restrained from realizing a grander plan. Laprade quoted Henri Sellier, whose successes in Suresnes gave a model for progressive urban renewal: "among us, it is necessary to employ a hundred times the effort to achieve a single result."[80] The second legacy might provide a valuable lesson to Parisians who talked a great deal but realized little of substance in urbanism. Whereas the example of Casablanca—a frightful village transformed into a magnificent city—might be salutary for Parisians, Porte Dorée itself displayed nothing praiseworthy. "One remains stupefied, in arriving at Vincennes, to see a superb esplanade begun and a little further a monumental edifice in stone (the Museum of the Colonies) positioned completely askew and outside the composition."[81]

The Exposition did not, therefore, successfully transplant the lesson of colonial urbanism to the Bois de Vincennes and these disadvantaged neighborhoods. The city's agenda for this site did not accommodate grand, Haussmannian visions on the scale of the redevelopment of Casablanca. Rather, the strategy used the Exposition for opportunistic appropriation of a limited terrain, satisfaction of the need for more middle-class housing, and creation of a slightly improved entrance to the Bois de Vincennes. One of the legacies of French colonial urbanism, according to Paul Rabinow, has been an impulse to evade democratic political structures in favor of legislative and administrative planning autonomy. He traced this inclination to French urbanists' frustration when they attempted to apply their colonies-tested urbanism to France and were thwarted by the participatory politics and public debate of Third Republic democracy.[82] Lyautey's sense of impotence and his inability to use the Exposition to reform the "red" quarters of eastern Paris through urbanism based on colonial models is, then, exemplary of colonists' experience at home.

As a result of its isolation from the city, the Exposition's site planning further mitigated against a radical transformation of eastern Paris. One of the consequences of Lyautey's constant agitation for more land was that the final configuration allowed for complete enclosure of its periphery. The only gap in this unified boundary was avenue Daumesnil, which penetrated the Porte d'Honneur and necessitated construction of an overpass link between the Section Métropolitaine and Cité des Informations. The Exposition was like a satellite to Paris that depended on the city, but kept its distance, effectively segregating the two in the manner of French urbanism in the colonies.

Along with this isolation, the placement of the Section Métropolitaine and Cité des Informations on the boundary tended to diffuse potential contrast between Parisian apartment houses and the Angkor Wat
temple, for example. From the tops of the tallest pavilions, such as the
West French Africa tower, a visitor could gain a view incorporating the
"surreal" juxtaposition of exotic pavilions with Parisian buildings, but
these viewpoints were rare (fig. 4.17). Within the precincts, however, Paris
was invisible and the consistent, if eclectic, march of colonial pavilions
surrounded the visitor. The strange internal juxtapositions of colonial
pavilions seem to have had very little impact on the average visitor.

We can read the Colonial Exposition as an attempt to create a whole
out of disparate fragments, as a collage, but it was not legible as such to
contemporary observers. They saw the difference between the pavilions as
representative of the diversity of the French colonial empire, not as a disjunction in the representational systems of the Exposition. Raymond
Cogniat recognized that the juxtaposition of the different colonies' pavilions posed a problem to chief architect Tournaire, but he felt that sepa-
rating the pavilions with vegetation sufficed to solve the dilemma.[83] The
pavilions were read as singular entities in and of themselves, not as elements in a larger composition, and the juxtaposition to Paris was short-
circuited by the wall they created along the fortifications zone.

The Exposition took colonized people and things out of their contexts and placed them into a new, constructed environment that was
carefully quarantined from Paris. The organizers resisted collage's
defamiliarization effect in favor of a spurious authenticity based on a hermetic, internalized logic of display. The exhibition of colonial peoples
and products reinforced the myths of colonialism, rather than calling
them into question by comparison with Paris. Leiris's ethnographic taxonomy denoted the layered marginality of the site, but this history and
these associations were not registered at the Exposition. In a translation
of French colonial urbanism to Paris, the fair and the metropolitan city

4.17 View of the Exposition from the Angkor pavilion (from Construction moderne, Aug. 16, 1931, 727)

were kept distinct. Lyautey's failure to "Haussmannize" eastern Paris was consistent with the segregationist logic of colonial urbanism, not with his desire to transform these districts. He at once wanted to create an internally coherent colonial environment and to renovate eastern Paris as he had done in Casablanca and Rabat. As long as the segregationist tactics of colonial planning determined the Exposition's relationship to Paris, he could have no impact on the city. This was a paradoxical program, one that could not be resolved by the Exposition plan.

The relationship of fair to city was equivalent to a Cubist collage in which, according to Marjorie Perloff, "the introjected fragment—say, the newspaper page or the violin *f*—retains its alterity even as that alterity is subordinated to the compositional arrangement of the whole."[84] The fragment introjected into the Bois de Vincennes retained and reinforced the alterity of the representations of the colonies by detaching them from metropolitan space. James Clifford's theory of collage posits a "Surrealist moment" in ethnography when "the possibility of comparison exists in unmediated tension with sheer incongruity," which serves to make "newly incomprehensible" the ethnographer's own culture.[85] In this sense, the Exposition was not a Surrealist moment: its purpose, and the basis for its vast popular success, was generation of a convincing colonial domain conceived by the colonizer. This goal depended on radical distinction of colonies from the *Métropole*. Neither the zoniers nor the impoverished workers of "red" Paris figured in the new world that Lyautey envisaged for France and her empire, just as colonized natives could participate in the Exposition only as servile accessories to its pavilions.

THE CIVILIZING MISSION
OF ARCHITECTURE

THE COLONIAL EXPOSITION IS PRESENTED TO US AS AN EXPOSITION OF COMPARATIVE ARCHITECTURE. THE CONSTRUCTIONS GROUPED IN ITS COMPOUND ARE SOMETIMES FAITHFUL TRANSLATIONS OF INDIGENOUS EDIFICES EXECUTED IN STUCCO, SOMETIMES EVOCATIONS, SOMETIMES VARIATIONS EXECUTED ON A COLONIAL THEME. . . . THE TRUE MISSION OF THE ARCHITECTS WAS TO OFFER TO US A PRECISE IMAGE OF THE STATES OF ART AND CONSTRUCTION IN EACH COLONY.

—MARCEL ZAHAR[1]

5.1   Algerian pavilion, 1900 Universal Exposition, Paris (Resource Collections of the Getty Research Institute, Los Angeles)

Architecture at the Colonial Exposition had numerous, even contradictory purposes. Maréchal Lyautey and his colleagues envisioned a grand exhibit of the *mission civilisatrice*, the specifically French imperative to colonize and civilize less advanced countries. *La plus grande France*, the France of 100 million inhabitants, required an architectural and artistic expression different from that of previous expositions. Colonial sections in 1878, 1889, and 1900 expositions established exotic conventions for pavilions, decorative programs, entertainment sections, landscaping, exhibits, and native displays[2] (fig. 5.1). The eclecticism and carnival atmosphere of those sections were rejected by Lyautey's group, who sought instead to promote authenticity of form and detail in the pavilions and a serious, if entertaining, significance in the exhibits.

5.2 Ulysse Moussali, Syria and Lebanon pavilion (from L'Illustration, special issue [July 1931], n.p.)

The architectural representation had another purpose: to exemplify the relative primitivism and degeneracy of the colonized peoples and to reinforce "ranks, hierarchies, and ancient places," in Lyautey's words, into which people and things were organized under French colonialism (fig. 5.2). To this aim, the architects and organizers emphasized the authenticity of the colonial pavilions and their fidelity to native architecture in general form and detail. The pavilions emphasized the strangeness and primitiveness of native cultures to make more apparent their need for colonization by the superior French civilization.

This constituted one half of the mission. Architecture was also responsible for housing exhibitions on the "benefits" of colonization, good works that resulted from France's benevolent intervention into evolution's progress. Interiors of the pavilions contained evidence of the positive influence brought to the colonies by the French. The difficulty reconciling these two tasks lay in their mutually exclusive character, a contradiction at the heart of colonialism: colonized peoples had to be proved barbarous to justify their colonization, but the *mission civilisatrice* required that they be raised above savagery. If they acquired too much civilization and became truly assimilated to France, colonization could no longer be defended, having fulfilled its mission. The ways in which the architects of the pavilions negotiated this contradiction is the subject of this chapter.

FRENCH HUMAN SCIENCES, COLONIAL POLICY, AND ARCHITECTURE

The form of the pavilions derived from the influence of French social science, colonial policy, and long-established stereotypes of various colonized peoples. Architecture was one of the gauges by which French social scientists judged a society's evolutionary status. Physical signs of racial difference—in body, technology, and material culture—between whites and other races formed the basis of French ethnology and anthropolgy until the 1930s. The Colonial Exposition actualized the racist biologism of French social science, which viewed physical differences as primary means of distinguishing races and the cause of their divergent civilizations.[3] From exclusive concern with physical anthropology, French social science shifted to the study of cultures and ethnography in the twentieth century. The physical manifestations of a society's evolutionary level formed a central subject for French sociology, geography, ethnography, and other human sciences. As a prominent element of material culture, architecture constituted essential evidence of a society's degree of civilization and its position on the evolutionary hierarchy. French colonial policy and practice was predicated on principles of scientific racism and the social sciences that buttressed it, which were defined by their usefulness to colonialism. George Stocking maintained that after World War I, when European colonial power was secure, "what was required was no longer simply the justification of dominance in terms of difference, but the more detailed knowledge of functioning societies that would facilitate and maintain an economical and trouble-free colonial administration—with a stress on the values of traditional native culture or social organization serving as a counterweight to urbanizing progressive natives who identified too closely with European models of equality and democracy."[4]

Following the hypotheses of scientific, racist social science, the pavilions incarnated the precise evolutionary standing of each colony, thereby placing their people within the French colonial order. Marcel Olivier, one of the Exposition's commissioners, described the role of architecture as an instantiation of colonialism's principles: "Colonization is legitimate. It is beneficial. These are the truths that, for several more months, are inscribed on the walls of the pavilions at Vincennes."[5] The pavilions were meant to be "read" as the record of the artistic achievements of each indigenous culture, ranked according to European standards. Architecture, as a complex response to the geographic and cultural environment, served as one of the chief indicators of the "advancement" of a society, a kind of precis of evolutionary development (fig. 5.3).

Architecture critic Marcel Zahar explained how architecture revealed "essential facts" about the civilizations on exhibit:

The house is one of the essential facts of human geography.

—(Jean Brunhes)

These wall combinations, these roof profiles, these portals, window and column outlines, express in architectonic equivalents the aspirations of a people, their intimate mentality, their religious beliefs, their faculties of adaptation and evolution, their strength of ambition . . . The plans of edifices and the plans of villages represent, like diagrams, the laws that regulate the communal life of peoples and the nature of climates. The materials employed inform us about the riches of the

5.3   Charles A. Wulfleff, Somalia pavilion (from Trillat)

earth; perfection of techniques is a sign indicating the degree of in-
genuousness and intelligence of the workers and artisans; the wall
cladding, the decorations attest to the progress of industry and art.
Architecture presents the synthesis of the potential of a race and the
resources of a region.[6]

In this statement, Zahar explicated the basic premises of human geography and their application to the analysis of architectural form. The
pavilions of the Colonial Exposition were, in this theory, physical demonstrations of each colony's native culture. In these terms, the Exposition
was the public, architectural equivalent of Jean Brunhes's collection at the
Archives de la Planète as a record of the world.

Of the various disciplines (ethnography, sociology, anthropology,
geography, and so on) that recorded and classified differences between
Europe and the rest of the world, human geography gave architecture the
most central role in determining evolutionary hierarchies. Paul Vidal de
la Blache, the leading French geographer, defined geography as the scientific study of places and human geography as the study of humans within
those places.[7] Brunhes, Vidal's disciple, gave a slightly different formulation: "The object of human geography is the study of the relationships
between human activity and the phenomena of physical geography."[8]
According to Vidal's theory, each society (or civilization, in his terms) developed through the interaction of the racial characteristics of its people
and their response to their *milieu* ("environment").[9] Every civilization has
produced a characteristic adaptation to its physical environment, manifested in its social forms or *genres de vie* ("modes of life"): "The equipment
that the Krighiz devised to meet the requirements of his unsettled life—
the shape of his tent and the cut of his clothes—is a perfectly integrated
whole, in which everything has its place, the materialization of a mode of
life."[10] For human geographers, architecture was a valuable indicator of
the interaction of humans with their milieu, visible in their *genres de vie*, and

of the comparative evolution of a given human group. Milieu, as defined by Vidal, included contact with other societies as well as geographic features of a society's environment. The most fruitful milieu provided its occupants frequent contact with other peoples, life in a temperate climate, and natural resources with which to develop technology and agriculture at a high level.

The Mediterranean basin met these criteria most completely, in Vidal's view. He placed the world's societies in an evolutionary order, with European, Mediterranean civilization at the pinnacle. In addition to climate, geography, and contact with other groups, the "essential racial quality" of a people could influence its development; some people were more "vital" than others and, therefore, progressed further. Europe exhibited almost continuous development because of the consonance of all these requirements. Vidal maintained that other societies' intellectual and cultural development were retarded or arrested by the limitations inherent in their race, by physical isolation from other societies, or by lack of natural resources or a beneficial climate in their milieu: "The African village whose site may be changed by a mere accident, and the European village whose history is traceable for thousands of years, is as widely different as the city of antiquity and the immense metropolis of today. The distance is that between a rudimentary and an advanced stage of civilisation."[11] African civilizations had a lower level of progress than certain Asian peoples, who attained a high level of civilization before lapsing into the decadence and degeneracy produced by isolation from new cultural influences and stimuli. He stated, "Western Europe has had an almost continuous development. This has not been the case in Northern Africa nor in Asia bordering the zone of desert and steppe. . . . Fully half the countries on earth today have learned nothing for thousands of years."[12] This reiterated Count Gobineau's contention that history was generated exclusively by the white race and by its "fertile marriage" with other races, whereas black peoples remained "immersed in a profound inertia."[13]

These theories posed a problem for French colonization: how best to perform the uplifting of backward races? The manner in which this work could be effected bore directly on the formulation of French colonial policy and its manifestation in colonial architecture and urbanism. French colonial policy affirmed the principle of a *mission civilisatrice,* a mentality that its colonial practice never fully repudiated despite alterations in official colonial policy. The mission had its origins in the ideology of the French Revolution: the perfectibility of man and the superiority of French culture were its precepts. Alice Conklin wrote a detailed analysis of the history of the mission and its application in French West Africa, in which she linked the phrase with the concept of civilization itself. According to Conklin, French notions of civilization were intimately connected with republican ideas of personal and political mastery, which were revived and extended under the Third Republic. On the basis of republican ideals, the French understood their role in the world as to civilize indigenous peoples of the colonies (who were primitive but capable of progress) and to maintain their own civilized, democratic institutions and culture.[14]

Nineteenth-century colonial policy of assimilation was derived from these republican ideologies and from the French conviction of their inherent cultural superiority. Assimilation was also based on the supposition that colonized peoples would only benefit by adopting French civilization and jettisoning their own. As Raymond Betts notes, assimilation policy aimed at the union of France and her colonies, such that each possession was to "become an integral if noncontiguous, part of the mother country, with its society and population made over—to whatever extent possible— in her image."[15] Under this policy, a single legislative body, the *Parlement,* was promulgated for both the *Métropole* and the colonies. France and her colonies were conceived as a united country, ruled under the same flag, with one language, despite differences in origins of its disparate peoples.[16]

The practical consequences of assimilation can be seen in Algeria, which was colonized in 1830 as one of France's first nineteenth-century

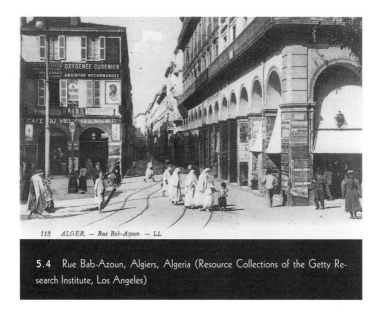

5.4 Rue Bab-Azoun, Algiers, Algeria (Resource Collections of the Getty Research Institute, Los Angeles)

acquisitions. During the "pacification" or military subjugation of the country in the 1830s and 1840s, Maréchal Thomas Bugeaud practiced *razzia,* the military destruction of people, property, and land in order to control territory.[17] His native policy established the general method of colonization in Algeria and the basis for assimilating the country into France. David Prochaska, in his account of French colonialism in Bône, summarized the early process. First the French occupied the buildings in Bône; second, they appropriated the land on the plain outside the city; third, they took over the cork oak forests; fourth, they mined the area for minerals; and fifth, they displaced the Algerians and peopled Bône with Europeans.[18] Under this assimilation policy, indigenous Algerian cities and towns were destroyed and rebuilt in French styles, French was taught in schools established by French authorities, and a French government was installed with the authority of a French province[19] (fig. 5.4).

Association

At the turn of the century, new French colonial policies emerged from the experiences of previous colonial administrations, from social Darwinian theories of racial evolution, and from examples of British and Dutch native policies.[20] The practice of assimilation was not entirely abandoned, but it remained the implicit agenda of French colonization and was pursued most vigorously in colonies where its techniques were already established. Government and cultural structures established under the assimilationist regime endured in Algeria, Senegal, and other "old" colonies.[21]

The Colonial Exposition displayed a different trend in colonial theory and policy, that of association between France and her colonies. By the turn of the century, the experience of several decades of colonization, new theories of nationality, and new tendencies in French politics worked to undermine faith in assimilation's potential success. By contrast with eighteenth-century optimism about colonialism's efficacy in transmuting native populations, twentieth-century theorists became less sanguine regarding the possibility of metamorphosing *indigènes* into French citizens. In addition, British "indirect rule," by which native elites administered British colonial policy, was greatly admired by advocates such as Jules Harmand and Paul Leroy-Beaulieu and served as a model for French colonial governance.[22] Darwin's and Spencer's theories of evolution served as the basis for relativistic concepts of race and social structure that determined more rigid relations between civilizations. Dr. Georges Papillault's "scientific laws" of the races and the theories of Alfred Fouillée exemplified this evolutionary thinking.

Fouillée wrote treatises on evolution as applied to education, nationality, and social structure that were representative of social Darwinism in France.[23] Although a staunch republican, he did not believe that all nations and races were equal and found proof of this inequality in the principles of evolution. Hereditary ethnic attributes of the races were the foundation of his theory of social evolution and he believed that they were modifiable, but only congruent with the sluggish pace of evolution. Differences among white, black, and yellow races were therefore relatively immutable because of evolution's slow working. As he put it, races were like runners on the "field of civilization" with those already in front (European white race) able to run proportionally faster and those already behind (black and yellow races) falling farther and farther to the rear. Only two methods of modifying the "inferior races" existed: education and cross-breeding with "superior races."[24]

According to Fouillée, the processes of selection and heredity, which have operated over immense stretches of time to differentiate the races, circumscribed a civilization's degree of evolution. This difference was precisely what could not be overcome in the sprint among the races: "We have seen that the inferior races and the superior races have each acquired quite different qualities and tendencies because of their evolution at different rates. . . . For the children of the inferior races, the work of centuries cannot be replaced by a simple stimulus of some years."[25] In a few years, education could not give the inferior races the superior intelligence (measured by brain capacity) and civilization (gauged by technological and artistic accomplishment) attained by the white race.[26]

The same evolutionary conundrum undermined cross-breeding as a means of uplifting black and yellow races, according to Fouillée: the fixity of racial characteristics multiplied by the "law of regression" caused the worst aspects of the two dissimilar races to predominate in their mixed progeny. On the other hand, the positive effect of education would be to raise the average from which the "inferior races" started their slow ascent toward civilization: "If heredity tends to restore the average equilibrium, education can raise the point of equilibrium. . . . If heredity is the great force of conservation, ideas are the great force of progress."[27] Since the "inferior races," could not be significantly improved, Fouillée believed that it was the responsibility of the white race to see that civilization's forward motion was not retarded by rising black and yellow populations. The intellectual elite of the white race, who formed the basis for its superiority over all other races, would have the edge in scientific invention, which would ensure its ascendancy.[28]

The logical conclusion of this theory as applied to colonial policy was that assimilation could not work, that the African could never truly become a Frenchman. If indigenous societies had their own organic structure, how could French civilization succeed in imposing its character on them? Furthermore, this result should not be sought when it might endanger the preeminence of "civilized" nations. The "natural aristocracy" that Fouillée saw in the white race *should*, according to exigencies of evolution, maintain its predominant position, even while educating lesser races. In response to these new theories of race and evolution, along with negative results from assimilationist policy in the colonies, the French embraced the new native policy of association. Strict physical, political, and cultural segregation of natives from the French grounded this policy. The world of colonial association was predicated on the precise and subtle differentiation of peoples, societies, and cultures into race-based hierarchies.

Albert Sarraut, a prominent advocate of association and former Minister of the Colonies, summarized the relation of the colonies to France as that of pupils to their teacher: "Instead of adapting all our protégés by force to the conditions of the Metropole, according to the old assimilationist error, it must be understood that, under our tutelage, their evolution should be pursued in keeping with their civilization, their traditions, their milieu, their social life, their secular institutions."[29] Sarraut indicated that, for example, indigenous policy could be more "educative" in Indochina and Madagascar, because more "civilized" natives inhabited those colonies, whereas French colonial policy must be more "medical and alimentary" in equatorial Africa because the natives in this colony were less intelligent.[30] Papillault codified the application of his racial theories to French *politique indigène* in the following outline:

1) North Africa, Syria, etc. are peopled by *white races* of a very evolved condition. Their progressive assimilation to French civilization is possible and desirable; 2) The Negroids of Africa and of the Pacific can be, in a certain degree, educated, not assimilated; 3) The Malagasy natives are Negroid cross-breeds [*métis*]. They can be educated, not assimilated; 4) The Indochinese natives are cross-breeds of Veddoids and Negroids. They can be educated, not assimilated; 5) Among these three last groups, a slow assimilation can be made by more and more frequent cross-breeding with the French.[31]

Each people required a suitable form of colonial rule predicated on its fixed place in the hierarchy.

Ostensibly, association still aspired to eventually uplift the "inferior" races, but the moment when this goal might be achieved was far in the future due to evolution's slow working. As a result of the beneficial influence of milieu and by means of a slow process that other races could never hope to attain, the white race had evolved into the superior people. This formula dictated fixed relations between the France and her colonies, especially in the realm of culture. Segregation was advantageous for the natives, by this logic, in allowing them to progress at their own level, without detrimental pressure to advance too fast. It also ensured that the negative effects of *métissage* could be prevented for the colonizers.

The Moroccan Protectorate of Maréchal Lyautey, established in 1912, enacted the fullest application of association policy, which dictated the strict physical, political, and cultural segregation of natives from the French.[32] As Morocco's "pacifier" and first French governor general, he founded his *politique indigène* ("native policy") on associative principles of colonization and his own respect for Moroccan society and culture. Lyautey believed that by preserving local ways of life, association could sponsor the renewal of indigenous culture and the creation of a modern, prosperous colonial state. To this end, he left existing Moroccan cities intact and built new European cities contiguous to them; he retained the traditional Moroccan government, although under indirect French control; and he encouraged indigenous arts and crafts through schools and workshops set up by the French.[33] The visible differences between the French district and the native town, for example, reinforced the primacy of French culture and power. Under the guise of preserving indigenous culture, association mummified native society like a taxidermist's specimen as permanent evidence of its primitiveness, "saved" from detrimental European influences and dangerous political ideas such as democratic representation and self-determination. Lyautey promulgated an architectural policy based directly on native precedents, of which Laprade's New Medina in Casablanca, 1916 is an excellent example (fig. 5.5).

Regionalism

The associationist philosophy of conserving traditional culture had its corollary in the regionalist movement in France, which exerted a strong influence on the representational systems of the Colonial Exposition. During the Third Republic, regionalists advocated the revival of regional culture, contested the cultural ascendancy of Paris, and valorized regional differences effaced by the post-Revolution program to build national solidarity.[34] Romy Golan linked landscape painting's revival after World War I with the regionalist return to provincial culture. "For its ultimate goal—the reaffirmation of French cultural supremacy after the ravages of World War I—was inextricably part of the larger history of French nationalism ... [Landscape painting] participated in a specific regionalist ideology that linked France's cultural vitality to the strength of its rootedness in the soil."[35] Prominent regionalist critic Léandre Vaillat characterized architectural regionalism as neither a masquerade nor the perpetual copying of past styles, but "a formula of conciliation between the counsels of the past and the demands of the present."[36] As Vaillat saw it, it was a doctrine of adaptation: "To practice regionalism is not to seek

5.5 Albert Laprade, Edmund Brion, and Albert Cadet, Nouvelle Médina, Casablanca, Morocco (from Léandre Vaillat, Le Visage français du Maroc [Paris: Horizons de France, 1931], [14 bis])

with a sweet obstinacy that which is definitively lost, nor to wrap oneself in a majestic and provincial mourning, but to continue the past by following the methods which belong to us."[37]

The link among regionalism, culture, and nationalism was made through reference to the principles of Maurice Barrès and Charles Maurras, what Zeev Sternhell designated "organic nationalism."[38] Barrès, a native of Lorraine and follower of Taine, attacked republican ideology and institutions as deracinating and valorized a cultural nationalism rooted in Catholicism, the monarchy, respect for ancestors, blood, and soil. He likened the conscious continuity felt by the individual with his or her ancestors, on which his nationalism was based, to an architectural order or a house passed from generation to generation.[39] François Jean-Desthieux, a theorist of conservative regionalism, credited Maurras with extending the nineteenth-century regionalism of Mistral into a modern doctrine of decentralization and antirepublican, royalist "integral" nationalism.[40] Lyautey himself came under the sway of social Catholic, monarchist thinking as a youth.[41]

Further links between right-wing nationalism and regionalism were forged by means of human geography. The Fédération Régionaliste Française, founded in 1900 Jean Charles-Brun, counted Barrès, Vidal de la Blache, and Brunhes among its members.[42] Regionalists integrated the geographers' theories into their concept of nationalism and sought to revive the arts and styles that corresponded to each region of the French nation, while still relating them to the larger whole of France. Vaillat interpreted nationalism as "the desire to localize, to situate an art, to adapt it and to harmonize it with what Taine has called the 'milieu.'"[43] "National unity and provincial diversity" was his credo.[44] Regionalist architects such as Charles Letrosne and Gustave Umbdenstock championed traditional forms while employing modern materials and construction methods.[45] They sought to create an authentically regional modern architecture by building in the "character" of a region, not in imitation of lo-

5.6 Charles Letrosne, *La Mairie normande* (from Charles Letrosne, *Murs et toits pour les pays de chez-nous* (Paris: Niestle, 19231926), vol. 1, 71)

cal buildings, but rather through abstraction of regional architectural forms into a new, modern synthesis (figs. 5.6 and 5.7).

Reproduction of native architectural styles, as in Morocco and at the 1931 Exposition, was explicitly linked to the regionalist movement by critics such as Vaillat, who saw preservation of indigenous art and architecture as an extension of regionalism. In an article on the "renaissance of indigenous art," critic Robert de la Sizeranne decried the death of French regional art and celebrated the local art of "*La plus grande France*," the France of the colonies. Sizeranne characterized the colonies as regions or provinces that possessed an art distinct from that of the *Métropole*, found in minor and applied arts such as ceramics, weaving, and leatherworking. This art deserved preservation as the regional culture of La plus grande France.[46] Just as the climates of Europe dictated its architecture, so nature in the colonies implacably brought the artisan or architect to a certain

5.7 Gustave Umbdenstock, Salle de Réunion, Lille-Délivrance (from Gustave Umbdenstock, *Gustave Umbdenstock: oeuvres architecturales, 1897 à 1933* [Strasbourg: EDARI, (1935)], 54)

ensemble of lines and masses, according to Vaillat. Writing on regionalism and the colonies at the 1925 Decorative Arts Exposition, he declared that "the French colonies, in the form they have given to their pavilions, have shown us that they intend to develop modern civilization following the traces and the path of ancient civilization."[47] This stylistic determinism fixed the type of architecture appropriate for the *Métropole* and for the colonies, respectively, just as association dictated different forms of government for each colony.

The Exposition, under Lyautey's leadership, served as an illustration of association's method. Its architecture depicted the human geography of the colonized peoples and their implantation in their "natural" places within the colonial hierarchy, to demonstrate the existing state of the colonies and the hopeless distance between them and France. The conservative doctrine of tradition and racination, promulgated by domestic regionalists, had resonance with colonial administrators and architects, an inflection mirrored in the "indigenous" architecture built for the Exposition.

HYBRIDITY AND ARCHITECTURE
AT THE COLONIAL EXPOSITION

Under the stucco of the fragile pavilions of Vincennes, it will be easy for the visitor to discover the solid edifice that the colonialists of all periods and of all races have cemented with their blood. There is not a room, not a stand in these pavilions that does not translate some substantial victory of colonization over ignorance, fanaticism, violence, the miseries of the body and of the soul.[48]

Architecture was one of the primary realms in which colonial politics was enacted and tested, as exemplified by the pavilions. The Exposition illustrated association policy by means of "authentic, accurate" reproductions of native architecture that were visually distinct from the metropolitan pavilions, thereby serving as a gauge of the "evolution" of each colonized people, in human geographic terms. Following this logic, the pavilions maintained an architectural hierarchy consisting of Art Deco for the metropolitan ones and "native" styles for those of the colonies. The distinction between them mirrored association policy, as practiced by Maréchal Lyautey during his service as governor of Morocco. Part of architecture's mission at the Exposition was to represent differences and to heighten the contrast between white and colored worlds. Architecture was also, however, responsible for housing exhibitions on the "benefits" of colonization, good works that resulted from France's benevolent intervention.

The architects faced the task of presenting "a precise image of the states of art and of construction of each colony," as Marcel Zahar

5.8   Charles and Gabriel Blanche, Angkor Wat, interior (Archives d'Outre-Mer, Aix-en-Provence)

described it, which depicted each colony in its state before colonization, as if colonialism's civilizing mission had left it untouched.[49] To negotiate this contradiction, the pavilions represented the colonies on the *exterior* as if unchanged and still savage, and on the *interior* displayed the didactic exhibits of civilization's progress. This split between inside and outside was efficacious only to the extent that it could be systematically maintained, such that each representational realm was perceptually and conceptually isolated (fig. 5.8).

The architects also had to answer the imperatives of designing buildings appropriate for Paris. They altered the scale, massing, construction, details, and internal organization of the indigenous models to create structures of a size and dignity befitting the grandeur of the capital of

France. Using Beaux-Arts planning techniques and monumental scale, combined with decorative elements signifying native culture, they created a hybrid architecture that negotiated the obligatory division of the metropolitan and the colonial. This mingling of representational vocabularies brought architecture at the Exposition into the dangerous territory of cross-breeding, so terrifying to colonialists.

Under the policy of assimilation, a mixture of metropolitan and colonial styles was considered an appropriate representation of French colonial policy, as seen in Algerian cities. With the shift to association—and the concomitant separation of metropolitan culture from indigenous culture—mixture carried the negative connotations of *métissage*, the cross-breeding of races and cultures that should remain isolated from each other. Association and Lyautey's concern for preserving Moroccan traditions, although inherently conservative in its aim to conserve hierarchies, translated into widespread adaptation of native architectural forms with French programs and planning, such as the New Medina in Casablanca. Lyautey's own policies, therefore, produced hybrids as well as segregation in Morocco.

Over the decades of contact between France and her colonies, new cultural expressions, neither French nor indigenous, emerged in the colonies and in the *Métropole*. Segregation of the two proved impossible on both sides, resulting in hybrid productions. These half-breed manufactures undermined the separation and differentiation of French culture from colonial culture to the detriment of the mission assigned to architecture. By 1931 the colonies and their assigned visual signs were well known to most Europeans as a result of over two centuries of representations. These myriad means had already *interpreted* the colonies for the French public. That is, specific stereotypes and visual images were attached to particular colonies over centuries of colonial rule. The interpretations created particular images of their empire in the minds of the French people. A large body of work studied Orientalism in Western architecture and documented hybrid structures that dot the European landscape.[50] Jacques Marseille analyzed the proliferation of colonial images in the *Métropole* as integral with the process of "conquering the heads" of the French. According to Marseille, the French had to be immersed in images so that "a lower class exoticism," made up of popular images of *la Tonkiki, la Tonkinoise,* and *la Fille du Bédouin,* would "sink into the senses of the popular soul"[51] (fig. 5.9).

There was, however, resistance to these images and their integration into French culture. As Raymond Cogniat indicated in his review of the Exposition, the architecture of Asia and Africa could affect the French like "a too strong drink, whose merits we appreciate, but that leaves us stupefied."[52] Metropolitan fear of hybridity and mixing with the native generated this attitude of distaste for the "too strong drink" of primitive culture. Two coexisting attitudes governed French relations to native culture. On the one hand, advocates of exoticism and Orientalism valorized a mixture of French and native culture as a means of rejuvenating French culture with the "new blood" of indigenous art and creating a modern colonial art and architecture. Albert Sarraut, for example, saw colonial art as an inspiration for the dissipated art of Europe:

> Form and color, technique and material connect and combine their infinite diversity to propose, for the inspiration of the Occident, the research and discovery of new interpretations that will regenerate the old blood of its esthetics. . . . Our antique and illustrious Europe, having burned with too many ardors in all matters of art and of the spirit, has need of an influx of young vigor into the network of its desiccated arteries.[53]

On the other hand, others, such as Bayard, Cogniat, and Papillault, were afraid of this mixing, which risked diluting French culture with degenerate art produced by inferior peoples. For them, *art nègre* was undesirable, a

5.9   Cover of a special issue on the 1906 National Colonial Exposition, Marseille (from La Dépêche coloniale illustrée, December 31, 1905)

threat to metropolitan superiority and intelligence. By conflating racial and cultural hybrids, these thinkers focused attention on the negative attributes of cultural hybridity.

Metropolitan hybridity was excluded from the Colonial Exposition to prevent a dangerous confusion between the French fascination with the exotic and the "scientific" representation of native culture. The latter demanded a fixed, frozen stereotype of each colony as a primitive society; the former—which generated jazz, primitivism, *bals nègres,* and avant-garde negrophilia—was too ambiguous and belonged to cosmopolitan, decadent culture, not the ordered, tradition-based world envisioned by Lyautey and his fellow conservatives. What was appropriate for Paris was deemed inappropriate for the colonies and the Exposition. Lyautey's own practices reveal a deep ambivalence toward Moroccan culture, consisting of genuine respect for Arab society and culture and a conviction that French civilization was superior to and should, therefore, guide Moroccan culture to new levels of evolution.

Hybrids were necessary for the functioning of colonial power, as mediators between colonized and colonizer. They are signs of a "mutually productive culture contact," in Annie Coombs's words, as exchanges between Europeans and natives rather than one-way domination.[54] The hybrid was, however, one of colonialism's illegitimate offspring. It was the horror of racist fantasies, the mixture of European populations with non-whites that produced progeny neither European nor native. The hybrid is a "mutation" for postcolonial theorist Homi Bhabha, an unintentional effect of colonial power that produces a split between the authoritative, European original and its ambivalent, "other" repetition.[55] It poses a threat in those contexts in which separation of its progenitors is most urgently required to maintain a system of power relations. The consequences of hybridization are erasure and blurring of boundaries between races, and dissolution of the codes of difference established by colonialism. The hybrid "terrorizes authority with the ruse of recognition, its mimicry, its mockery," according to Bhabha.[56]

Webster's Dictionary defines the hybrid as follows: I. an offspring of two animals or plants of different races, breeds, varieties, species, or genera; 2. a person produced by the blending of two diverse cultures or traditions; and 3. something heterogeneous in origin or composition, composite.[57] It is a new entity created when two dissimilar things are combined. As Robert Young points out, it implies making one from two distinct things, like grafting a vine or rose onto a different root stock. The process of making difference into sameness is not, however, permanent in this type of hybrid; the plant can revert to its original state if not pruned and maintained.[58]

The hybrid is nothing new or specific to the colonial context. The melding of cultures has occurred throughout history in largely unacknowledged processes of appropriation and assimilation. According to Ella Shohat and Robert Stam, hybridity is "an unending, unfinalizable process which preceded colonialism and will continue after it."[59] What distinguished twentieth-century French colonialism and its hybrids from earlier precedents were the pseudo-scientific, social Darwinian discourse that accompanied the interdiction against cross-breeding, and the violence and fear with which hybridity was resisted. Alfred Fouillée, for example, believed that intermarriage would reduce its product to the common denominator of primitive instincts. Moral and physical disharmony was the only possible result from mixed unions.[60] In other words, hybridity could never produce more vigorous offspring when applied to humans. It represented a degeneration of the stronger side of the mixture, a threat to those qualities that made it superior. The paradox inherent in French colonialism is that its practices produced hybrids even while repudiating them. The arts and disciplines of representation brought the non-European world to the West in images that enabled the colonizing powers better to see, control, and hold their colonies. The 1931 Colonial

5.10   Rue des Nations, Universal Exposition, Paris, 1878 (Resource Collections of the Getty Research Institute, Los Angeles)

Exposition was the successor to previous world's fairs and their colonial sections, which were prime devices for disseminating these images to the *Métropole* by means of human displays, pavilions, and exhibits of native culture, such as at the 1878 Rue des Nations (fig. 5.10) and the 1889 Rue du Caire. Whereas imperialist systems attempted to control miscegenation, the melding of native with metropolitan, the very process of translating non-Western cultures into representations that were legible to Western audiences spawned these impure products.

Segregation between French and native had to be visible and obvious to maintain the authority of the colonizing power. The colonial state aspired to create "a human landscape of perfect visibility," as Benedict Anderson describes it, in which everything and everyone has its place defined by the classificatory systems of colonialism.[61] The visual order of colonialism required the immediate tangibility of authority and its distinction from what it was not, which it relegated to the space of otherness. According to Robert Young, "The principle of opposition, between civilization and barbarism or savagery, was nothing less than the ordering principle of civilization as such. . . . Fear of miscegenation can be related to the notion that without such hierarchy, civilization would, in a literal as well as a technical sense, collapse."[62] Emphasis on physical difference as a gauge of civilization dictated separation of the colonizer's and colonized's material worlds and culture.

Similar principles on the divisions between races informed the Colonial Exposition's exhibitions and the design of its pavilions. In a report on the organization of the physical anthropology section, Dr. Papillault summarized the "scientific laws" that organized the anthropological displays, based on extensive anthropological observations of the human races. Anthropology, for Papillault, could furnish conceptions that explain the aptitudes and value of the colonized races and their relations with the *Métropole*:

> 1) The diverse human races that people our globe demonstrate, in their morphological constitution, evolutive characters that are currently fixed at very different levels; 2) In a very general fashion, their aptitudes for intellectual and moral effort are in narrow correlation with the progress of their organic evolution; 3) The hybrid products of cross-breeding . . . possess a value intermediate to those who engender them. Cross-breeding results in elevating a less evolved population and lowering a very evolved population; 4) The differences of level in morphological and functional evolution of the human races are sometimes quite marked enough to create an irreducible opposition to all attempt at assimilation and unification . . . [63]

The races occupied permanent places in this evolutionary hierarchy that were related to their capacity for development and to their current achievements. Papillault maintained that the various races could exhibit such diverse levels of evolution that they could never unite without damage to the more evolved race.

To make the logic of colonial authority visible, the "superiority" of metropolitan culture had to be rigorously opposed to the "degeneracy" of indigenous culture. The transparency of colonial authority "is the action of the distribution and arrangement of differential spaces, positions, knowledges in relation to each other, relative to a differential, not inherent, sense of order."[64] In this late colonial order, the claim to authority made by colonizers was dependent on the relative superiority of metropolitan culture rather than the innate right of Europeans to colonize other peoples. The change in French policy from assimilation (the prerogative of colonizers to colonize based on their absolute superiority) to association (predicated on the contingent, if definitive, superiority of colonizers) clearly delineates this shift from innate right to relative order. Preservation of this order of things was based on visual classification of the colonial landscape, etiquette, body language, architecture, clothing, and other outward signs of authority.

Visible signs of difference are one of the structures that established colonial hierarchy and order. In The *Wretched of the Earth*, Franz Fanon described these signs and their operation in the colonial world: "a world cut in two" manifested by the division of the settlers' world and the natives' world. The zone where the natives live is not complementary to the zone inhabited by the settlers. The two zones oppose each other, but not in the service of a higher unity. Obedient to rules of pure Aristotelian logic, they both follow the principle of reciprocal exclusivity.[65] The settlers' quarter is strongly built of stone and steel, brightly lit, clean, and populated by people whose feet are never visible since they are protected in strong shoes. "The settlers' town is a well-fed town, an easygoing town ... a town of white people, of foreigners." By contrast, "men of evil repute" fill the natives' town, "a world without spaciousness," a hungry town filled with barefoot natives, "a crouching village, a town on its knees, a town wallowing in the mire." Signs of dominance and prosperity—the settler's table, his bed, his wife, his hygienic and capacious district—are the focus of the native's envy as well as the locus of his or her subjection[66] (fig. 5.11).

5.11   Governor general's palace, Saigon (from Exposition coloniale international de Paris, Commissariat général, Indochine. Documents officiels [Paris: Editions Géographiques, Maritimes, et Coloniales, 1931], Pl. 1)

What Bhabha calls the "rules of recognition" of colonial authority
govern this double universe: "those social texts of epistemic, ethnocentric,
nationalist intelligibility."[67] Signs of authority are as distinct as possible
to make colonialist supremacy a self-evident proposition, so that it is immediately recognizable, and so that it seems to be a natural part of the
physical and political landscape. Colonizers intended the signs of difference to obey these rules of recognition, so that the "proper places" of
things and people reinforced colonial authority. Difference had, therefore, its visual code on which the structure of colonial power relations was
predicated.

The pavilions at the Exposition could not maintain opposition between colonizer and colonized while meeting requirements for both savage imagery and civilized amenities. These structures contained a mixture

of vocabularies and spaces that broke down visual barriers between colonial and metropolitan zones. They were hybrids that had been many years in the making through the mass of "interpretations" of native culture presented to metropolitan audiences. According to Pierre Courthion, they came in three types: original creations, stylized interpretations, and reconstitutions.[68] In each case, specific native building types and styles were the referents for these pavilions, but they reproduced the colonial exemplar with relatively greater or lesser accuracy according to the value held by the French for the indigenous culture. Architects altered scale, massing, construction, details, siting, and internal organization of the indigenous models, but Zahar still claimed that these buildings were "precise" representations of the "art and construction of each colony."[69] By means of French planning techniques combined with physical signs derived from the native architecture of each colony, the architects created a hybrid architecture, metropolitan and colonial.

The Exposition was a different context than either the colonies, where colonial authority employed many structures of power, or France. The organizers intended the Exposition to be a purified and clarified demonstration of how French colonialism *should* operate, a simulacrum of a perfect colonial world that existed nowhere except in the Bois de Vincennes. Relations between France and her colonies, therefore, had to be represented as clearly as possible in the architecture. Hybrids generated in the colonies were of relatively little threat to this project, but the pastiches and eclectic constructions of metropolitan Oriental fashion were dangerous because they admitted the possibility of cultural cross-breeding in the *Métropole* itself.

Contemporary commentators recognized and acknowledged that the pavilions were hybrids, not pure expressions of native culture. Pierre Mille described The Netherlands section as "a city... made of authentic Javanese and Balinese habitations and overlooked by a pink and black building, with several superimposed roofs: one of the most successful things of this Exposition and it is not a servile copy, but an adaptation, a *hybridization.*"[70] The exigencies of designing pavilions for exhibitions, panoramas, and disparate displays necessitated adaptations and alterations to "primitive" native styles. These changes produced "stylized interpretations" and "original creations." Zahar identified the modifications produced by French architects when they designed the pavilions in "authentic" indigenous styles: "For the requirements of product presentation, it was necessary to amplify the volume of the residences of certain regions (Madagascar, West Africa, Cameroon, the Belgian Congo...)."[71]

Authenticity was the gauge of separation of colonial from metropolitan culture, the index of difference at the Colonial Exposition. Too great a deviation from the original indigenous model endangered the claim that these buildings represented "precise images" of native cultures and undermined accepted stereotypes and images of the colonies. The degree to which contemporary observers were troubled by the pavilions' hybridity can be gauged by their criticisms. Marcel Zahar reproved Charles Wulfleff for the "fantasy" with which he designed the Somali pavilion, "in arrangements of a dubious aesthetic, seeking to make his own decorative invention prevail over the true style of the region."[72] Zahar maintained the fiction that a "true native style" could be represented by these pavilions, despite the obvious contradiction in monumentalizing a native style (making it appropriate for Paris) and still "preserving its original character."

The most efficacious means for reinforcing the apparent authenticity of the pavilions was the native, engaged in his or her "primitive" crafts, rituals, and performances. Natives inhabited the pavilions and performed their daily activities, expurgated of European habits, clothing, and technology, as if they were in fact occupying authentic reproductions of indigenous buildings in a precolonial pastoral. In a further effort to make the Exposition seem as if it transparently represented the colonies, many architectural perspectives depicted natives inhabiting the pavilions, surrounded by flora and fauna appropriate to the colony, rather than European visitors. The discrepancy between the Exposition as virtual

5.12   Léon Bazin, Porte d'Honneur, Colonial Exposition, Paris, 1931, perspective (from L'Illustration, special issue [July 1931], n.p.)

replication of a "voyage around the world in one day" and these syncretic
constructions is evident in analysis of these perspectives.

The Porte d'Honneur by Léon Bazin provides an instructive example
of a hybrid design that aided the imaginative abstraction from Paris to
more exotic locales (fig. 5.12). This was the main entrance, and Bazin
worked diligently to give it both a monumentality appropriate to Paris and
a suitably Oriental flavor. The ambiguity between its Art Deco pillars and
vaguely Middle Eastern fountain produced some uneasiness in contemporary commentary. In a review, critic Raymond Cogniat wondered what
gave the Porte d'Honneur its indefinably exotic character, its evocation of
"sunny countries" when nothing in the architecture was explicitly Negro,
Arab, or Indochinese.[73] Bazin's perspective drawing of the entrance makes
this mysterious evocation of the tropics more explicit: it depicts a crowd of

5.13 Louis-Hippolyte Boileau et Léon Carrière, Cameroon and Togo pavilions, perspective (Archives d'Outre-Mer, Aix-en-Provence)

"Arabs" walking through the pylons and palm trees on their way, perhaps, to a market, but certainly not visiting a world's fair in a European capital.

By contrast, the Togo and Cameroon pavilions, designed by Louis-Hippolyte Boileau and Léon Carrière, referred to a more explicit repertoire of images of "black Africa" (fig. 5.13). They reproduced native huts from coastal Africa, enlarged to monumental proportions. This amplification and adaptation of indigenous houses produced a more suitable pavilion, as Cogniat explained, because Togo and Cameroon lacked a monumental architecture, such as that found in French West Africa.[74] In the perspective drawing of this section, African natives populate the precinct amid trees and mountains of the sub-Saharan savanna, natives and flora added for verisimilitude.

Like many of the pavilions, the French West African section was a schizophrenic collection of buildings that recalled "barbarian" dwellings

at the same time that they contained exhibitions on mining in Senegal. The painting by Roger Robert Nivelt in *L'Illustration's* special issue depicts the West African lake village as if it were in the African brush, inhabited by natives, rather than located in the Bois de Vincennes and occupied by Parisians[75] (fig. 5.14). It is typical of renderings that appeared in *L'Illustration* and other contemporary periodicals: painted in a style derived from Gauguin and Orientalist artists, it evoked the exotic atmosphere of other climates, architectures, and peoples with hot colors and impressionistic brushwork.

Although the Martinique pavilion used a French classical style, a perspective in *L'Illustration* showed it as if it were in the colonies, not on the

5.15   Charles A. Wulfleff, Martinique pavilion, perspective (from L'Illustration, special issue [July 1931], n.p.)

edge of Paris. Nighttime views of Wulfleff's pavilion show a group of natives entering the building clad in serapes and floppy hats (fig. 5.15) and,
inside, dancing with bewigged colonists (fig. 5.16). Rather than representing Parisians in modern European dress in and around the buildings,
they show natives of the colonies inhabiting the pavilions, surrounded by
"native" flora and fauna. Although visitors did come to the Exposition
from the colonies, including the Sultan of Morocco and the Emperor of
Annam, a desire to make the Exposition seem as if it *is* the colonies, not
just a reproduction of them in Paris, motivated the rendering of *indigènes*
associated with the pavilions.

These perspective renderings reveal the degree to which a scenographic, surface representation of native culture determined the architecture of the colonial pavilions. The perspective renderings showed the

5.16   Charles A. Wulffleff, Martinique pavilion, perspective of interior (from
L'Illustration, special issue [July 1931], n.p.)

pavilions as if they occupied a purely exotic, colonial space, not the heterogeneous environment of an urban exposition. The hybrid nature of structures with native exteriors and metropolitan interiors was effaced in these images in favor of an overdetermined, stereotyped reading of each culture. Hybridity, if confined to the colonies themselves, could be accommodated in the service of racial uplifting or opportunistic governance. At the Exposition, however, it undermined the codes of difference established by French preconceptions and colonialist propaganda, blurring rules of recognition that controlled the colonial order.

The mixture of colonial exteriors with metropolitan interiors produced an undesirable hybridity that threatened the Exposition's goal of representing the absolute difference between the colonized and the colonizer. This hybridity was magnified by the monumentality and European details of the pavilions. It could be tolerated as long as the exteriors remained within the accepted vocabularies assigned to the colonies, which signified primitiveness and degeneracy. As the architectural perspectives indicate, this task was not adequately fulfilled, since the pavilions combined metropolitan monumentality with native savagery, and they required supplements of authenticity in the form of human displays.

This hybridity, and its potential threat to the Exposition's representational order, was not recognized as such by contemporary commentators, except when it too blatantly transgressed the distinction between metropolitan and colonial. The Guadeloupe pavilion, for example, attracted the ire of Lyautey as too modern and as a distraction from the nearby Angkor temple's exotic allure. In February 1931 Lyautey attempted to have the Guadeloupe lighthouse tower reduced in size on the grounds that it visually conflicted with the neighboring Indochinese pavilions, but the Guadeloupan commission succeeded in retaining the tower intact.[76] Blurring the boundary between metropolitan and colonial formed the most grievous and dangerous threat to the coherence of the Colonial Exposition's *decor.*

5.17   Nestlé kiosk (from Olivier, Rapport général, vol. 6, pt. 1, 260)

Albert Laprade recognized this fact when he attacked the messy eclecticism of the many small kiosks that dotted the site:

> At Vincennes, in these admirable surroundings, it is likely that, despite the efforts of the chief architect, all will be spoiled at the last minute by abominable little kiosks that will wipe out any colonial ambiance. Already like mushrooms, ultra-modern vulgarities appear, so-called colonial kiosks that begin to disgust one with all colonial art! They submit us to these abominable pear-shaped or sugar-loaf domes, to those pseudo-Algero-Tunisian keyhole arches! This congenital indiscipline is a very great subject of sadness for our enterprise.[77]

Laprade identified qualities that made the kiosks' hybridity regrettable: promiscuously mixed exotic styles contrasted with "ultramodern" constructions, all of which deviated from the standardized "colonial ambiance" cultivated at the Exposition (fig. 5.17). The objectionable hybridity of the kiosks and commercial pavilions seems a matter of degree rather than principle since the official colonial pavilions were, themselves, mixtures of native and French architecture. Although the colonial pavilions were hybrids, their hybridity followed long-established codes for the representation of non-French cultures. They were part of a program contained within French colonization; this program generated serviceable, efficacious hybrids that facilitated subjugation to France.

AN ARCHITECTURAL PHYSIOGNOMY OF THE COLONIES

At the Colonial Exposition, architecture can be classed as one of three genres: original creations more or less independent of milieu; stylized interpretations of certain groups of habitations and edifices aimed at forming a characteristic ensemble; exact copies and reconstitutions of indigenous houses and palaces. The first of these categories will satisfy the artists, the second will be the joy of the dilettantes, and the last, the admiration of the ethnographers.

—Pierre Courthion[1]

The external appearance of the colonial pavilions was determined by a physiognomy of architectural features that represented each colony's racial and cultural character. Like the science that catalogued corporeal differences between races, architectural physiognomy detailed physical indicators of difference among cultures that allowed them to be allotted places in an evolutionary hierarchy. Nineteenth-century physiognomy and the related science of phrenology recorded the body and its external indicators of character and temperament. By revealing inner qualities through their outward expression, they were thought to document innate racial character, criminality, or atavism. According to Robert Young, "the study of the physical differences between different races was developed in the second half of the nineteenth century into an obsessive delineation of British (and European) people into 'types' in the science of 'physiognomy'"[2] (fig. 6.1).

Physiognomic science enumerated racial distinctions in aesthetics and material culture as well as body. In the *Métropole*, disciplines that recorded and classified differences between European and non-European civilizations—together with literature, film, painting, travel accounts, advertising, world's fairs, and museum exhibits—constructed a visual code of physical differences among the races. Human geography, for example, recorded what Jean Brunhes termed "material human works," in relationship to geography and climate, as indicators of the character of a people. Human geographers, and critics influenced by human geography, drew parallels between bodily and architectural physiognomy on the basis of the physical evidence of material culture and architecture. Brunhes, in his human geographic study of the Swiss Val d'Anniviers, described the "physiognomy" of the houses and their spatial orientation within the valley as the result of physical, social, and economic considerations.[3] Emile Bayard applied human geographic principles to native architecture in the colonies. Bayard, inspector general of artistic education and museums at the Ministry of Fine Arts, wrote a series of books on various French styles

6.1   Types Coloniaux, 1922 Colonial Exposition, Marseilles (from Exposition nationale coloniale de Marseille décrite par ses auteurs [Marseille: Commissariat général de l'exposition, 1922], 77)

from Louis XIII to moderne; French regionalism and human geography strongly influenced his theories of art and architecture. In the introductory chapter to his treatise on colonial art and architecture, *L'Art de reconnaître les styles coloniaux*, Bayard likened the "architecture" of animals—an adaptive response to their milieu—to that of the primitive hut and cabin. He maintained that climate, topography, and other environmental factors of a region ordain the "lines and forms of architecture," just as it determined specialized physiognomies of the animals who inhabit that region. Arabs, he maintained, created an architecture whose "essentially geometric decor" corresponded to the aridity of their country, with its limited vegetation and the strong flat line of horizon.[4]

The pavilions were, therefore, equivalent to racial "types" produced by physiognomy. They represented the stereotypical character of a colonized people, as understood by French social science and colonial administration, by means of synthetic architectural signifiers. Architects used various strategies to represent this character. In a few cases, such as the Angkor pavilion, the colony was depicted by a representative monument that was reconstituted with considerable accuracy of detail and massing. Most other pavilions were original creations or stylized interpretations of native architecture, in Courthion's formulation. They were composites of typical details and generalized characteristics that conformed to the architectural type associated with that colony.

In this respect, they were analogous to Sir Francis Galton's composite photographs, which superimposed many individual photographs into a typical physiognomic image. Galton developed the composite photograph as a method for discerning hereditary characteristics of various categories of humans, such as criminals and different races. His object was to "improve" human stock through eugenics, and eliminate undesirable or harmful traits by selective breeding and choose only the fittest, most superior humans for reproduction.[5] Galton held that innate moral and intellectual faculties were closely bound up with physical ones. The "ideal, typical form" of a race or class of individuals determined, according to his theory, the mean toward which eugenic improvement should be directed, and this central physiognomic type could best be determined by composite portraiture.[6] He criticized the usual method for determining physiognomic types by selecting representative individuals as not trustworthy because "the judgment itself is fallacious. It is swayed by exceptional and grotesque features more than ordinary ones, and the portraits supposed to be typical are likely to be caricatures."[7]

As a means of producing truly representative faces, Galton used many portraits of individuals in the same pose, reduced to the same size, and superimposed photographically on a single plate. "The effect of composite portraiture is to bring into evidence all the traits in which there is agreement, and to leave but a ghost of a trace of individual peculiarities. There are so many traits in common in all faces that the composite picture when made from many components is far from being a blur; it has altogether the look of an ideal composition."[8] The result was what Alan Sekula designates the "collapsed version of the archive," the average of photographic archives' many individual images into one typical image of criminal, class, or racial characteristics.[9]

The colonial pavilions portrayed native cultures in a similar manner by reproducing a plethora of typical details in a composite architecture that elicited general characteristics of a race, rather than specific components of native monuments. Their authenticity was generated by the *typical* nature of the architecture, not their accuracy or correspondence with an actual building in the colony. Pierre Guesde, head of the Indochinese section, described the Angkor pavilion as a precise copy of the original: "Charles Blanche, the architect, has striven to recreate the exact physiognomy of this masterpiece of Cambodian art, as remarkable for the grandeur of its conception and the harmony of its forms as for the magnificence of its decoration."[10] Jean Gallotti described the French West African section as typical of the architecture of the Sahara: "Everything here is constructed in this Saharan style derived, it seems, from the Berber style of Morocco and South Algeria, which gives its physiognomy to great cities in the Sudan like Timbuktu."[11] The result was a similar set of types to that French physical anthropology produced for racialized human bodies.

Like the physiognomic, composite portrait, each pavilion reproduced the external appearance of a culture's architecture as indicators of its inherent, racial character. Accumulation of detail reinforced the interpretation as a truly accurate reflection, if not literal reproduction, of a race's civilization and its place on the cultural hierarchy. The pavilions of Madagascar, Morocco, Indochina, and French West Africa provide case studies of this architectural physiognomy and the process by which French architects interpreted native cultures. They represented stereotypes based on precedents established at earlier expositions and a graduated scale of representational accuracy. The following case studies investigate how the civilizations were rendered in architectural terms, and how hybrids of French and native architecture came to represent the architectural physiognomy of the colonies.

MADAGASCAR

A royal Malagasy house, situated next to the Tour des Bucrânes and flanked by a stair of ravishing curves, such as one sees in Tananarive, completes our impression of *Madagascar:* it is an interpreted copy of the native hut of the king Andrianampoënimerina.[12]

The hybridity of Madagascar's section resulted from the fact that the colony had no real architecture to emulate and very little indigenous culture, according to French historians (fig. 6.2). Emile Bayard stated: "There is no Malagasy art. The autochthon seems a stranger to the artistic idea. . . . There is nothing, in this immense country, nothing of art, except nature. . . . Here, the fetishes do not even have the barbaric attraction

6.2   Tour des Bucrânes and main pavilion, Madagascar section (from Trillat)

that we find in Sudanese fetishes. No originality, no instinct."[13] Marcel
Zahar summarized the dilemma that designing the pavilion posed for its
architect, Gabriel Veissière: "In order to represent Madagascar with a
palace of substantial dimensions, Mr. Veissière had a subtle problem to
resolve. No model offered itself to him because, in the nineteenth century,
occupying English and French troops took care to devastate the royal
palace of the sixteenth century, and the architects who were mandated to
repair the deterioration judged it best to adorn these edifices with Renaissance facades."[14] As a result of this lack of authentic precedents, Veissière was forced to concoct a suitable "native" architecture out of vestiges
of royal Malagasy houses and a variety of other traditional sources. At
previous colonial expositions, the Madagascar pavilion was conventionally eclectic and exotic, without distinguishing features that marked it as
Malagasy.[15] The 1922 Marseilles National Colonial Exposition, for ex-

6.3   Madagascar pavilion, Colonial Exposition, Marseilles, 1922 (from Exposition nationale coloniale de Marseille décrite par ses auteurs, 124)

ample, included a pavilion that reproduced only two "characteristic traits" of Madagascar architecture: a large roof and the red color of the walls[16] (fig. 6.3).

The imperative to achieve authenticity at the 1931 Exposition, however, dictated that Veissière devise a set of structures closely related to existing Madagascar culture (fig. 6.4). "The architect designed a tower, enlarging the Betsileo raised stone by twelve times, and added to it the skulls of zebus placed face to face, beasts possessing a sacred character. As for the palace, it evokes the spirit of Malagasy construction by its simple and massive forms; the ramp of the monumental stair conforms to the designs of the ramps which curve along the houses of Tananarive."[17] The tower borrowed elements from the tombs of the Betsileo, Mahafaly, and Bara tribes. It was a monumental version of the carved stone posts in Betsileo tombs, which are called *trano manara* or "cold houses" because they

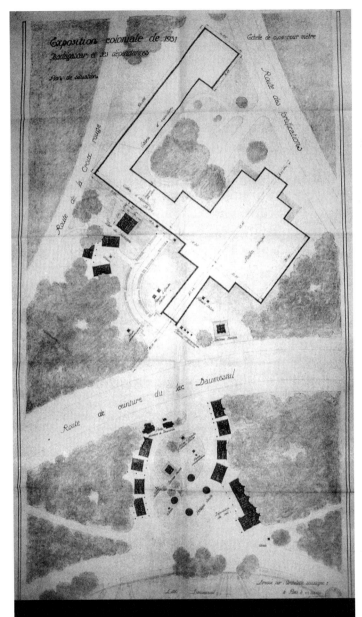

6.4   Plan, Madagascar section (Archives de Paris, Paris)

are never illuminated by fire.[18] The incised carvings on the tower evolved from those on the Betsileo tombs. The zebu heads, however, appear to derive from Mahafaly tomb poles called *aloalos*, which are wood pillars adorned by carvings of zebu heads, doves, or human figures, or from Bara funerary poles on which sit the skulls of zebus.[19] Veissière united various Madagascar precedents, appropriated from disparate ethnic sources, into the massive *Tour des Bucrânes*, Tower of Skulls.

In the main pavilion, Veissière alluded to the high roof and exterior gallery of the royal residence in Tananarive, the Manjakamiadana, and to the ramps that ascend Tananarive's central hill to the Rova, the royal compound. A Frenchman, Jean Laborde, designed the original Manjakamiadana for Queen Ranavalona I in 1839. This structure, a wood palace with a steep roof and arcades on the sides, was an enlarged rendition of the traditional royal house in Madagascar.[20] In 1872 Queen Ranavalona II commissioned Scottish missionary and architect James Cameron to clad the Manjakamiadana in stone, thereby giving it a more prestigious allure and producing the "Renaissance" facade to which Zahar alluded.[21] The wooden edifice constructed by Laborde was preserved within Cameron's stone shell, and the massive timber column that supports the roof can still be seen inside the dwelling.[22] Another royal building within the royal compound, the Tranovola or Silver Palace, bears an even closer resemblance to Veissière's pavilion, particularly in the arcade columns that support the enormous hipped roof. Queen Ranavalona I ordered its construction in 1841 for conferences and receptions.[23]

The interior contained a skylit atrium space illuminated by glazing set into the roof (fig. 6.5). Through an ingenious system of skylights and light monitors, Veissière created a modern space that abstracted references to the balustrades of tropical houses without making literal copies of any particular native type. Around the atrium, galleries housed exhibitions consisting of art objects made by indigenous artists, murals, graphs, and detailed informational diagrams on idustrial production, raw

6.5   Main pavilion, Madagascar section, interior (from Construction moderne, Sept. 27, 1931, 794)

materials, and so on.[24] The contrast between urbanity and sophistication of these spaces and fabricated barbarity of the exterior further marked the hybridity of this edifice.

The main Madagascar pavilion and the Tour des Bucrânes approximated some ethnographic accuracy of detail, but these elements were authentic only in isolation. As wholes, the structures registered the intermixture of European and Malagasy culture produced by three centuries of contact. Some precedents on which Veissière based his designs, such as Laborde and Cameron's royal residence, were already mixtures, hybrids of Malagasy imperial architecture and imported references to European buildings. Other sources, such as the Mahafaly *aloalos*, originated in authentic cultural manifestations, but their accuracy was compromised when combined with elements from divergent ethnic traditions.

Unlike other colonies, for which a plethora of images circulated in the *Métropole*, Madagascar was relatively unknown to French audiences. This was due partly to the island's isolation from Europe during the nineteenth century until the French conquered it in 1895, and partly to the heterogeneous, European culture sponsored by the Malagasy nobility, which had very little exotic appeal. By comparison with Angkor Wat or the mosque at Djenné, Madagascar provided no easily conjured images of cultural monuments or iconic figures. A monograph on native habitation in the French colonies by Augustin Bernard and other eminent geographers described a wide variety of indigenous dwelling types in Madagascar, but that they were of the hut category, not monumental structures.[25] Period guide books and monographs contain photographs and drawings of native culture that are scarcely more than safari-style pictures of hunting trophies and scenes of "primitive" life.[26] In the introduction to the official Colonial Exposition monograph, Mr. Delélée-Desloges characterized it as "a sort of 'Unknown Island.'"[27] The production of a largely fabricated architecture at the Exposition would not have been contradicted by widely held conceptions of that island's indigenous culture.

MOROCCO

Morocco was one of the best-known French colonies, widely depicted in every medium. In travel accounts such as Eugène Delacroix's *Voyage au Maroc*, 1832, and Pierre Loti's journal *Au Maroc*, and films such as *Le Sange d'Allah*, Morocco served as the exotic setting for numerous French fantasies.[28] In their studies of French colonial literature, literary critics Georges Hardy and Roland Lebel listed dozens of travel accounts, tourist guides, poems, military memoirs, scientific monographs, and novels on the country.[29] Even before its "pacification" in 1912 by Maréchal Lyautey, it was the object of considerable interest in France, as witnessed by the mass of literature produced on Moroccan themes before this date.

Zahar reiterated the common images while describing the north African pavilions at the Colonial Exposition:

> In Islamic lands, Algeria, Morocco, buildings present the same dominant features, imposed by religion and the Arab temperament. White and smooth walls, which protect from enemies, which protect from indiscretions, which close on the family, on the women above all, like a paradise and a prison! All the attractions are reunited in the central court: the trees, the flowers, the softly bubbling basins, finally the shadow. And the roofs space themselves out in terraces where the natives stretch out for long meditations.[30]

The Moroccan section, designed by Robert Fournez and Albert Laprade, consisted of a central garden with souks on either side, terminated by a pavilion modeled after garden kiosks in houses (fig. 6.6). Behind this pavilion, a series of rooms designed with carved wood and plaster ornament contained exhibits on the French protectorate (fig. 6.7). Novelist Pierre Mille captured its integrated, hybrid quality: "Morocco: here the building is more than a copy: a hybridization of styles recently created by our architects and of the Moroccan style."[31]

6.6 Moroccan section, bird's-eye perspective (from L'Architecture, April 1931, 115)

This structure was the successor to a concentrated effort to assemble a colonial architecture specific to the indigenous culture and architectural traditions. Earlier pavilions, before Morocco came under French control in 1912, conformed to the eclectic standard of nineteenth-century world's fairs and included few elements derived directly from traditional monuments. The first such exhibition occurred at the 1867 Universal Exposition in Paris and consisted of a large imperial tent, two smaller tents, and a stable grouped around the Tunisian pavilion, the palace of the Bey.

6.7   Courtyard, main pavilion, Moroccan section (from *Construction moderne*, Nov. 15, 1931, pl. 27)

In 1878 the Moroccans erected another tent, shops, and a main pavilion, designed by French architect Jacques Drévet, that contained four rooms around a courtyard. Moroccan pavilions at subsequent Parisian world's fairs tended to follow this precedent of abstracted reference to north African architecture without specific sources. In 1889 and 1900 the pavilions included square towers modeled after minarets, courtyards, and shops.[32] After Morocco became a French protectorate, the 1922 French Colonial Exposition in Marseilles included an elaborate Moroccan section that encompassed a courtyard pavilion with minaret, augmented by a monumental gate to the Casbah, and extensive souks.[33]

The Moroccan section exemplified what François Béguin called the *arabisance* of French colonial architecture in North Africa (fig. 6.8). Béguin characterized *arabisance* as "the numerous traces of the arabization of ar-

6.8 Main pavilion, Moroccan section (from Construction moderne, Nov. 15, 1931, 101)

chitectural forms imported from Europe" to North Africa and extended the term to include a general "climate" of sympathy to the Arab world that propagates these "operations of hybridization." For Béguin, not one but rather many architectural *arabisances* developed over the course of French colonization.[34] Lyautey's administration sponsored considerable research into indigenous culture. This effort to document native art, customs, and social structure was an essential part of his *politique indigène*. He disdained the clumsy attempts to recreate French architecture and urbanism in Algeria, and advocated a colonial style that combined the best of modern planning with traditional forms.

The Moroccan section at the 1931 Exposition was the culmination of Lyautey's program to develop an appropriate French colonial style. One of its architects, Albert Laprade, had worked for Lyautey during his governorship and helped design two of its best known monuments: the residence general in Rabat and the new medina in Casablanca.[35] Laprade also collaborated with Jean Gallotti, a French critic, on an intensive study of Moroccan houses and gardens.[36] Gallotti contributed text, Laprade line drawings, and Lucien Vogel photographs of a variety of traditional residences (fig. 6.9). According to Gallotti, these two volumes provided a primer of Moroccan domestic architecture as interpreted by sympathetic, observant Frenchmen, as well as a guide for foreigners on methods for designing houses in the traditional manner. By examining the plates and text of *Le Jardin et la maison arabes au Maroc,* contemporary accounts of the Exposition, and other sources on north African architecture, it is possible to trace the provenance of Fournez and Laprade's design for the pavilion.

In an article for *Vu* magazine, Gallotti described the Moroccan section in terms of its north African precedents:

> One senses that the architects Mr. Fournez and Laprade thought of the eminent dignity of the Hispano-Moorish art of Fez . . . The mirror of water that stretches to the central dome, between the trellises sheltering the boutiques, recalls to us what this art owes to Persia. The general disposition of the plan will recall Bab Dekaken to those who have visited Fez. And on the rear facade, next to the monument to the Overseas Armies, those who have visited Rabat will recognize Bab-Rouah in the great entrance gate.[37]

The long promenade along a basin of water, beginning at the Place de l'Afrique du Nord and lined with souks on either side, culminated in a hexagonal cupola attached to the main building (fig. 6.10). This hexagonal structure was modeled after the reception building at Dar-El-Beida in Marrakech, for which Gallotti's book includes a plan and several photographs, and the crenelated towers and picturesque massing of the main

6.9   Albert Laprade, perspective of a Moroccan house (from Jean Gallotti, Le Jardin et la maison arabes au Maroc [Paris: Albert Levy, 1924], vol. 2, pl. 111)

6.10 Moroccan souks, Moroccan section (from Trillat)

building were also closely patterned after Dar-El-Beida (fig. 6.11). In the main exhibition room the ceiling constructed of wooden slats was strongly reminiscent of the ceiling in a "Berchla"-type residence illustrated in *Le Jardin et maison* (fig. 6.12). Laprade and Fournez recombined these elements into a new synthesis that created a unified amalgam, a true hybrid architecture (fig. 6.13).

INDOCHINA

Indochinese art lives in an eternal mode of expression. It has not at all evolved since its birth because it is the slave of a severe symbolic tradition and must resist, consequentially, any individual agitation. If the art of Indochina has not at all developed, if it does not at all vary, it must be gratefully acknowledged, at least, to never have known decadence. This is due to the temperament of a calm and obstinate race,

6.11   Dar-El-Beida, Marrakech, Morocco (from Gallotti, Le Jardin et la maison arabes au Maroc vol 2, pl. 116)

faithful to ritual like an ancestral rule, to a race whose manual skill matches patience of execution without equal.

—Émile Bayard[38]

The Angkor pavilion and other Indochinese pavilions resonated with decades of representations that had been promulgated in the *Métropole* (fig. 6.14). The overabundance of popularized images and scholarly erudition that proliferated after Angkor Wat's "discovery" in the mid-nineteenth century made Indochina one of the best-known French colonies.[39] Central to the stereotype was the notion of the Khmer as a formerly advanced but presently degenerate society, a conception articulated by Pierre Loti in his travel account, *Un Pèlerin d'Angkor:* "The barely recognizable ruins of the temple before me represent the spontaneous conception, naive and

6.12   Main pavilion, Moroccan section, interior (from *Construction moderne,* Nov. 15, 1931, 100)

savagely powerful, of an isolated people, without analog in the world and without neighbors: the Khmer people, a detached branch of the great Aryan race, who settled here by chance and developed far from the original stock, isolated from everything by immense stretches of forests and swamps."[40]

The Khmer civilization that created the great stone temples of Angkor, including Angkor Wat, represented the type of isolated, stagnant culture that Vidal de la Blache characterized as having "learned nothing for thousands of years." In his account, it achieved greatness at a distant moment in the past, from which it had not at all advanced since it ceased contact with the Indian and Chinese civilizations that enriched it and "civilized" it.[41] Loti reiterated this convention in his romanticized impressions of the ruins at Angkor. The Khmer potential for greatness, Loti

6.13   Léon Bazin, perspective of courtyard, Moroccan pavilion (from L'Illustration, special issue [July 1931], n.p.)

believed, lay in their racial kinship with the Aryan race, European stock,
but their lack of intercourse with other centers of advanced civilization
caused their decline. Loti and Vidal were typical of French thinkers in
presuming that what they saw as the stagnant character of Indochinese art
revealed lack of evolution in Khmer civilization. According to these views,
it was proof of the Khmer's current decadence that they were ignorant of
the origins of the ruins in their country, knowledge that the French would
restore through archaeology and epigraphy. By reconstructing the Khmer
past and restoring its masterpieces, the French lay claim to Khmer monuments as their own.[42]

At the beginning of *Un Pèlerin d'Angkor*, Loti rehearsed the long
French fascination with monuments of Indochina that fed this propri-
etary attitude. When his brother died in Indochina and his personal

6.14 Indochinese section, aerial view (from Olivier, Rapport général, vol. 2, part 1, 32)

effects were sent back to his family in France, Loti found among them a colonial magazine devoted to Angkor. He put this journal in his "petit musée," a collection of seashells, birds, and anything that seemed to come from far-off lands. As he leafed through the magazine, Loti halted, with a shiver, at the image of colossal ruins lost in the forests of Siam: "great, strange towers all parts enlaced with exotic foliage, the temples of mysterious Angkor!" Thirty-five years later, in 1901, he made the journey to Angkor foreseen in his childhood fantasies.[43] Like many tourists to Indochina, he took his preconceptions as his guide and had little recourse to scientific experts—Henri Dufour and Charles Carpeaux—in residence at the Angkor ruins, preferring to construct his own fantasies[44]:

These colossal walls and these towers, that have just appeared to us like some mirage of the torrid heat, this is not the village itself, but only *Angkor-Vat*, its principal temple.... Leading to this phantom basilica, a bridge of ancient ages, constructed in cyclopean blocks, traverses the lake crowded with reeds and water-lilies; two monsters, gnawed by time and bearded by lichen, guard the entrance to it.... And, this door cleared, we are here inside the first wall, which has more than a league of tower: a mournful solitude encloses, simulating an abandoned garden.[45]

The 1931 version of Angkor Wat was the successor to this long tradition of images transmitted by explorers, archeologists, and exoticist writers. Through these representations, Angkor became an emblem of "lost" Khmer civilization and the glories of French colonialism. Architects of the Indochinese section could have employed various scholarly treatises, photographs, and a set of molds taken at Angkor (housed at the Musée Indochinois) to construct their version. They might have also drawn on Indochinese pavilions at previous French world and national fairs, including Auguste Delaval's reconstitution of Angkor Wat at the 1922 National Colonial Exposition.

The earliest set of comprehensive and detailed drawings of Angkor were the work of Louis Delaporte, who accompanied Ernest Doudart de Lagrée and Francis Garnier on the 1866 mission that sought a navigable route into China up the Mekong River.[46] Doudart and his colleagues also took plaster molds as well as measurements and photographs of the monument.[47] In 1873 Garnier published an account of the commission's work, *Voyage d'exploration en Indo-Chine,* with two volumes of text (description and annexes) and two portfolios of drawings (scientific documents, such as maps and measured drawings of the monuments, and a picturesque album of drawings by Delaporte).[48] These volumes furthered the multiplication of images of Angkor in French culture that began with Henri Mouhot, its French "discoverer."[49]

The first exhibition of Indochinese art and architecture was at the 1878 Exposition Universelle in Paris; it included sculpture, molds, and drawings from Delaporte's voyages and a model of Angkor Wat by Emile Soldé.[50] Louis Delaporte, as director of the Musée Indochinois at the Trocadéro, created models for the 1889 Exposition that combined details from molds taken at Angkor and generic Khmer details at full scale. Although the models corresponded to no particular Indochinese monument, they were direct predecessors of the "reconstituted" Angkor Wat at the 1931 Exposition. The first full-size reconstruction was produced for the 1889 Exposition Universelle (fig. 6.15), along with pavilions for Cochinchina and Annam and a Tonkinese village.[51] The Temple d'Angkor at the 1889 Exposition was a fantastic amalgam of motifs rather than an accurate reconstruction of any particular building. It roughly corresponded to the central tower, with its repeating pediments over the doorways, and featured a pinnacle that recalled Indian stupas. The proportions and many details were quite divergent from the original, even from drawings available in 1889, but critics of the time saw it as a perfect reflection of Khmer art. At the 1900 Exposition Universelle, Angkor Wat was the ostensible referent for a pavilion that actually resembled nothing found in Cambodia (fig. 6.16). The 1900 Exposition included several other Indochinese pavilions, such as one that was modeled on Tonkinese architecture, and a Khmer royal pagoda by architect Alexandre Marcel.[52]

The 1906 National Colonial Exposition in Marseilles continued this tradition of generic Indochinese architecture; it included a Cambodian pavilion that was allegedly a reproduction of the "Bayon temple at Angkor-Wat" [sic][53] (fig. 6.17). The Bayon is actually the principal structure of the Angkor Thom precinct adjacent to Angkor Wat.[54] Angkor Thom is famous for towers carrying four faces of Lokeshvara, the Universal Buddha, which represents the omnipotence of the supreme being looking in the four cardinal directions. The version of the Bayon reconstructed at the Marseilles exposition, designed by Vildieu and Lagisquet,

6.15   Pagode d'Angkor, Universal Exposition, Paris, 1889 (Resource Collections of the Getty Research Institute, Los Angeles)

6.16   Angkor pavilion, Universal Exposition, Paris, 1900 (Resource Collections of the Getty Research Institute, Los Angeles)

6.17   Cambodian pavilion, Colonial Exposition, Marseilles, 1906 (Resource Collections of the Getty Research Institute, Los Angeles)

was a crude fabrication in oversimplified forms, devoid of ornament and detail by comparison with the 1889 and 1900 Indochinese pavilions. The 1922 Exposition in Marseilles reproduced the central mass of Angkor Wat in more detail than at any previous exhibition, as well as an extensive Annamite quarter and Laotian village (fig. 6.18). Designed by Auguste-Émile-Joseph Delaval, it consisted of a raised platform flanked with two basins of water that approximated the long causeway to the temple. Two long pavilions located in these basins replicated part of the compound's first wall and gate. The complex layers of Angkor's walls and gateways did not exist; the structure recreated only the five-towered tower at the very center without precincts that surround the central mass.

Pierre Guesde, head of the Indochinese section at the 1931 Exposition, intended that the reconstituted Angkor Wat surpass previous ones in authenticity and detail. When asked by a reporter if the latest

6.18 Angkor pavilion, Colonial Exposition, Marseilles, 1922 (postcard: collection of the author)

reconstruction was a repetition of pavilions already admired at the Marseilles expositions, he replied that it was similar, but that there was no other choice of monumental architecture in Indochina except that of the Khmer. In addition, the Marseilles pavilion had been merely "a vague interpretation" of Angkor Wat, whereas the monument at Vincennes would be its "faithful reproduction."[55] Successor to previous Indochinese pavilions, this hybrid of Angkor and of French architectural conventions was hardly the "faithful reproduction" that Guesde claimed. Parts of the temple formed set views that recreated celebrated tableaus of Angkor and the interior contained exhibits on native education.

Even in cases of "exact copies and reconstitutions, "such as the Angkor pavilion, the dichotomy between interior and exterior was considered less transgressive than consistent with a physiognomic architecture (fig. 6.19). In an interview published in *La Dépêche coloniale et maritime,* Guesde described the exterior as an exact copy of Angkor, but the interior

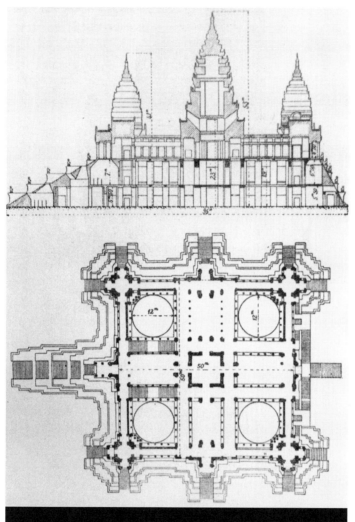

6.19 Angkor pavilion, section and plan (from *Construction moderne*, Aug. 16, 1931, pl. 182)

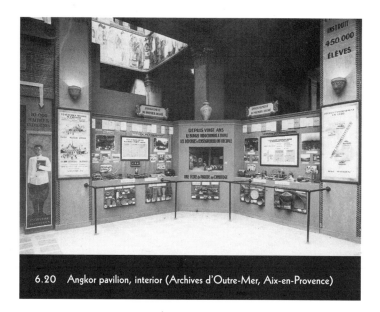

6.20   Angkor pavilion, interior (Archives d'Outre-Mer, Aix-en-Provence)

was altered: "The palace will preserve its two floors, its 150 meters of extension of facade and its 60 meters of height, the dimension of the Notre-Dame towers in Paris. The interior of the monument, by contrast, will be resolutely modern and perfectly adapted to its ends, with vast halls where air and light will penetrate abundantly, spacious passageways, wide staircases permitting an easy circulation of the crowds"[56] (fig. 6.20). Here he summed up the strategy for constructing an externally accurate reconstitution of the Angkor complex, while conceding the interior to requirements of modern exhibition spaces.

Courthion referred to exact copies or reconstitutions of indigenous house and palaces as one category of pavilion. In French, the word *reconstitution* means the action of forming anew something that has vanished, reestablishing it to its original condition so that the lost thing is recreated to its former and normal state. This process can occur in reality or by thought, according to *Le Petit Robert* (dictionary): the plan of a monument can be reconstituted according to archeological excavations, or facts reconstituted after an inquiry.[57] In English, "reconstitution" is the method of restoring something to a former condition. This presupposes an original state to which the thing can return and that we can determine it.

Bayard summarized the dominant image of Angkor and the French conception of its principal characteristics in terms of its plastic complexity and "hallucinogenic" surface ornament: "Nothing, outside of an engraving, could give some idea of this fantastic accumulation of columns, portals and stairs, tiaras of stone, galleries and terraces extending out of sight, so bordered by statues and cut by passages and projections that the imagination finds itself stupefied."[58] This stereotype dictated that the Blanches give most attention to Angkor's ornament in its reproduction at the Exposition. This reconstitution had recourse to the Cambodian temple only to the extent that it reproduced (and refined) its moldings and roughly approximated its massing. The plaster ornament was reconstituted by means of molds taken at Angkor and shipped to Paris, from which accumulated defects were removed during fabrication of the new ornament. The added qualities were technical perfection, hygiene, and functionality (figs. 6.21).

> Certain parts of the Angkor-Vat temple at Vincennes are as faithful as molds; the part including the highest tower and the four adjacent towers is a vision of the central part of the Cambodian temple. This reconstitution was conceived on the basis of archeological discoveries carried out by Charles and Gabriel Blanche, architects. The profiles and architectural details, executed by Auberlet, are reproduced as minutely as possible, at their real scale. The porticos encircling this central part, as well as the towers in the foreground, have been planned more liberally for practical reasons, because the original ensemble comprises three encircling precincts, the exterior precinct having a perimeter of several kilometers.[59]

6.21   Angkor pavilion, construction photo (from L'Architecture 53/4, 138)

The molds had extraordinary value as representations of the truth in making this claim of authenticity, as we see in this statement by Marcel Zahar. They were taken under the supervision of Victor Goloubew, member of the Ecole française d'Extrême-Orient and an eminent archeologist of Cambodian antiquities. In a memorandum on the molds, Guesde described the advice he gave to Auberlet, the stucco contractor.[60] Auberlet had constructed the Indochinese pavilions at the 1922 Marseilles exposition and retained the molds that he used there. Guesde advised him that the work of "Mouhot, Doudart de Lagrée, Delaporte, Aymonier, and other explorers who have published their studies on Angkor Wat," together with existing molds in the Musée Guimet at the Trocadéro Museum, contained all the architectural and archeological documentation that he would need (fig. 6.22). Although Auberlet's experience and the

6.22   Angkor pavilion, detail of ornament (from Construction moderne, Aug. 23, 1931, cover)

documentation he had collected for the Marseilles pavilion might be sufficient, Guesde thought it profitable to obtain some new molds to take advantage of the most recent work of the Ecole française d'Extrême-Orient.
In June 1930, therefore, five cases containing twelve plaster molds arrived
in Paris from Cambodia and were opened by a delegation including
Goloubew, Philippe Stern, conservator at the Musée Guimet, and officials
from the Indochinese section.[61] Guesde noted that, just as at Marseilles,

there had been no question of sending the tons of molds necessary to re-produce the monument in its smallest details. Rather, the dimensions and architectural proportions could be the same without reconstituting all the sculptural and decorative programs in their complete verity. This was not "a work of archeological and historical science, but a simple interpreta-tion" approaching reality while actually giving an illusion of it.[62]

By his own admission, however, Guesde acknowledged that the re-constituted temple was not enough to constitute a full representation of Indochina and its colonization:

> The exhibition must give an idea of the whole of the collective life of the
> Indochinese Union; the life of the countries will be, therefore, manifested
> in six pavilions arranged around the central palace and built according to
> the traditional architecture of each of these regions. . . . A whole native
> population will live in these edifices and these villages. Annamite artists
> will give frequent presentations and we dream on this occasion of the cel-
> ebrated Cambodian dancers. Add daily cinematographic sessions, lec-
> tures, an abundant documentation. Nothing will be lacking, as we see, to
> give to the world's public a magnificent and exact vision of Indochina.[63]

The result was an idealized version of an Angkor Wat that never existed. The reconstitution recreated the temple as a shell, elaborately detailed in the Khmer manner, but fragmented and reassembled into a picturesque com-position. It was a scenographic fabrication rather than the purely authentic reconstitution (the temple restored to its original state) that its creators claimed (fig. 6.23). The architects added interior spaces where none existed, and reorganized its components into a picturesque ensemble that was both more accessible to its audience and a more effective pavilion. Whereas the original Angkor Wat is solid below its stepped towers and terraces, the Blanches created a hollow building filled with exhibition halls and lit with glass block ceilings (fig. 6.24). Although allegedly conceived on the basis of

6.23 Angkor pavilion, glass block skylight in courtyard (from Construction moderne, Aug. 23, 1931, 747)

archeological discoveries, the architects felt free to alter the temple into a more functional pavilion by reconfiguring its elements along a Beaux-Arts axis and creating interior spaces for the pedagogical exhibits.[64]

WEST FRENCH AFRICA

At certain points of the Exposition, one meets curious effects of contrast: thus, the central part of the Temple of Angkor-Vat, a stratified block cut like a jewel, covered all over its surface with admirable chiseled motifs, is next to a quarter of Djenné, a West French Africa village where huts of a primitive art appear summoned from enormous chignons of clay run through with stakes.

—Marcel Zahar[65]

6.24 Angkor pavilion (from Construction moderne, Aug. 16, 1931, pl. 182)

The French West African section, by architects Germaine Olivier and Jacques-Georges Lambert, was a large collection of pavilions based on a mélange of African styles (fig. 6.25). This collection of pavilions in simulated red clay stucco (*pisé*) were meant to represent a *tata* or Sudanese fortified palace. Two hundred natives came to inhabit these pavilions and work in its displays and shops (fig. 6.26). This section contrasted sharply with the more civilized style of neighboring Angkor Wat. Within the social Darwinian hierarchies established at the Exposition, juxtaposition of these structures heightened the contrast between the "higher" achievements of certain cultures and the more "primitive" productions of others. As Jean Gallotti described it, the French West African section was a large but monotonous collection of pavilions based on a mélange of African styles. The uniformity of the architecture is an indication of the lack of importance attached to individual cultures of Dahomey, Senegal, the Sudan, Guinea, Mauritania, Upper Volta, Nigeria, and the Ivory Coast, all

6.25   French West Africa section, aerial view (from Olivier, Rapport général, vol 2, pt. 1, 32)

countries grouped under the appellation French West Africa (*L'Afrique occidentale française*). These countries all belonged to what was known as "Black Africa," sweepingly defined as the home of the black race in a French geography textbook from the 1930s.[66] Although the Exposition's *General Report* paid homage to the individuality of the eight countries and to the need to present this "heterogeneous mosaic" in its diversity, the architecture did not render this variety.[67]

This tendency to conflate all the cultures and peoples of "Black Africa" typified contemporary attitudes toward *art nègre* (Negro art), as can be seen in a contemporary work, Georges Hardy's *L'Art nègre: l'art animiste des Noirs d'Afrique*. In his introduction, Hardy decried then-current talk of an *art nègre*, saying that Europeans did not speak of a corresponding *art blanc*. He

6.26   Natives, French West Africa section (from Trillat)

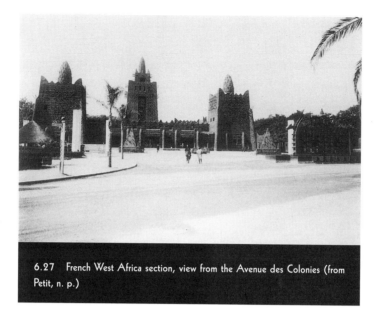

6.27   French West Africa section, view from the Avenue des Colonies (from Petit, n. p.)

warned the reader against simplistic ideas and adoption of a synthetic view of Black Africa, since it was an immense world populated by 100 million people. Whereas he insisted that the Negro did not exist in the sense of the "animal-man" of popular imagination, however, he continued to perpetuate the very stereotypes of a unified "black race" and its art that he seemed to repudiate at the beginning of his book. The limited climatic and geographical resources of the African continent, the "unity of Negro-African languages," and the "common preferences of the race" conspired to produce a uniformity of cultural expression that Hardy called "animism." Having made these generalizations, he continued his study of "Negro art" without further differentiating among the peoples of Black Africa.[68]

The Colonial Exposition similarly homogenized French West Africa into a unitary architectural entity (fig. 6.27). The architects previously designed west African pavilions at the 1922 Exposition in

Marseilles and the 1925 Decorative Arts Exposition in Paris. At the 1931 Exposition, the section included a main pavilion, an indigenous village, a mosque from the Sudan, a "fetishist" village of straw huts, a restaurant, and huts housing natives.[69] A series of small pavilions recreated a street from Djenné (*la rue de Djenné*), a picturesque, narrow path lined with didactic exhibits and shops assembled to give the impression of an African town (fig. 6.28). In front of the whole ensemble, a large esplanade provided an open area for indigenous dance performances, parades, and other ceremonies. The architectural whole formed the backdrop for the human displays, which Louis Valent called "as perfect as possible a reconstruction of the indigenous life in the black countries."[70]

Olivier and Lambert planned the main pavilion as a courtyard building with a tall central tower and two smaller towers surmounted by "enormous sugar loafs"[71] (fig. 6.29). A grand galerie or grand vestibule occupied the front section. Galleries on either side of the patio courtyard opened onto rooms behind the courtyard's walls; they contained an exhibit of indigenous art, including collections of jewelry. Around the patio, each country had its own room of its raw materials, cultural products, and colonial projects (fig. 6.30). At the back of the patio, the Hall of Products held exhibits on textiles, oils, colonial farming, food crops, forestry products, hunting, and fishing. Exhibits on economic resources and social action, along with a series of photos of modern African architecture, surrounded the hall. The West African committee commissioned a series of dioramas by French artists to illustrate scenes in each colony and the characteristic activity in each locale.[72]

Bas-reliefs by Carlos Sarrabezolles in African motifs decorated the exterior walls of the main pavilion: hippopotamus heads, vultures, fish, banana fronds, and figures derived from "fetishes" (fig. 6.31). Sarrabezolles also sculpted two tableaus of life in West Africa that ornamented either side of the entrance facade near the end towers. To the side of the central door, Anna Quinquaud had two sculptures of typical African

6.28   Rue de Djenné, French West Africa section from L'Illustration, special issue [July 1931], n.p.)

6.29   Tower, main pavilion, French West Africa section (from Construction moderne, July 26, 1931, pl. 169)

6.30   Main pavilion, interior, French West Africa section (from Edna Nicoll, A travers l'Exposition coloniale [Paris: Eds. Edna Nicoll, 1931], 144)

6.31   Main pavilion, entrance, French West Africa section (from Construction moderne, July 26, 1931, 679)

women.[73] Charles Garnier sculpted the doors themselves and decorated the interior of the pavilion. The internal patio, at the entrance to the main tower, contained a large fountain with sculpted lions by Georges Saupique. Over the tower door, panels with the heads of African *types* by Emile Monnier graced the lintel. The Salon de Dakar included two decorative panels by Jeanne Thil: "Le Débarquement à Dakar en 1900" and "Le Débarquement à Dakar en 1930."[74]

The reconstructed Djenné street housed workshops run by the *Pères blancs* of Ségou and Ouagadougou, as well as shops where artisans plied such traditional crafts as weaving fine wool tapestries. A group of tents from Adrar was erected around the walls of the main pavilion, evoking the desert with its camels and warriors, and completing the presentation of a slice of West African life.[75] While the Djenné street had pretensions to archeological accuracy and architectonic unity, the fetishist village, consisting of straw huts grouped around the lake and an African restaurant, produced an image more picturesque than exact (fig. 6.32). The exterior of the mosque was reputedly an accurate reproduction of the Djenné mosque, but it housed a cinema that showed documentary films on West Africa .

According to Louis Valent, Olivier and Lambert patterned the central pavilion after Sudanese *tatas*, houses of kings, and after mosques of Djenné and Timbuktu, of "pure Sudanese style, the only truly original style of the Nigerian countries." Valent described this style as fourteenth-century Berber.[76] Other contemporary sources described it as Moorish or Egyptian in origin because of the trapezoidal form of its porticos and its pyramidal minarets.[77] André Maurois traced this style to Moroccan influences—the Casbahs of the Atlas—on the one hand, and to Egypt and Chaldea, on the other.[78] The *General Report* simply attributed it to the typical Black African house, "in earth or *pisé*, a sort of clay mixed with cut straw, a low habitation, with a flat roof, forming a terrace."[79] In a letter to Lyautey, Camille Guy, commissioner of the section, indicated that the principal pavilion would generally be modeled after the architecture of Timbuktu and Djenné and would borrow its decorative details from the various colonies of West Africa.[80]

The commissioner and his architects chose the tata to represent all the architecture of this vast and complex territory because it coincided with the popular image of the architecture of Djenné and Timbuktu. Zahar explained the juxtaposition and dichotomy as indicative of each "race's" level of civilization: "After work coming from the genius of a refined race [the Indochinese], we discern the summary constructions of tribes that have not yet surpassed the primitive stage. What is simpler, more artless, than this Djenné village of French West Africa, composed of huts in mud surmounted by a dome crossed with wood beams, like a

6.32 Village lacustre, French West Africa section (from Olivier, Rapport général, vol. 5, pt. 2, 300)

chignon run through with pins. . . . Here, for the needs of the Exposition, the residences have been considerably enlarged."[81] Zahar's last remark verifies the fact that this section was not an archeologically correct reproduction of a *tata*, but rather a composite of west African architecture, altered to produce the requisite impression of grandeur and monumentality. Jean Gallotti insisted that it was only an "exaggeration," not a fantasy, and that it was "imprinted with a strong character, with a sober grandeur, with a barbarian strangeness."[82] Antony Goissaud stated that French West Africa was a "personal architectural composition inspired by Sudanese architecture without copying any edifice."[83] An ambiance of exoticism was, however, more important to this section than accurate replication of architectural details, a marked disparity with the concern for detail exhibited by Angkor Wat's architects.

In 1931 west African architecture was less familiar in France than the architecture of other French colonies, although monuments such as the Great Mosque at Djenné, the ostensible source for the mosque in the section, were well known. Although it is not possible to reconstruct the references that architects of the section used or had access to, I projected a partial bibliography of popular and scholarly sources available at the time and traced a genealogy of previous pavilions.[84]

European contact with west Africa dates from the fifteenth century when Portuguese explorers traveled down the coast and landed at Senegal, Cap-Vert, Sierra Leone, and other locations.[85] These men brought the earliest images of West African art and culture to Europe in the form of small, portable objects such as horns, ivory spoons, and forks, objects that were often commissioned by Europeans and inspired by European art.[86] Early accounts of African culture by Europeans depicted societies with well-structured states, prosperous people, and wealthy, commodious cities.[87] This vision changed in the sixteenth century with the advent of slaving, replaced by the myth of what Sally Price calls "primitive man" and Jean Laude refers to as the "wicked savage."[88] During the sixteenth and seventeenth centuries, French commercial development was largely limited to the coast around Saint-Louis and Gorée, with a few other ports of call at which trading companies concentrated their outposts.[89] A number of French, Dutch, and German explorers did undertake missions to parts of west Africa, including Jannequin in 1643, André Brue, Dapper, and Müller in the late seventeenth century, and Le Maire and Froger in the mid-eighteenth century.[90]

Travel accounts and their illustrations served to make "mysterious" west Africa less enigmatic, but also promulgated stereotypical images of the architecture. In addition to travel and exploration, literature, painting, photography, and advertising reinforced these images of primitive huts made of earth and straw.[91] As Labelle Prussin points out, after the period of conquest began, Europeans categorized West African geography and the culture of its inhabitants under two general rubrics: that of the savanna or Saharan sahel, associated with Islam and civilization, and that of the rain forest, associated with paganism and savagery.[92] When French commentators attributed a higher degree of civilization to West Africa, they often evoked the architecture of Djenné and Timbuktu as typical for the entire region, whereas their reference to the straw huts of the jungle areas depicted the natives as barbarian savages[93] (fig. 6.33).

The French universal and colonial expositions were one of the means for promulgating these images. The first displays were auxiliary to the French sections, as at the 1855 Exposition Universelle in Paris where the exhibit consisted of products from the colonies without didactic or thematic organization.[94] The exhibits continued to be minor elements of French colonial sections until 1889 when two small mosques within a Senagalese village appeared at a universal exposition.[95] The 1889 exposition was also notable for Charles Garnier's *Histoire de l'Habitation Humaine*, in which he recreated twenty-three full-scale houses including several cabanes du Soudan and a maison au Soudan.[96] The 1896 Rouen exposition

6.33 Village in Mangbetou, Belgian Congo (from Georges-Marie Haardt and Louis Audouin-Dubreuil, *La Croisière noire*, Expedition Citroën Centre-Afrique [Paris: Plon, 1927], 224)

featured a Village noirs (fig. 6.34) and the 1897 exposition at Brussels included a Village Sénégalais.

With the 1900 pavilion, the West African exhibit achieved its most recognizable form: the Sudanese mosque. Louis Scellier de Gisors, architect for the Sudan, Congo, and Senegal pavilions, found inspiration in Timbuktu, probably the mosque of Sankouré or Djingarey-Ber.[97] At the end of the nineteenth century, after the conquest of western Sudan by Marshal Faidherbe, the newspaper *Le Figaro* sent Félix Dubois to Timbuktu to document this new territory and its secrets. The result was the overnight best seller, *Tombouctou, la Mystèrieuse*, combining journalistic "objectivity" with Orientalist sensationalism.[98] Dubois' accounts of architecture in Djenné and Timbuktu made images of these earth constructions widely known in France and probably influenced Scellier de Gisor's design. The West African pavilion at the 1906

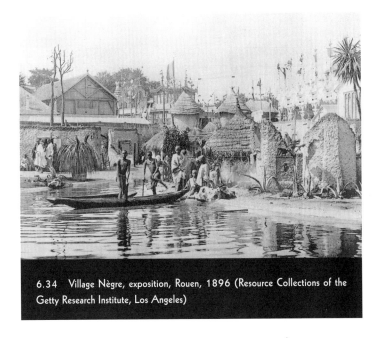

6.34   Village Nègre, exposition, Rouen, 1896 (Resource Collections of the Getty Research Institute, Los Angeles)

exposition in Marseilles followed similar precedents in its "neo-Sudanese" style, or style *sahélo-soudanienne*, as Nadine Beauthéac calls it, made from an amalgam of domestic and religious sources[99] (fig. 6.35). The African pavilions at the 1910 Brussels Universal Exposition, the 1911 Roubaix Colonial Exposition, the 1922 Marseilles exposition, and the 1925 Paris Decorative Arts Exposition adopted this mode.[100]

Each successive exposition constructed higher towers, from the relatively small 35-meter one at Marseilles in 1906 to the 57-meter colossus of 1922 (fig. 6.36). By contrast, the highest tata in Timbuktu was only 15 to 20 meters.[101] The scale and monumentality of the Olivier and Wulffleff's section at the 1922 Colonial Exposition provoked a surprised reaction in the press: "The great interest of the French West Africa palace was that, for the first time, the public has had a brusque revelation of the

6.35   French West Africa pavilion, Colonial Exposition, Marseilles, 1906
(Resource Collections of the Getty Research Institute, Los Angeles)

existence, in our West African empire, of an original architecture having its own traditions, methods, and typical character, and the impression that the Blacks, whom we have wrongly considered until now as incapable of having an idea of beauty and proportion, have been sensitive for centuries to the joy of constructing symbolic and grandiose monuments."[102] The pavilion to which the astonished French public responded was not the "original architecture" of West Africa, but the hybrid product of French architectural monumentality and a mixture of Sudanese forms that became associated with "authentic" West African architecture.

Olivier and Lambert employed this formula in their complex for the 1931 Exposition, although they reduced the tower to 45 meters[103] (fig. 6.37). The contrast between the tata derived from Sudanese residences and mosques and the two village complexes—the lake village of straw huts and the Djenné street in simulated earth—placed the relatively

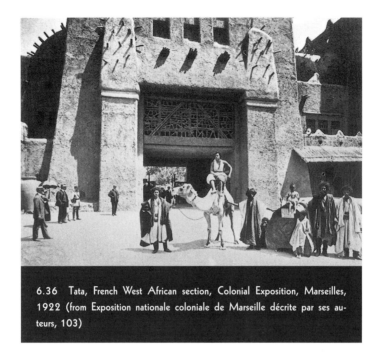

6.36 Tata, French West African section, Colonial Exposition, Marseilles, 1922 (from Exposition nationale coloniale de Marseille décrite par ses auteurs, 103)

civilized architecture of the desert and savanna in opposition to that of the jungle. The conflation of all west Africa into an image of red towers bristling with stakes and a swarm of primitive huts indicates the architects' relative lack of detailed knowledge of the area's architecture and their willingness to substitute picturesque effect for accuracy.

What this version of West Africa also effaced was the brutality and violence of colonization in West Africa. Pacified natives who worked their crafts in the shops and rowed their boats at Vincennes were forced at home to labor on rubber plantations and railway projects in huge numbers. In *Voyage au Congo*, André Gide documented the horrors of forced labor and maltreatment during construction of the Brazzaville-Pointe Noire railway.[104] Albert Londres wrote a series of articles enumerating the disgrace of virtual slavery in French Equatorial and West Africa that cul-

6.37   Main pavilion and Village lacustre, French West Africa section (from Construction moderne, July 26, 1931, 680)

minated in his exposé, *Terre d'ébène*.[105] For those who wanted to know the results of colonialism, the only images they would have found at the Exposition depicted the raw materials exported and infrastructure projects constructed by the French, not the cost of these "benefits" in human lives and suffering. The idealized picture of happy savages in their indigenous environment effaced the realities of French colonization and its savagery and violence.

ON ARCHITECTURAL PHYSIOGNOMY

In representing souks, a minaret, the huts of a native village, it is appropriate to be at the same time faithful to reality and to add to them, thanks to the magic of sunset and night scenery, that which they evoke of dream and mystery . . . The decorative architecture of the interiors, containing equally the museum stands and documentary dioramas capable of reproducing the atmosphere of a historic scene . . . must be more or less inspired by local color. But, at the same time, it must respond to the need to logically explain . . . with exact inventories and precise recapitulations, the victorious evolution of the civilizing idea across the world.[106]

The rhetoric of authenticity espoused by Colonial Exposition's *General Report* was belied by the hybridity of the pavilions. As opposed to the unselfconsciously eclectic hybrids displayed at nineteenth-century expositions, the pavilions at the 1931 Exposition endeavored to represent the actual condition of each colonized people's culture. The mixture of colonial exteriors with metropolitan interiors produced an unintended hybridity that subverted the goal of representing the absolute difference between colonized and colonizer. The monumentality and European details magnified this hybridity. Blurring the boundary between metropolitan and colonial formed the most grievous and dangerous threat to the coherence of the Exposition's decor.

These pavilions embodied the simultaneous creation of and denial of hybridity by twentieth-century French colonial practice. The Madagascar section encapsulated the type of hybrid produced by earlier Parisian world's fairs and Orientalist fantasies, a hybrid dominated by the exotic and the spectacular, what Edward Said calls "latent Orientalism."[107] This form of hybrid was disavowed under the principle of association that attempted to enforce the separation of French and indigenous representational forms. Fournet and Laprade's design for the Moroccan pavilion originated in the *arabisance* of the protector, the Arabic style of associationist segregation. Yet, it too was a mix of many Magrebian monuments. The Indochinese and French West African sections made an instructive contrast of refinement and primitiveness. There was no question about the provenance of the Angkor Wat reconstitution: however much it was reconfigured and altered, the pavilion clearly referred to an original monument that gave it authority and authenticity. The West African pavilions, especially the tata structures, had no such clear genealogy in indigenous monuments, but were, instead, interpreted mixtures of various Sudanese sources.

As physiognomies of native culture, the pavilions were required only to maintain authenticity on the exterior. By combining disparate architectural elements and recognizable images from native architecture, the architects designed composite physiognomic types that represented the evolutionary status of a colonized people. The split between interior and exterior was not problematic or threatening to the requirement for authenticity as long as the exteriors conformed to established stereotypes for respective colonies. Furthermore, the standards of authenticity were fluid, dependent on the respect with which the French held a given indigenous culture, the type of visual knowledge available to the architects, and the standards fixed by antecedent expositions.

The attempt to constitute a consistent, hierarchized environment in which the division between colonizer and colonized would be fully lisible can be judged by the discrepancy between interiors and exteriors of the pavilions and the composite nature of their external architectural vocabularies. Courthion's categories of "exact reconstitution," stylized interpretation," and "original creation" connote the degrees of hybridity. The Moroccan section was the most successful in this respect, because it integrated metropolitan elements (exhibits and interior spaces) with indigenous elements (Maghrebian details, massing, and planning), while maintaining a uniformly Moroccan appearance. No discordant metropolitan element appeared to destroy its illusion of an exotic realm apart or seemed to spoil that separation required by association and social Darwinism. This most hybrid production seemed to be the most native. The Exposition blended indigenous styles with metropolitan grandeur, "savage" vocabularies with "civilized" monumentality, to generate an architectural representation of French authority. The pavilions placed emphasis on the indigenous half of this formula, but in a dangerously ambiguous manner that skirted the boundary between exotic and civilized.

NATIONAL OR COLONIAL ARCHITECTURE: THE MUSEE DES COLONIES

IN REALITY, PARIS IS ESSENTIALLY A CLASSICAL AND FRENCH CITY; THAT IS ITS GLORY AND ITS FULL EXTENT. THE POINT OF PERFECTION WAS REACHED AROUND ABOUT THE MIDDLE OF THE EIGHTEENTH CENTURY, AFTER THE EXCESSES OF ROCOCO TENDERNESS, AND BEFORE THE RIGIDITIES OF ULTRA-CLASSICISM, WHICH LED IT TO PERISH FROM A KIND OF SCLEROSIS OF THE ARTERIES.
—ALBERT GUÉRARD[1]

IT IS OUT OF THE QUESTION, CERTAINLY, TO ORIENTALIZE OR "AFRICANIZE" OCCIDENTAL ART, NOR WOULD IT BE APPROPRIATE TO DISTORT

NATIVE ART WITH THE OPPRESSIVE STAMP OF THE OCCIDENTAL AES-
THETIC.... UT OUR ANTIQUE AND ILLUSTRIOUS EUROPE, HAVING BURNED
WITH TOO MANY ARDORS IN ALL MATTERS OF ART AND THE SPIRIT, NEEDS
AN INFLUX OF YOUTHFUL VIGOR INTO ITS DESICCATED ARTERIES.
—ALBERT SARRAULT[2]

The Musée des Colonies provides a case study of contested discourses in French architecture between the wars. French classicism had become, in the views of architect Guérard and colonialist Sarrault, a feeble and exhausted tradition. For architects and theorists concerned with renovating this tradition into a modern French architecture, the Orient offered a potential source of revitalization, but one with complicating consequences. Sarrault posited a vague rejuvenation of European culture by injection of "youthful vigor" from the colonies, a reanimation that stopped short of "Orientalization" of Western culture. He did not, however, divulge the precise formal and symbolic content of that vigor, and left in suspension the means by which colonial art might transform European art.

Questions raised by this indeterminate rejuvenation, inspired by native culture, were intrinsic to the program and design of the museum. The museum was unique at the 1931 Colonial Exposition as the only pavilion built as a permanent edifice and the only one that represented both France and her colonies. Its architects faced such issues as whether the museum should have inspiration from colonial architecture and, if so, what form that inspiration should take. How could the museum represent the relationship between the *Métropole* and the colonies without compromising French cultural superiority, particularly if it represented La plus grande France, the amalgam of France and her colonies? Could French architecture borrow from naive and primitive styles of colonized cultures without becoming dangerously hybrid? The conflict between France as an integrated unity of *Métropole* and colonies, as opposed to France as a loose association of provinces and colonies, underlay an ambiguity in the museum's purpose and design. These contradictions reveal disparities within French national identity, her colonial policies, and practices that could not be neatly resolved in a single building.

"A DISCREET EXOTIC SAVOR": THE MUSEUM'S PROGRAM AND DESIGN

The Museum of the Colonies, as described in the Exposition's *General Report,* was to "symbolize, in its structure, its decoration and its installations, the entire work realized in the colonies by the French genius, in the past and the present."[3] It was conceived on the model of the Tervueren Museum in Brussels, the Colonial Institute in Amsterdam, and the Imperial Institute in London as a clearing-house for information on the results and techniques of French colonization. During the Exposition, the museum housed historic and synthetic exhibits of France's colonial empire and, from 1935 to 1960, served as the Parisian museum of colonialism.[4] Its exhibits were a microcosm of ethnographic artifacts, historical objects, statistical displays, and recreated native environments found in the Exposition as a whole. The museum now serves as the Musée des Arts Africains et Océaniens, a pedagogic institution with limited collections.

The first laws relative to the Exposition included provisions for a permanent Museum of the Colonies. The law of March 17, 1920, authorized organization of an *Exposition colonial interalliée* with a permanent museum that, during the Exposition, would house exhibitions for the minister of the colonies Algeria, Morocco, and Tunisia.[5] The 1920 law envisaged an ambitious complex of natural and manufactured exhibits, together with a park containing colonial fauna and flora.[6] The eventual site for the museum, established in 1927, was a rectangle of land belonging to the School of Arboriculture and Horticulture adjacent to the Porte Dorée. At the same time, offices for the North African colonies were removed from the museum's program and located in separate pavilions for Morocco, Algeria, and Tunisia.[7]

7.1   Aerial view, Porte d'Honneur, Section Métropolitaine, and Musée des Colonies (from Olivier, *Rapport général*, vol. 2, part 1, 90)

With this change, the museum became part of an ensemble of metropolitan buildings around the Exposition's main entrance at Porte Dorée (fig. 7.1). The other metropolitan pavilions at the Porte d'Honneur were unmistakably French as signified by the Art Deco style. The Cité des Informations contained a long reflecting pool that might have made reference to water elements in Moroccan gardens, but its structure was unambiguously modern and European. Audoul's Section Métropolitaine anticipated the classicizing style of the 1930s, with its massive tower and stepped massing. It was featured in the modernist journal, *L'Architecte,* as a progressive design at the Colonial Exposition, along with the Cité des Informations and Togo and Cameroon, Madagascar, and Guadeloupe pavilions.[8] The museum had a different function as the site of colonial exhibits, the aquarium, and the future monument of French colonialism in Paris; therefore, it required a distinct character.

7.2   Léon Jaussely, Proposed elevation, Musée des Colonies, 1927 (Archives d'Outre-Mer, Aix-en-Provence)

The initial scheme was designed by Léon Jaussely, a winner of the Ecole des Beaux-Arts Grand Prix de Rome in 1903 who was best known for his urban plans.[9] He was director of architecture (*architecte en chef*) for the Exposition from 1921 to 1927 and in this capacity produced various schemes for its site plan and for other aspects of the Exposition.[10] His scheme for the museum, at the time intended to house the North African exhibits, was designed in a pastiche of exotic styles variously described as "mixed North African" or "Algero-Tunisian" (fig. 7.2). In May 1927 he presented his design to the Comité Technique, the administrative body charged with overseeing architectural and engineering matters at the Exposition. The committee members did not favorably receive Jaussely's project. They sharply attacked its colonial style and declared that there was no reason to adopt a "North-African" style rather than an "Indo-Chinese" or "Sudanese" style, and even less reason to mix them.[11] The pastiche of exotic styles was considered inappropriate for an edifice meant to represent France as well as her colonial empire.

Léandre Vaillat succinctly summarized the problem in a 1928 review of the Exposition and its architecture. He stated that the evocation of Andalusian gardens and Moorish cafes in a "determined style" might be suitable for the Moroccan pavilion, but the museum had to endure the Parisian light and ambiance. A little tact was, therefore, essential. "It was necessary to proceed by equivalence, to transpose, in some way, the taste for exoticism without localizing its evocation."[12] He made the problem clear: the museum had to be a national *and* a colonial monument, a task complicated by debates over aesthetic definitions of "national" and "colonial" architecture at the time.

Nationalism in this case meant the nationalism of *La plus grande France.* Questions of national identity, including integration of provinces and colonies into a nation, collective cultural expressions of the Republic, and the basis of national unity, were vexed issues throughout the nineteenth and early twentieth centuries. After the 1789 Revolution, efforts to define the nation evolved as a reaction to the loss of collective identity that came with the monarchy's fall. The diverse cultures and peoples of republican France had few common political or cultural points of reference once the king, who had personified France, was toppled.[13] A new definition of the nation was constructed by the Republic's leaders through the invention of a new national image, traditions, and institutions founded on the nation, rather than the king, as the source of political legitimacy.[14] A matrix of unifying republican organizations was founded on monarchical institutions that had, in the seventeenth century, begun to forge a relative community out of language and culture. Subsequent regimes extended the homogenization of France through uniform administration, territorial division, and scholastic and cultural systems.[15]

The definition and character of the new nation were still difficult problems even after the institutional structure of republican France was determined.[16] For example, in 1882, Ernest Renan gave a lecture at the Sorbonne, *Qu'est-ce qu'une nation?* in which he formulated a theory to counter the German system of nationhood based on race, language, religion, and state. He systematically repudiated each of these categories as based on errors, mistakes of confusing race and dynasty with nation, and of giving a false importance to language, religion, and geography. " Man is slave neither of his race nor his language nor of his religion, nor of the course of rivers nor of the direction taken by mountain chains. A large aggregate of men, healthy in mind and warm of heart, creates the kind of moral conscience which we call a nation."[17] He proposed instead that *patrie* was founded on "forgetting," a "legacy of memories," "present-day consent" or the will to live together, and a "spiritual principle" that formed the conscience of the nation.[18]

In the absence of a more "fundamental" cohesiveness, leaders of the Republic and subsequent governments constructed a conceptual unity based on the claim that France was the "Queen of Civilization," the most civilized nation in the world, and that it was the "civilizing instinct" or *mission civilisatrice* that united all Frenchmen.[19] This unity was fictitious, an invention that attempted to counter the country's lack of geographic and cultural homogeneity. As Eugen Weber pointed out, Bretons, Provençals, and Alsatians had no common language, traditions, or "race," and their traditional government had been eliminated by the Revolution.[20] The arts were primary carriers of Frenchness since they were one of the bases for the claim to be the seat of civilization, not to mention one of the chief means of nationalist propaganda. Museums formed one of the principal means for promulgating national ideologies in France and other nation states. According to Carol Duncan: "Art museums ... appeared just at the moment when notions of the public and public space were first being defined throughout Western Europe. ... If the various capitals of Europe and, later, America, ended up with similarly conceived art museums, it was because, from the start, those nation-states and cities had similar ideo-

7.3 Le Tableau des Races (from Atlas colonial illustré [Paris: L'Illustration, 1922])

logical needs, and public art museums afforded them similar ideological benefits."[21] Museums promulgated unified conceptions of French culture, language, and arts, unifying factors that provided a common national identity for the disparate peoples, although this identity was conceived and disseminated from Paris and the central government without reference to local traditions.

The problem of integrating the diverse cultures of metropolitan France into a republican nation was given additional scope when the nation acquired a new colonial empire in the late nineteenth century (fig. 7.3). Nationalist thinkers linked France's place among the great nations of the world and her economic well-being with the acquisition of a colonial empire. In his treatise on colonization, *De la colonisation chez les peuples modernes,* Paul Leroy-Beaulieu alleged that, "*Le peuple qui colonise le plus est le premier peuple*" ("The people that colonizes the most is the premier people"). Furthermore, he believed that colonization "is the expansive force of a people, its reproductive strength, its dilation and multiplication across space; it is the submission of the universe, or a vast part [of it], to its customs, its ideas, and its laws."[22] Jules Ferry, great advocate of French colonialism, linked French colonial and industrial policy and saw exportation of French goods to the colonies as the key to prosperity for the manufacturing states of Europe. Without an expansionist foreign policy, he predicted that France would descend from the first to the third or fourth rank of European powers. Her destiny was to be "a great country . . . she must carry everywhere where she can her language, her customs, her flag, her arms, her genius."[23]

If culture was the universal glue that held the nation together, how could divergent cultures from the colonies be integrated into the nation? *La plus grande France* required a new definition that would articulate the new form of associative imperialism. The premise of France as civilizer demanded that the colonies be encompassed into the metropolitan culture, since the concept that Africans or other natives could not be integrated threatened the theoretical structure on which republican national unity had been built.

This conundrum had its correlate in the Museum of the Colonies, a structure that embodies both the colonial empire and the *Métropole* itself. The Comité Technique rejected Jaussely's mixture of North African styles because it referred too strongly to the nation's colonial side. The museum's design had to represent *La plus grande France* while staying within the representational hierarchies established at the Exposition.

Albert Laprade, another Beaux-Arts-trained architect, provided the solution to designing a nonspecifically colonial museum appropriate to the capital.[24] At the same Comité Technique meeting in which Jaussely's scheme was rejected, Laprade presented several perspective sketches for an alternative design. According to his notes, the committee responded with approbation to one sketch that showed "a great tapestry of stone in warm tonalities . . . a tapestry sheltered by a sort of light canopy, evoking the

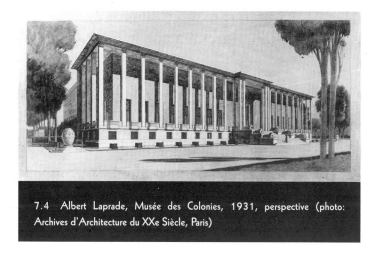

7.4   Albert Laprade, Musée des Colonies, 1931, perspective (photo: Archives d'Architecture du XXe Siècle, Paris)

countries of the sun in a neutral and modern note"[25] (fig. 7.4). He claimed that he avoided an archeological colonial style—"the elephants with hanging trunks, the whole warehouse of Khmer, Negro or Arab accessories"[26]—in favor of a "simple, noble, very calm, very neutral" architecture that "left to the sculpture the concern for evoking the Empire dispersed over the globe."[27] Laprade stated that this approach was "the only solution possible because it would have been illogical to adopt an architecture more Asiatic than African, or the inverse."[28] His desire was "to evoke far off countries while remaining in harmony with the atmosphere of Paris."[29] Laprade was adept at designing in adaptations of indigenous styles to modern planning, having built the new medina in Casablanca under Lyautey, but he shunned this approach for the museum.

Although the attenuated columns and abstracted Ionic capitals of his scheme belong to the classical vocabulary, he denied any explicit connection between his design and "Neo-Greek tradition" or "Greco-Latin canons."[30] Instead, he saw this composition as classical only in its "great simplicity" and described it as "a synthesis of the spirit of the primitive civilizations."[31] Furthermore, he claimed a place for his design in contemporary architectural debates, saying it proceeded a little from the *Esprit nouveau,* but with moderation, so that it was both "of its time" and for eternity.[32] He felt that his project balanced the exigencies of monumental building in Paris, with its obligatory references to the classical language, and the new modern aesthetics of thinner proportions and abstract ornamentation.

In these terms, Laprade's design belonged to the general movement toward classicism prevalent in French architecture between the wars, a corresponding shift to the *rappel à l'ordre* in post–World War I art. The phrase *rappel à l'ordre* was coined by Jean Cocteau in an essay written in 1926, but is commonly used to refer to a return to traditional, especially classical, art forms after World War I. As Romy Golan observed, post-1914 European art was characterized by the desire to restore prewar conventions.[33] What Franco Borsi designated the "monumental order" was the dominant trend in France in the 1930s, such as Auguste Perret's later work, interiors for transatlantic liners like the *Normandie,* and diplomatic and exposition buildings by Roger-Henri Expert. "Order," according to Borsi, implied classicism and tradition as opposed avant-garde and internationalism.[34] Revisionist historian Bernard Lemoine focused on this efflorescence of classical buildings to the exclusion of avant-garde production, and labeled it the *style des années 30,* the thirties style. Architectural historian Jean-Claude Vigato distinguished between the classicizing modernism of Art Deco and the conventional classicism taught at the Ecole des Beaux-Arts. Vigato linked Art Deco with a progressive tendency within mainstream Parisian design, one opposed by traditionalist forces at the Ecole.[35] The French turn toward a classical order is conspicuous in such monuments as Tony Garnier's Boulogne-Billancourt Town Hall (1934), the Palais Chaillot (Carlu, Boileau, and Azéma, 1937), and Auguste Perret's Musée des Travaux Publics (1937–1939). The Museum of the Colonies was one of the first of these overtly classical buildings.

Yet another designation for the modernism of the interwar period was devised by Michel Roux-Spitz: the Paris School. This consisted of a group of architects who complied with principles of the modern movement, exemplified by the Congrès internationaux d'architecture moderne (CIAM), but did not adhere to the austere, "purist" style advocated by Le Corbusier. Their work accommodated the conventions of the Haussmannian block and Parisian zoning laws and maintained recognizably Parisian massing, proportions, and materials within a geometric modernism.[36] Roux-Spitz summarized the dilemma faced by Ecole des Beaux-Arts architects who, like Laprade, sought to balance the dictates of traditional training and the *Esprit nouveau* of functional modernism: "An architect's success, that is to say both commercial and social success, lies in the proportion he manages to maintain between trends and tradition. Between what he perceives as a fashion and the knowledge that comes from an academic education in the fine arts."[37] Although Laprade situated his work for the museum within the *Esprit nouveau,* it was more properly associated with the Paris School and its moderate modernism. In 1929, he designed one identifiably modern structure, a garage on rue Marbeuf, that had won praise as a masterpiece of its kind and proof of his "great talent and audacious initiative."[38] Laprade was associated with the Société des Artistes Décorateurs, a more conservative group than the Union des Artistes Moderne, which was founded in 1929 by Frantz Jourdain, Rob Mallet-Stevens, and Pierre Chareau.[39] He was firmly ensconced in this group, and by 1931 had made a reputation as a talented architect working in the *style moderne.*

As Albert Guérard indicated in his synoptic description of Parisian architecture, however, classicism was the predominant style for public institutions such as the Museum of the Colonies. Marcel Zahar observed that Parisian monuments seemed to require the classical language to achieve the correct degree of dignity:

The Permanent Museum is a curious example of the survival of traditions. Most monuments of past centuries appear with a decoration of colonnades; one concludes from this that no monument can decently appear in public without its colonnade, even if its presence proves to be perfectly useless. The Permanent Museum thus appears like stone architecture. It seems that this makes it more noble, more dignified . . . Without Mr. Laprade, from what picturesque and humorous vision would we have perhaps benefited, what "elephant's trunk" or "pagoda" aesthetic genre? . . . We estimate ourselves fortunate.[40]

For Zahar, the choice of classicism was obviously preferable to a vulgar colonial or Oriental style of dubious taste. Compared with Jaussely's direct reference to North African architecture, Laprade's classicism better suited the program and dignity of the museum. Whereas the classical character of its front facade placed the museum within the monumental French tradition, however, its colonnade is not its primary expressive element. The columns are too tall and slender to dominate. Instead, they form a permeable screen in front of the bas-relief, which performs most of the building's symbolic duty.

Jean Gallotti provided a nonclassical interpretation of the museum's antecedents, one that gave it a more explicitly colonial heritage.[41] In a review of Laprade's design, Gallotti praised its "eternal qualities of beauty in architecture"—simplicity, order, equilibrium, harmony of proportions—as the ingredients of the *style 1930*.[42] He also pointed to specific details that gave it "a discreet exotic savor": "The delicacy of the facade columns, is it a souvenir of the wood porches of equatorial huts? The capitals, have they been borrowed from certain Moroccan houses? The geometrical ornaments, are they from Negro or Berber art?"[43] For Gallotti, Laprade's scheme evoked the colonial world through these elements while being far from a reconstitution or even an adaptation of any colonial style, in contrast to Jaussely's proposal.

7.5   Palais des Colonies, Universal Exposition, 1889 (Resource Collections of the Getty Research Institute, Los Angeles)

The problem of evoking the colonial world in a metropolitan building was original to the 1931 Exposition. At previous fairs, pavilions equivalent to the Musée des Colonies in function were designed in eclectic, exotic, but distinctly European styles. Gabriel Davioud designed the Trocadéro, for example, for the 1878 Exposition Universelle in an Oriental, "Moorish" style. As the backdrop for the colonial section and future home of the Musée d'Ethnographie, the Trocadéro's function was analogous to that of the Musée des Colonies. Although it contained retrospective exhibits for the Exposition and served as the permanent monument of the Exposition after its closure, Davioud made no attempt to characterize it as either a specifically colonial or metropolitan building. The Palais des Colonies at the 1889 fair (fig. 7.5) was identifiably

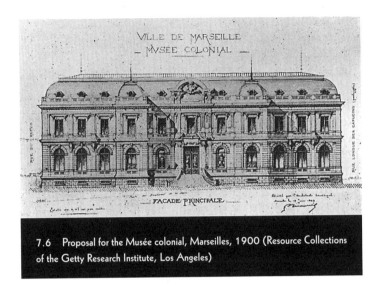

7.6   Proposal for the Musée colonial, Marseilles, 1900 (Resource Collections of the Getty Research Institute, Los Angeles)

metropolitan, designed in an eclectic style native to no particular country. Similarly, the Musée des Colonies proposed for Marseilles in 1900 had no colonial details or motifs and was a strictly Beaux-Arts classical structure (fig. 7.6). The Grand Palais de l'Exportation for the 1906 Marseilles Exposition Coloniale consisted of a classical colonnade with a central monumental arch. At the 1922 Marseilles exposition, the Grand Palais was an eclectic confection, similar to that of the 1906 exposition in its lack of definite stylistic references to colonial architecture (fig. 7.7).

In Paris, few buildings carried explicitly colonial motifs unless they housed functions linked with colonial finance, business, or administration, such as the Ecole Coloniale, or were entertainment buildings, such as theaters, cinemas, zoos, casinos, and park kiosks. Many of these edifices were constructed during the nineteenth-century passion for Japanese and Egyptian styles.[44] The rue du Caire, for example, was decorated with Egyptian motifs in reference to its function as an arcade for rug dealers. Although specific functions were associated with certain exotic styles,

7.7   Muller and Bentz, Grand Palais, Colonial Exposition, Marseilles, 1906
(Resource Collections of the Getty Research Institute, Los Angeles)

such as cemeteries with the Egyptian mode, they were rarely applied to other Parisian building types.

Colonial styles, however, made considerable impact on French decorative arts. Emile Bayard's *L'Art de reconnaître les styles coloniaux de la France* contains a diatribe against the influence of primitive styles on French design, but his objections are largely confined to interior decoration. In the introduction, Bayard denounced what he saw as an excessive admiration for colonial styles applied to contemporary design in a "frenzy of exoticism" and with lack of knowledge. Although the French had a taste for the "captivating naiveté" of primitive art, it should not prevail over the "solid foundation, the manifest genius that the great classical aesthetic currents have propagated across the world."[45] The "savage hut and Arab hovel, the rough idol," could only offer an originality "often without any character other than barbarity."[46] Europeans might admire the "definitive" beauty of primitive art, but they did so without connecting it with the cultures of indigenous peoples. That is, they viewed this beauty simply in aesthetic terms without considering its propriety for French art. Exotic art might "revitalize" French culture, but should do so without fundamentally altering its classical basis and reference to European traditions.

This attitude was typical of the conservative official architecture establishment in France between the wars and conformed to the policy of association. Architectural design education at the Ecole des Beaux-Arts was largely untouched by the vogue for the primitive, as can be seen in a survey of programs assigned for design prizes and of winning entries for the years 1900–1939. Of the Grand Prix programs for these years, only three explicitly related to the French colonial empire or could be designed in a "colonial" style: *Un Palais colonial* in 1909, *Une Résidence du représentant de la France au Maroc* in 1923, and *Le Palais de l'empire coloniale* in 1939.[47] By contrast, painters and sculptors in the Ecole des Beaux-Arts were encouraged to work in colonial styles and were offered various prizes and scholarships to travel to the colonies and to foundations such as the Villa Abd El Tif in Algeria.[48] The "reproductive strength," in Paul Leroy-Beaulieu's words, of French art might be reinforced by colonization, but her architecture remained pure.[49]

Parisian buildings most relevant to the design of the Musée des Colonies were the Ecole Coloniale by Maurice Yvon, 1898, and the Institut d'Art et d'Archéologie by Paul Bigot, 1925–1927. The French colonial ministry founded the Ecole Coloniale in the late nineteenth century to prepare both French and native students for colonial administration.[50] Yvon designed the school on classical principles, but used various Oriental motifs on the facade to indicate the building's colonial function. The Institut d'Art et d'Archéologie was designed in a Moorish style.

A few buildings in colonial styles were erected for the immigrant native populations of European cities. The Mosques of Paris, Fréjus, and Berlin, for example, were Moslem cultural centers as well as religious edi-

7.8   Maurice Mantout, Institut Musulman, Paris, 1926, view under construction (from L'Illustration, Nov. 14, 1925, 518)

fices for the Arab residents[51] (fig. 7.8). The Mosque of Paris, or Institut musulman, was a Moslem cultural center as well as the main religious edifice for the Arab residents, who numbered about 25,000 in the mid–1920s, according to a contemporary source.[52] It served as a symbol of the North African presence in France and as point of contact between immigrant Arab communities and natives of Paris. Its architect was Maurice Mantout, of the firm Heubés, Fournez and Mantout. The Mosque is a rare Parisian example of the North African architectural style that developed under association policy.

In the context of the Colonial Exposition, the hybrid retained its negative significance for Lyautey and his colleagues, as indicated by the reception of Jaussely's scheme for the museum. A hybrid *arabisance* might be acceptable for the Paris mosque within the conventions of what the French could read as Arab, but hybridization between French and native cultures and peoples was generally anathema to colonial authority. Laprade's design for the museum muted its colonial traits and deferred the representation of the colonies to the sculptural program, thereby sufficiently distancing the museum from the taint of hybridity to satisfy the Comité Technique.

"CONCRETIZING THE SENTIMENT" IN THE MUSEUM'S DECORATIVE PROGRAMS

As opposed to the pavilions, in which the architecture itself exemplified the indigenous culture of each colony, the museum's design relied on sculpture and other decorative arts to represent the colonial empire. As Laprade himself stated, sculpture carried the entire responsibility for evoking the specificities of life in the colonies.[53] In Jean Gallotti's words, the bas-relief by Alfred Janniot "concretized the sentiment" expressed in the museum while evoking the colonial world.[54] Given the pressure on the architecture of the Musée des Colonies to provide a suitably monumental and civilized representation of France herself, the decorative programs were the best medium for representing the colonies.

Exterior decorative programs by the foremost classicizing Art Deco practitioners of the day supplemented the museum's architectural expression with abstract colonial motifs. Jean Prouvé, who later became an outspoken advocate of prefabricated construction, designed and built the African cast iron entrance gate at the foot of the monumental front staircase. Four primitive lion figures carved in granite by Navarre flank the gate. During the Exposition, a statue of "France bringing Peace and Prosperity to the Colonies" by Ernest Drivier was placed in the middle of the ceremonial staircase[55] (fig. 7.9). Ornamental grills on the windows at the gallery level and in the base were fabricated by Edgar Brandt and Schenck, respectively. These elements belonged to the subtly colonial, classical vocabulary of Laprade's building.

7.9   Laprade, Musée des Colonies, 1931, front facade (from Trillat)

Although it was the least visible aspect of the facade, the inscription on the side wall toward Paris carries one of the museum's most important messages. It reads:

A ses Fils qui ont étendu l'Empire de son Génie et fait aimer son nom au delà des Mers, la France reconnaissante.

(To her sons who have extended the empire of her genius and made her name loved beyond the seas, France is grateful.)

A list of the names of all the men who furthered the establishment of the French colonial empire, from the Crusades to the twentieth century, lies below this dedication. This genealogy establishes the fictional continuity of French colonial efforts as well as the nobility of its cause, linked with holy wars and voyages of exploration. The military and warlike character of this litany made it unacceptable material for the front facade of the museum, since the Exposition's theme was ostensibly "French peace" brought to the colonies. One proposal for the statue at the museum's entrance was a work by Bouchard on the theme of the colonial army, but it was rejected as too martial. The carved list of Crusaders and "pacifiers," a similarly bellicose reminder of the force required to acquire the colonial empire, was relegated to the museum's side facade.

The bas-relief is conventionally Beaux-Arts in its techniques and forms. It portrays the contributions made by colonies to the *Métropole*— goods, materials, and images given to France. It was conceived and sculpted by Albert Janniot, Prix de Rome winner in 1919 and a prominent Art Deco sculptor of the classical school.[56] His previous commissions included a sculptural group and a bas-relief for the Pavillon du Collectioneur (Pierre Patout, architect, Emile Ruhlmann, decorator) at the 1925 Exposition des Arts Décoratifs and bas-reliefs for the *Ile de France* ocean liner. The design and sculpting process for the museum took three years, which was considered a prodigious feat given the size of the bas-relief: 100 by 13 meters. Janniot devoted the first year to drawing the composition at various scales, another to making a clay model of the whole at half scale, and the third to sculpting the stone with his assistants. Two hundred fifty "personages and animals" are depicted.[57] Janniot's theory of the work was described as a choice of two methods: "the Assyrian-Greek bas-relief where the white void is more important than the sculpted part or the Oriental Hindu-Khmer (or Javanese) bas-relief in which the voids are almost nonexistent and the composition fills the architectural surrounding almost to bursting." For the Musée des Colonies, Janniot chose the latter since "the Assyrian conception was not suitable under our gray sky."[58] His creation also harkens back to a medieval tradition, that of the tympanum above the doors of cathedrals. The tradition of Jean Goujon (to whom his sculpture at the Decorative Arts Exposition was dedicated) and other medieval masters is evoked in the density of the sculpted forms over the surface of the wall and in the relative shallowness of the relief. The plethora of forms and borrowed motifs, from Egyptian profiles to Asian vegetation, attests to the breadth of Janniot's conception of the bas-relief.

This "stone tapestry" was separated into sections by continents, with France at the center of the front facade, Africa to the left, Asia to the right, Oceania on the return side toward Paris, and the American colonies on the other return. A contemporary account described the figures assembling around the pivotal image of France: "The products of all these countries converge with the sailing ships, the freighters, the transatlantic ships toward the central door, surrounded by Marseilles, Bordeaux, Saint-Nazaire, Le Havre, Bourget and surmounted by the figures of abundance and of peace."[59] This "vivid swarming mass" evoked the "potent, but still confused, activity of the less evolved countries" of the French colonial domain, particularly its people at work.[60]

7.10 Alfred Janniot, bas-relief, Musée des Colonies, 1927–31, detail: entrance (from Jean Charnonneaux, Le bas-relief du Musée des Colonies [Paris: L. Reynaud, 1931], pl. 33)

These scenes of colonial life contrast with the allegorical figures of France, her great ports and her virtues that circumscribe the entrance doors (fig. 7.10). Terra Mater or Abundance appears in the center, raising her hand in a gesture of blessing, with figures from mythology—Ceres, Pomona, and the Sun—below her. Peace and Liberty flank her, above figures symbolizing work and leisure. Below them, the great French port cities are illustrated by seminude women and architectural monuments of each metropolis. In figures depicting French ports, racial characteristics of natives are spurned in favor of features and poses of Beaux-Arts classical beauty. Natives of the colonies are portrayed busy in their traditional occupations, primarily agricultural and artisan work (fig. 7.11). In this account, the contribution of the colonies to France consisted of the materials and goods produced by (French) exploitation of the colony's natural bounty, including the labor of its population. Frozen into a productive relation to France, the *indigène* is the "good savage" who labors for

7.11   Janniot, bas-relief, Musée des Colonies, 1927–31, detail: Dahomey
(from Charnonneaux, pl. 6)

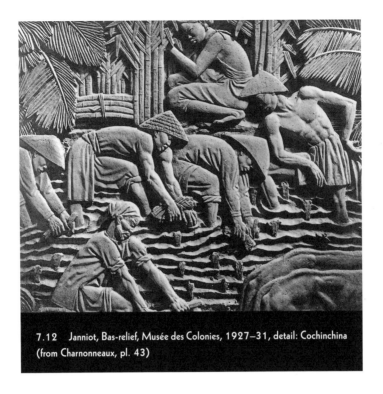

7.12   Janniot, Bas-relief, Musée des Colonies, 1927–31, detail: Cochinchina (from Charbonneaux, pl. 43)

the good of the *Métropole* in his or her organic relation to the earth and labor (fig. 7.12).

The interior decoration of the museum strengthened this lesson on the hierarchies of civilization and evolution in the French colonial domain. For the interiors, Laprade assembled a group of designers who exemplified the conservative strain of French modernism.[61] They worked together on pavilions for the 1925 Exposition des Arts Décoratifs where their variant of classical modernism had great success. Many of these designers, such as Jean Dunand and Jean Dupas, collaborated on the decoration of the *Ile de France* (1927), the *Atlantique* (1931), and the *Normandie* (1935) ocean liners.[62] French ocean liners were part of what Romy Golan

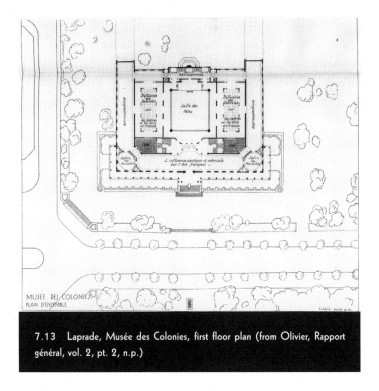

7.13 Laprade, Musée des Colonies, first floor plan (from Olivier, Rapport général, vol. 2, pt. 2, n.p.)

calls a "propaganda machine" launched between the wars to spur interest in the colonies.[63] Many of the museum's designers had, therefore, considerable experience designing in colonial modes as a result of their work on the liners.

Laprade divided the museum into four floors: basement, entrance level (fig. 7.13), mezzanine, and second floor. The entrance level contained a heterogeneous group of rooms and exhibits including the Salle des Fêtes and rooms devoted to exhibits of the influence of the colonies on French arts and letters.

The Salle des Fêtes, an auditorium where lectures, congresses, and performances took place, was the most important space (fig. 7.14).

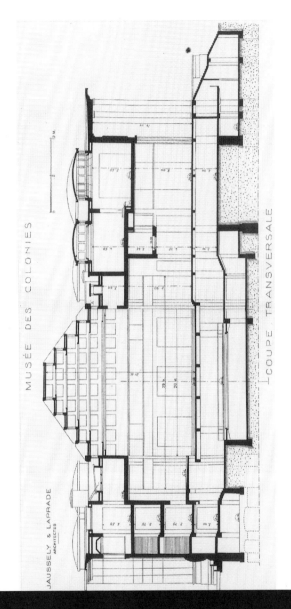

7.14 Laprade, Musée des Colonies, section (from Olivier, *Rapport général*, vol. 2, pt. 2, n.p.)

7.15 Ducos de la Haille, Salle des Fêtes, Musée des Colonies, 1931, mural (photo: Musée des Arts Africains et Océaniens, Paris)

Rising the entire height of the museum, it is a 29-meter square room with a peripheral gallery around a sunken, central area. Laprade placed a small stage at the back for performances and speeches. At the mezzanine level, balconies on each side overlook the central space. Except for the stepped cupola with scalloped edges, the architecture is sober, even plain.

Frescoes are the primary decorative ingredient in the Salle. Pierre Ducos de la Haille, professor at the Ecole des Beaux-Arts and master fresco painter, painted them. They illustrate the overall theme of the contribution of France to the colonies. At the back of the stage, the most important panel depicts "France offering the Dove of Peace to the Five Continents"[64] (fig. 7.15). The figure of France is represented by a fully clothed white woman, holding the hand of a monumental Europe at her side. She dispenses the benefits of civilization to Asia to the left and Africa to the right, which are portrayed by seminude women of appropriate colors lounging on white and black elephants, respectively. A cupid sits at her feet, perched on the grapevine that gives wine to France. A cortege of natives swarms around the figures of Asia and Africa, bearing goods as offerings to the Métropole. Below, Oceania lies on a hippocampus to the left and America sits on another seahorse to the right, pointing to the skyscrapers of dynamic Manhattan.[65] The latter figure recalls those that appear on the column of Antonius Pius.[66]

Allegorical figures of Peace, Justice, Liberty, Science, Art, Commerce, Industry, and Work, mixed with symbols of the colonizers (such as the figure of Albert Laprade to the right of the stage), line the side walls. The rest of the walls are covered with paintings by Ducos de la Haille's students on related themes. The "laboring populations" of the colonies are included here, juxtaposed with the fruits of their labor: mines, construction sites, and railroads of the modern colonies. These frescoes represent what was omitted from the bas-relief—the results of colonial development, but the results are portrayed only as the product of *France's* contribution to the colonies, not as the effect of the natives' own effort and work. In this image of the empire, France, tutor of the colonies, has taught the natives how to reap the bounty of their countries for the benefit of France.

Two oval rooms, the Salon du Ministre (on the Saint Mandé side) and the Salon Lyautey (on the Paris side), occupy the corners of this floor and received the most intensive decoration of any space in the museum. The Salon du Ministre, Salon Paul Reynaud (named after the Minister of the Colonies) or the Salon de l'Afrique, was decorated to celebrate Africa's "contributions of an intellectual, literary, philosophical, and artistic order"[67] (fig. 7.16). The interior was allotted to Emile-Jacques Ruhlmann, one of the best-known Art Deco decorators of the time. The frescoes were awarded to Louis Bouquet (1885–1952), an Academy-trained artist

7.16   Emile Ruhlmann, interior design, and Louis Bouquet, mural, Salon du Ministre, Musée des Colonies, 1931 (from Nicoll, 116)

from Lyon. These images hark back to the Orientalism of Delacroix, Gérôme, and Ingres, which was briefly revived during the interwar period and exhibited at the Colonial Exposition.[68]

The Salon Lyautey, Salon du Maréchal, or Salon de l'Asie (fig. 7.17) was dedicated to the Orient's contributions to the Occident. Eugène Printz, another prominent, conservative practitioner, conceived the decoration. André-Hubert and Ivanna Lemaître, who specialized in decorating churches and were interested in Eastern religion, painted the frescoes. Figures in the frescoes were drawn from Asian myths and religious teachings, articulated around figures of Buddha, Confucius, and Krishna. In the largest panel, these characters appear in scenes from their lives, and other walls depict the music and theater of the Far East and celebrations of primordial elements of earth, water, and fire. The fact that the Lemaîtres were knowledgeable about Asian beliefs perhaps accounts for the relatively accurate and comprehensive pantheon. The Lemaîtres gave the spiritual contributions of the Far East a full description with neither the Orientalist conventions found in Delacroix, Ingres, or Renoir's paintings, nor the excessive stylization of the Art Deco exoticism of Georges Barbier or Erté.

The distinction between the cool sophistication of the decorative elements (furniture, flooring, lighting, etc.) and the writhing, sinuous forms in the frescoes is another instance of segregation of colonial from metropolitan by aesthetic means. The natives are illustrated in their "natural" state, with only the Apollo figure expressing the relationship between colonized and colonizer. The contrast between the refinement of modern furnishings (however much they were influenced by *l'art nègre*) and the primitive and enigmatic riot of colonial life in the frescoes evoked the difference between France and her colonies and the distance between them. As a contemporary account noted: "the strict order of metropolitan civilization, has arrived at a stage where the predominance of simplicity and practical sense feels repugnance for superfluous ornaments and uselessly

7.17 André-Hubert and Ivanna Lemaître, mural, and Eugène Printz, interior design, Salon Lyautey, Musée des Colonies, 1931 (from L'Architecture, 54/7, 236)

complicated forms."[69] This formula indicates that although Asian and African civilization might be "celebrated" in these frescoes, they were characterized in such as way as to reinforce their evolutionary retardation.

The exhibits displayed in the museum had their place in expressing this hierarchy as well. They were divided into three parts: history of French colonialism (Section Rétrospective), current state of colonization (Section de Synthèse), and the aquarium. The aquarium in the basement is the only part of the original exhibits to exist today in its initial place and close to its first configuration. Along with the displays of "colonial" fish, a luminous planisphere where "minuscule vessels ploughed the oceans in miniature" demonstrated "the development of our colonial empire, simultaneously explained by a cinematographic projection."[70] Exhibits of various means of transportation from airplanes to the trans-Saharan railway took up the rest of the basement.

On the first floor, the retrospective section (fig. 7.18) filled the two long galleries along the sides of the building and the gallery in the back. The section on the influence of the colonies on French arts and letters was located in the two halls next to the Salle des Fêtes and the Hall d'Honneur. The retrospective section consisted of displays of furniture and tapestries, paintings of the nineteenth-century Orientalist school, and more recent art works by artists such as Delacroix, Frometin, and Gauguin. Exhibits on the history of colonization from Godefroy de Bouillon to the nineteenth century took up the bulk of this section. Various artifacts and tableaus invoked Richelieu, Colbert, Choiseul, Vergennes, Napoleon, and Louis-Philippe: sculpted wood dating from François I, mannequins wearing uniforms of the first overseas regiments, flags, manuscripts, arms, relics.[71] One area illustrated scenes from *Paul et Virginie,* the famous colonial novel.

The synthesis section offered the most extensive array of the museum's exhibits, explaining the present realities of French colonization. On the mezzanine, "an evocation of the prehistory and of colonial

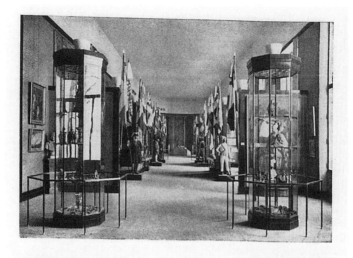

7.18   Laprade, Musée des Colonies, 1931, galleries, first floor (from Olivier, Rapport général, vol. 5, pt. 1, 151)

ethnography and of the indigenous arts" was assembled, along with an exhibit on "The Races," with statues by Founery.[72] This "study of colonial humanity" was filled with material loaned by the Museum of Ethnography at the Trocadéro and the Museum of Natural History.[73] Dr. Paupillault, director of the laboratory at the Ecole des hautes études and professor at the Ecole d'anthropologie, organized the anthropological section, which he defined as furnishing "explicative and practical conceptions" of the "aptitudes and value of the colonized races" to the *Métropole*.[74]

Having traversed the mezzanine and its lesson on "indigenous humanity," the visitor would to go to the first floor to be educated further about the "empire built under the Third Republic."[75] Here, the visitor found colonial products, presentations on the organization of the colonies during the contemporary period, and numerous didactic exhibits on colonial wood, the colonial army, tourism, public works and the like (fig. 7.19). Conquests of the different colonies were depicted with the efforts of "pacification:" "Après la conquête, la pacification totale" (After conquest, total pacification)[76] was the motto for this section. The lighting on this floor was a great technical innovation at the time: Laprade designed large circular and polygonal skylights with vertical glazing to prevent the light loss caused by the soot that typically accumulates on conventional skylights. A library, containing works on the colonies and inspired by the colonies, was included in this area to provide information for the casual or professional visitor. Two immense lacquer panels, *Les éléphants* and *La forêt vierge* (or *Tigre se désaltérant*), by Jean Dunand, famous for his work on the *Normandie*, decorated the two levels of the library (the second level is labeled Salon de Repos on the plan).

This eclectic collection of categories and objects recalls Michel Foucault's evocation of a "certain Chinese encyclopedia" described by Jorge Luis Borges, which Foucault employed to describe a heteroclite ordering of things.[77] Rather than the neat distinction between art works and artifacts, as in an art museum, or between historical and contemporary ob-

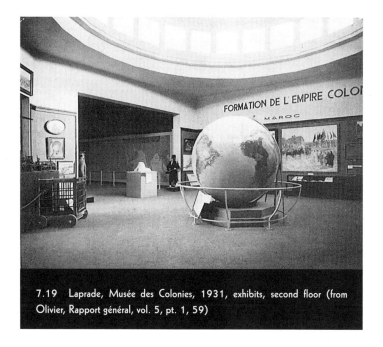

7.19 Laprade, Musée des Colonies, 1931, exhibits, second floor (from Olivier, Rapport général, vol. 5, pt. 1, 59)

jects, as in the natural history museum, the Museum of the Colonies mingled things of native and French, historical and modern, utilitarian and artistic provenance.[78] As Carol Breckenridge notes, the emotive, nonverbal forms of experiencing objects in the cabinet of curiosities were replaced, at the world's fair and in the museum, by more disciplinary languages concerned with authenticity, connoisseurship, provenance, and patronage.[79] These forms of knowledge were equally forms of control, methods with which a usable past could be constructed out of the colonies' messy history and present. The museum failed to fulfill this aspect of the modern museum's mission since it did not provide a lucid, determined ordering of history and the present.

The indistinct, overlapping mandates of the museum's two sections and the split authority for their organization produced a disordered, confusing "potpourri," according to Laprade. In a memo on the interior's organization, Laprade lamented the "bizarre" division of sections and lack of logic in the exhibits' layout. The "fabrics pasted on all the walls, great decorative motives in sculpture, arcades, pilasters in plasters, etc." destroyed the simplicity and harmony of the interiors and contributed to the visitor's confusion, in his estimation.[80] The disordered exhibits represented a collapse of the calibrated harmony and hierarchy that Laprade achieved on the exterior, thereby compromising the legibility of its order.

SOUVENIR DU MUSÉE DES COLONIES

The museum's contradictory program can be read in a painting by Louis Bouquet: *Souvenir du Musée des Colonies* (fig. 7.20). The painting depicts Albert Laprade surrounded by his representational partners: from left to right, Alfred Janniot, sculptor of the bas-relief on the façade; Bouquet, who painted frescoes in one of the Museum's salons; Emile Ruhlmann, who designed the interior decoration of that salon; and Léon Bazin, Laprade's assistant. One more person is in the painting, but she is neither identified nor does she belong to any of the "noble" professions represented by the men around her.[81] She is a bare-breasted, black woman who resembles Josephine Baker, patron saint of *négrophilie* between the wars. She embodies the primitive presence of the colonies in Paris at the Exposition.

This painting demonstrates the relative status of French art and architecture to that of the indigenous peoples of the colonies. The French artists have names and the civilized trappings of their professions, including appropriate clothing, paint brushes, and portfolios, whereas the black woman has no name and wears only a skirt and decorative ornaments for her hair and neck. She is anonymous and representative rather than identified and personal. The French arts are epitomized by white men and the indigenous arts of the colonies by a black woman; the equation of power and knowledge is clear in political, gender, and sexual terms. Native arts are rarely attributed to a particular artist or a precise moment

7.20 Bouquet, Souvenir du Musée des Colonies, c. 1931, private collection (photo: Musée des Arts Africains et Océaniens, Paris)

of creation when they are displayed in museums, at expositions, or in galleries.[82] They are feminine, sexual, intuitive, and traditional, according to this economy of power, whereas French art is virile, personal, upright, and the product of individual genius. This painting might have been made without reference to native, without the figure of the black woman, except that this is the "souvenir" of a building that was not just another monument in Paris: these men designed and decorated the Museum of the Colonies, the emblem of France's far-flung empire.

How well did Laprade's design respond to the task of providing a national *and* colonial monument (fig. 7.21)? As a symbol of association, in which the colonies are culturally autonomous but integral parts of La plus grande France, it failed to articulate adequately the individuality of the colonies and, instead, subsumed them to the homogeneity of the sculptural representation. The museum's architecture represented the metropolitan side of the empire, whereas the sculptural and decorative programs portrayed the colonies, thereby reinforcing both colonial and Beaux-Arts hierarchies. This split was intended to further the Exposition's program of fixing people and things in their proper places within colonial power hierarchies, which made the museum a success within that logic.

The desire to unify the colonies and France was countered by a correlative fear of mixing their separate representational norms. Yet, the museum does contain colonial elements: African motifs in the stone base, primitive sculptures and ironwork of window grills and at the entrance gate, attenuated columns that recall a tropical porch, and hybrid furniture. Like the black woman in Bouquet's painting, the colonized could not quite be relegated to their proper place. While the seamless colonial world fantasized by Laprade and Lyautey could be largely realized in the museum's stately architecture and decorative programs—imaged with docile, productive natives reaping the bounty of nature—it could not entirely resist the hybrid contamination feared by Papillault and Bayard. The Musée des Colonies embodied the national-colonial architecture sought by Laprade, within an uneasy commingling of conflicting images and conceptions of the *Métropole*, the colonies, and La plus grande France.

The decorative programs are therefore supplemental to the architecture. Within traditional architectural theory, as codified by theorists from Alberti to Kant, ornament is always additional to the inherent beauty of a building.[83] In *The Truth in Painting*, Jacques Derrida used this notion of a supplement to the work (the *parergon* to the *ergon*, in Kant's terms) in order to question this classical opposition between ornament and inherent

7.21   Laprade, Musée des Colonies, 1931, perspective of entrance (photo: Archives d'Architecture du XXe Siècle, Paris)

beauty.[84] For Derrida, the supplement is what appears extraneous and additional, but is actually *required* to define the work or entity to which it is added. One of his examples is the architectural frame. The frame cannot be detached from what it frames, as is typical of the supplement. A mutually dependent relationship exists between frame and framed, between center and margin, between the work and its supplement. The ostensibly weaker, less "central" term reveals the lack in the dominant term, but also provides the definition of its edges.

Ornamentation of the Musée des Colonies left intact the primacy of architecture as the true metropolitan expression, the true "civilized" art. It also preserved the opposition of colonized to colonizer. That Laprade abdicated the burden of representing the colonies in architectural terms reveals the degree to which the architecture was *incapable* of representing the colonies without compromising its status as metropolitan, dominant, and primary. The taint carried by the colonial was relegated to the supplement of ornament to contain its threat to that primacy.[85] This status of margin or supplement corresponds to the relative place given the colonies: as margins of French civilization, sites of the most threatening and alluring things, and sources of supplementary labor, materials, and sexuality.

CONCLUSION

No, this is not the future world, countries mingled, races mixed, vices and virtues crossed: it is the Colonial Exposition.
—Paul Morand[1]

The Exposition closed its gates on November 15, 1931, after six months of what Morand described as "butterflies, floating islands, affectionate lions, lightning bugs, aperitifs in rocking chairs, the measured breeze of the punkahs, sun couches, parrots, and orchids."[2] The pavilions, amusements, illuminations, kiosks, dancers, and artisans disappeared from the Bois de Vincennes, with the exception of the Musée des Colonies and the Togo and Cameroon pavilions, which remained as the Musée des Bois Coloniaux. More than thirty million tickets had been sold, making it the most popular French world's fair since the 1900 Universal Exposition. The Exposition featured scholarly conferences and lectures, musical and theatrical performances, special films on colonial subjects, and parades through the grounds. Not only was it an enormous popular success, it was a financial one, netting a profit of thirty three million francs.[3]

The antipodes' visit to Paris ended with a formal banquet at which Lyautey saluted the "good artisans of Greater France," the "Great Ancestors" of French colonial expansion who built her empire. In his final speech as Commissaire, he summarized the goals he had sought to achieve at this grandiose manifestation of colonial power. His first object was to give the "colonial sense" to the French, the "imperial sense" that they had too often lacked; the success of the Exposition was for him proof that it had achieved this aim. As "Lyauteyville, the magnificent résumé of all that which old Europe has made in the Universe,"[4] the Exposition was meant to sponsor greater French pride in colonial France and to generate wider knowledge of its constituent parts. Lyautey claimed that it had also made possible stronger ties between the colonial powers, which he hoped would translate into a charter or a common doctrine for all European colonial policies. This charter had to be based on the policy of association to ensure colonial economic development, endurance of the work already realized in colonization, and cooperation of colonized peoples. Reiterating the themes of his inaugural speech, Lyautey called for the "union of all France behind her possessions in the sentiment that her future is henceforth overseas," and the "union of all the colonizing nations in a policy of association for the greater moral and material profit of all."[5] The union that he promoted, however, actually consisted of strict separation of colonized peoples from colonizers, and concomitant division of their interests. It was this principle of segregation that the Colonial Exposition embodied.

In the preceding chapters I analyzed moments of strangeness and discontinuity within the apparently seamless discursive and representational fabric of the Exposition, those flashes of instability and failure that disrupted its seemingly consistent order. By returning to questions posed in the introduction, some provisional answers can be provided:

What happened when the colonies were brought to Paris in 1931?

Were unexpected meanings produced out of the juxtaposition of the colonies to Paris?

How were the colonies architecturally represented?

Was the Exposition a convincing colonial environment?

How was meaning generated by an architecture that served the dual function of representing French colonial power while it represented the colonized societies of the empire?

The answers lie in the Exposition's status as a collection of hybrid productions collaged onto Paris.

The Exposition constructed the French colonies into a new entity, a *collection*. It was a collection of colonial fragments, taken from their contexts, and reassembled into a new whole, an ideal colonial world based on the classification of visible difference. This collecting operation created a self-contained world that attempted to efface any temporal or spatial discontinuity with colonialism's hierarchies. Representative people, buildings, and objects collected from the antipodes were "evidence" that was frozen in the Exposition's time and space. Every person and thing was meant to occupy its "proper" place. The Colonial Exposition might have been based on Walter Benjamin's theory of historical materialism:

> Whoever has emerged victorious participates to this day in the triumphal procession in which the present rulers step over those who are lying prostrate. According to traditional practice, the spoils are carried along in this procession. They are called cultural treasures and a historical materialist views them with cautious detachment. For without exception the cultural treasures he surveys have an origin which he cannot contemplate without horror. They owe their existence not only to the efforts of the great minds and talents who have created them, but also to the anonymous toil of their contemporaries. There is no document of civilization which is not at the same time a document of barbarism.[6]

The Exposition was a procession of cultural treasures, spoils brought from the colonies to celebrate the victors' triumph.

By comparison with the ethnographic collection as Marcel Mauss defined it, the Exposition produced objects and evidence for "the needs of the case." Mauss based ethnography's claim to objectivity on the fact that it collected "authentic, autonomous objects that cannot have been fabricated for the needs of the case."[7] Paul Rivet and Georges-Henri Rivière exhibited ethnographic objects at the reorganized Trocadéro Museum with didactic explanations and field observations to situate them in their cultural contexts. They attempted to recreate the life of the people who made the artifacts, rather than isolating them as objets d'art or curiosities.[8] The Colonial Exposition, on the other hand, specifically created buildings, artwork, and displays for its purposes. To achieve the necessary degree of authenticity, this fabricated evidence required the exhibition of natives, the one aspect of indigenous life that could not be contrived. Although the Exposition presented a range of indigenous civilizations, it could not be considered an objective presentation. In this respect, it was the precursor of the theme park, which similarly constructs a complete, fictional world with specially created material. Both create ideal worlds that can exist nowhere except in their hermetic environments, isolated from contamination by political and economic realities, a world where differences between people are effaced under universalized Western culture and values.

Although the Exposition closely bordered eastern Paris, metropolitan pavilions screened the visual juxtaposition of Parisian buildings to colonial pavilions. This shield effectively canceled any collage effect that might have been produced by the proximity of native architecture to French edifices. Individual architectural representations further precluded a collage effect among pavilions since each pavilion was reduced to a sign representing a colony, thereby distilling its alterity into a visible record of difference. Unlike the collage effect produced by the ethnographic collection, the Exposition did not generate new meanings for the colonies or French colonialism. Whereas the ethnographic collection takes things out of context and places the proper arrangement of cultural symbols and artifacts in doubt, the Exposition attempted to evade any such problematization of its order.[9] Its isolation from contact with Paris and effacement of the site's history of marginality reinforced the "proper" arrangement of things and people as conceived by Lyautey and his royalist associates.

Yet, the strangeness of bringing the colonies to Paris was read and expressed by some observers. A journalist named Simon remarked on the oddity of mixing and opposing so many styles of architecture: "The reed cabin is next to the immaculate temple of Septimus Severus and the cow-blood red of Madagascar. Further on, the Cité des Informations appears, ultra-metropolitan and modern."[10] The Exposition was not the reproduction of the colonies, nor an accurate rendition of French colonialism's results. It was an idealized colonial world that could exist nowhere except within its precincts; it was a simulacrum of the French colonial empire. "To dissimulate is to feign not to have what one has. To simulate is to feign to have what one hasn't."[11] There was no domain such as was depicted, no basic reality that it accurately represented. The French colonial empire was never the perfectly controlled field that Lyautey and the other organizers hoped to represent. The Exposition was a fantasy, a "hyperreal" construct built out of a fictional vision of La plus grande France.

The Surrealist's Counter-Exposition provided an alternative politics of representation: they juxtaposed objects to heighten difference and to produce new cognitive entities. They juxtaposed *Fétiches européens* with non-Western sculptures to undermine the cultural hierarchies that founded Western stereotypes of primitive art and its degeneracy. They employed the collage technique as a method for calling into question the status of both high art and "barbarian" statues, although their attitude toward non-Western art was highly mystificatory. Even as they valorized intuitive, symbolic, and sensual qualities of non-Western art, they reinforced existing stereotypes of primitive peoples. In this sense, both the Surrealists and the Exposition's organizers took for granted the truth value of material culture as a signifier of cultural worth. The physiognomic categorization of primitive cultures was equally important to both groups as a metonymic manifestation of evolutionary development, but the Surrealists attached a positive value to these stereotypes. The imperialist value system was reversed without being subverted by their practices.

The lessons of Lyauteyville came in a variety of forms, but none was more important than architectural representation. The pavilions and didactic exhibitions that they housed embodied the principles of French colonization. On the basis of human geographic precepts, native architecture represented the evolutionary status of a people. Marcel Zahar placed heavy emphasis on architecture as the means through which "the visitor here receives an initial awareness of the colonies." Unlike a table of statistics, "the quality of the materials used (wood, thatch, clay, stone, etc. . . .) teach us about the vegetative and geological riches" of a country and "the technique of construction indicates to us the degree of intelligence and ingenuity of the builders, the appearance of the facades translates the refinement, the strength, or the naiveté of a race."[12] In the pavilions, the visitor could read the cultural and intellectual status of a colony's inhabitants and their degeneracy or ignorance relative to the superior French civilization indigenous to Paris. Accounts of the heroism of French colonists and colonization's progress in bringing material and moral improvements to benighted heathens regaled the visitor. The colonial pavilions embodied a dichotomy: the insubstantiality and barbarity of the native cultures were represented by exterior stucco shells in opposition to the solidity and enlightenment of French civilization, and exhibited in statistics and photographs within the interiors.

The mixture of colonial exteriors with metropolitan interiors produced an unintended hybridity in the pavilions that threatened the Exposition's goal. The monumentality and European details magnified this hybridity. Cross-breeding, as the melding of two different entities, produces a third thing with qualities of both parents, but its own, autonomous identity. The Exposition's associates, such as Dr. Papillault, saw cross-breeding in the most opprobrious light, as degradation of the white race and incapacitation of its power and progress. Michel Leiris, on the other hand, celebrated the mixtures created by contact between colonizer and colonized. He stated in a 1982 interview that he had: "always been attracted to the Other who is not totally Other, the Other who appears *chez vous.*"[13]

The hybrid does not "stay in its place" because it belongs to no strictly delineated category of phenomena. It cannot be identified easily by surface characteristics and therefore it confounds the physiognomy of difference with the camouflage of sameness. For Homi Bhabha, the hybrid "terrorizes authority with the ruse of recognition, its mimicry, its mockery."[14] Marcel Griaule, Leiris, and other contributors to *Documents* recognized the subversive potential of the hybrid when they valorized tourist art, jazz, and Creole culture, all impure products of the syncretic crossing of European and native arts. As Griaule noted in *Un Coup de fusil,* if Europeans denigrate black art that uses European motifs, "what is one to think of our blind borrowings from an exotic world about which we must proclaim in our defense that we know nothing?" For it is not just the ignorant native who makes hybrids out of scraps of imperfectly assimilated Western civilization melded with her indigenous culture. The Western world equally has a long history of appropriating motifs and knowledge from strange and distant civilizations.[15]

The hybrid cultures of the colonies were perfidious to colonialism because they dwelt within colonial systems, mimicking and mocking the colonizer's authority. As Leiris recognized, this anxious relationship threw both sides of the colonial divide into question:

> Two cultures seem to intermingle in a fascinating, ambiguous embrace only so that each can inflict on the other a more visible denial . . . to merge the *yes* and the *no,* to accept only what comes of an incessant putting in question, a perverse inclination to find enjoyment only in ambiguity and paradox.[16]

In the realms of politics and representation, the subversive premises of the *mission civilisatrice* disrupted the colonizers' carefully constructed world.

Natives' resistance to staying in their assigned place in the colonial world erupted around the Exposition in protests and anticolonial tracts. Natives' claim to the full promise of colonization in the form of self-representation, returned to the colonizer in anticolonial, nationalist resistance.

The theoretical tools with which we understand these complex phenomena are often quite crude. We need the concept of the hybrid to examine the complex mixings at the Colonial Exposition, but it is not entirely adequate. Postcolonial theories of the hybrid tend to favor one side of the colonizer-colonized equation. François Béguin's theory of *arabisance*, for example, leaves intact the myth of one-way influence, hegemonic European control over power and representational systems as ostensibly practiced and as mythologized by colonial discourse. The "Arabizing" of European architectural forms, as Béguin understands *arabisance*, remains consistent with this Orientalist logic. The hybrid as Bhabha theorizes it is characterized by the ambivalent desire to represent the Other while subsuming the Other to Europe's dominance. Although colonialism's ambivalence can be dissected by means of its hybrids, the general category of "hybrid" effaces the historical specificity of colonial discourse and its effects in particular places and times. Furthermore, the generation of hybrids operated in unexpected and strange ways; *arabisance*, for example, might be understood as the colonizer mimicking the colonized, in Leiris's ambivalent embrace of intermingling.

The repetition or mockery of colonial authority was not sufficient to subvert its efficacy. In her critique of *Paris Is Burning*, Judith Butler theorized drag balls as "repetitions of hegemonic forms of power which fail to repeat loyally." The subversion produced by this disloyal repetition is, she stated, always accompanied by uncritical appropriation, which produces ambivalence. Similarly, the hybrid products of colonialism can be read as both sincere attempts to replicate European culture and dangerously subversive mockeries of it. Subversive aspects of the hybrid are not, however, necessarily resistant. As Butler noted, regarding the drag ball, "the citing of the dominant norm does not, in this instance, displace that norm; rather it becomes the means by which that dominant norm is most painfully reiterated ..."[17] The "realness" of the dominant norm is performed by repetition, as can be witnessed in the Colonial Exposition's compulsive enactment of the "proper" roles for colonizer and colonized. The "realness" of its architecture overrode the potentially subversive effects of its hybridity. By repeating the norms of colonialism with sufficient authenticity, the Exposition compelled belief in its truths and reality. Only at those moments when the masquerade failed to conform to the norm, when hybridity came out of its camouflage as the real, was a subversive effect produced.

The Exposition's staging of difference was not totally successful in keeping the metropolitan and the colonial separate, untainted by contamination from each other. Unlike the fiction promulgated by the Exposition, neither France nor the colonies remained the same after colonization. "The linear time of the West or the project of modernity did not simply mummify or overlay the indigenous times of colonized countries, but was itself open to alteration and reentered into discrete cultural combinations," according to Kumkum Sangari.[18] Lyautey and his colleagues hoped that what could only exist in fragments in the colonies themselves—the Europeanized colony inhabited by docile, productive natives—could be realized in toto. This sanitized, unthreatening version of the colonies entertained and titillated its visitors within the safe confines of the Bois de Vincennes. The endeavor to segregate France and her colonies failed, at the Exposition and in Greater France, because it was constantly undermined by the hybrid mixtures that colonization itself produced. Despite Lyautey's efforts to create a unified, unambiguous lesson of European superiority and colonial inferiority, the Exposition was one of those places where colonized and colonizer danced in a fascinating, ambivalent embrace.

NOTES

Introduction

1. Colonial expositions enjoyed a vogue during the 1920s and 1930s, such as the British imperial fair in 1924–1925 at Wembley, the colonial expositions of 1924 in Strasbourg and 1930 in Anvers, and the 1937 Universal Exposition in Paris, which included an extensive colonial section. In 1922 the French hosted a grandiose display of their colonies at the National Colonial Exposition in Marseilles; in 1930, they celebrated the centennial of the Algerian conquest with elaborate festivals in Algeria and France. See Charles-Robert Ageron, *France coloniale ou parti colonial?* (Paris: Presses universitaires de France, 1978); "L'Exposition Coloniale." *Les Lieux de Mémoire,* vol. I, Pierre Nora, Ed. (Paris: Gallimard, 1984)

2. Louis Hubert Gonzalve Lyautey, "Discours à la cérémonie de la pose de la première pierre du Musée des Colonies, 5 novembre 1928," in Marcel Olivier, Ed. *Exposition coloniale internationale de Paris, Rapport général,* 7 vols. (Paris: Imprimerie Nationale, 193–934), 4: 364. All translations from the French are mine unless otherwise noted.

3. Marcel Zahar, "Batir! Informer!" *L'Art vivant* 7, no. 151 (1931): 384.

4. See Keith Walden, *Becoming Modern in Toronto: The Industrial Exhibition and the Shaping of a Late Victorian Culture* (Toronto: University of Toronto Press, 1997).

5. Mikhail Bakhtin, *Rabelais and His World,* trans. Helene Iswolsky (Bloomington: Indiana University Press, 1984), 10.

6. Louis Hubert Gonzalve Lyautey, "Inauguration de l'Exposition coloniale internationale de Paris (6 mai 1931)," in Olivier, *Rapport général,* 4: 374.

7. Barbara Maria Stafford, *Artful Science: Enlightenment Entertainment and the Eclipse of Visual Education* (Cambridge: MIT Press, 1994), xxiv, 1–3.

8. See Vanessa R. Schwartz, *Spectacular Realities: Early Mass Culture in Fin-de-Siècle Paris* (Berkeley: University of California Press, 1998).

9. Robert de Beauplan, *"Les Palais de l'Indochine," Exposition coloniale internationale de Paris* (Paris: L'Illustration, 1931), n.p. Herman Lebovics uses the phrase "seductions of the picturesque" to describe the environment at the Colonial Exposition. Herman Lebovics, *True France: The Wars over Cultural Identity, 1900–1945* (Ithaca, NY: Cornell University Press, 1992), 51–97.

10. André Maurois, *"Sur le Vif," L'Exposition coloniale* (Paris: Degorce, 1931), 24.

11. Louis-Hubert Gonzalve Lyautey. *Paroles d'action. Madagascars, Sud-Oranais, Oran, Maroc (1900–1926)* (Paris: Armand Colin, 1927), 195. Lyautey was the Commissaire Général of the 1931 Exposition as well as a hero of colonial military conquests.

12. Franz Fanon, *The Wretched of the Earth,* trans. Constance Farrington (New York: Grove Press, 1963), 52.

13. Homi K. Bhabha, "Signs Taken for Wonders: Questions of Ambivalence and Authority under a Tree Outside Delhi, May 1817," in *"Race," Writing, and Difference,* Henry Louis Gates, Jr., Ed. (Chicago: Chicago University Press, 1986), 171.

14. Benedict Anderson, *Imagined Communities: Reflections on the Origin and Spread of Nationalism* (London and New York: Verso, 1991), 185.

15. I use the word *Métropole* in the French sense of "mother country" and "metropolis." This term designates France herself, as opposed to *La plus grande France* (greater France) or *La France d'Outre-mer* (France overseas). In 1931 *Métropole* connoted Europe, home of the "white race," and its civilization.

16. Although Belgium, The Netherlands, Italy, the United States, Portugal, and Denmark participated in the 1931 Exposition, I interpreted it as a primarily French event. The French colonial administration set the policies, sponsored the publicity, and dictated the physical organization. I did not, therefore, elucidate differences between French colonial policies

and practices and those of her colonial partners, nor did I examine the foreign sections in detail. For extended analyses of the United States and The Netherlands sections, respectively, see Robert W. Rydell, *World of Fairs: The Century of Progress Expositions* (Chicago: University of Chicago Press, 1993); and Frances Gouda, *Dutch Culture Overseas: Colonial Practice in the Netherlands Indies, 1900–1942* (Amsterdam: Amsterdam University Press, 1995). On Italian colonial architecture and urbanism, see Giuliano Gresleri, Ed., *Architettura italiana d'oltremare 1870–1940* (Venezia: Marsilio, 1993); and Krystyna Clare von Hennenberg, "The Construction of Fascist Libya: Modern Colonial Architecture and Urban Planning in Italian North Africa (1922–1943)" (Ph.D. dissertation, University of California, Berkeley, 1996).

17. Charles Depincé, *La Quinzaine coloniale*, 25 September 1900, 501, quoted in Henri Brunschwig, *French Colonialism 1871–1914: Myth and Realities*, trans. William Glanville Brown (New York: Praeger, 1966), 169.

18. Walter Benjamin, *Das Passagen-Werk*, 2 vols., Rolf Tiedemann, Ed. (Frankfurt am Maine: Suhrkamp, 1982).

19. Walter Benjamin, "Paris—The Capital of the Nineteenth Century," in *Charles Baudelaire: A Lyric Poet in the Era of High Capitalism*, trans. Harry Zohn (London: Verso, 1973), 155–176.

20. Walter Benjamin, "N [Theoretics of Knowledge; Theory of Progress]" (from *Das Passagen-Werk*), trans. Leigh Hafrey and Richard Sieburth, *Philosophical Forum* 15, nos. 1–2 (198–984): 6 [N 9a, 8].

21. Many histories of France contain only the most marginal treatments of colonialism and the French empire, and even less on the Colonial Exposition. For example, Alfred Cobban's *A History of Modern France* has only short sections on the colonies and no mention of the Exposition. Colonialism in France is often consigned to political history or to specialized histories of the colonies and decolonization, such as the *Histoire de la France Coloniale, 1914–1990*, by Jacques Thobie et al. This approach assumes that the French empire had no presence in daily life or culture in the metropolis, that the two halves of the colonial system were, in fact, separate realms. Alfred Cobban, *A History of Modern France* 3 vols. (New York: Viking Penguin, 1965); Jacques Thobie, Gilbert Meynier, Catherine Coquery-Vidrovitch, and Charles-Robert Ageron, *Histoire de la France coloniale, 1914–1990* (Paris: Armand Colin, 1990).

22. See *Albert Kahn 1860–1940: realités d'une utopie* (Boulogne: Musée Albert-Kahn, 1995); Pascal de Blignieres, *Albert Kahn, les jardins d'une idée* (Paris: Editions La Bibliothèque, [1995]); and Jeanne Beausoleil, *Autour du Monde: Jean Brunhes, regards d'un géographe/regards de la géographie* (Boulogne: Musée Albert Kahn, 1993).

23. Kumkum Sangari, "The Politics of the Possible," in *The Post-Colonial Studies Reader*, Bill Ashcroft et al., Eds. (London and New York: Routledge, 1995), 144.

24. James Clifford, *The Predicament of Culture: Twentieth-Century Ethnography, Literature and Art* (Cambridge: Harvard University Press, 1988), 145–146.

25. Michel Leiris, "The Sacred in Everyday Life," in *The College of Sociology*, Denis Hollier, Ed. (Minneapolis: Minnesota University Press, 1988), 27.

26. Homi K. Bhabha, *The Location of Culture* (London and New York: Routledge, 1994), 1–18.

Chapter 1

1. Maurice Tranchant, *Le Tour du monde en un jour à l'Exposition coloniale* (Paris: Studio du Palmier Nain, 1931), 21.

2. Marcel Olivier, ed. *Exposition coloniale internationale de Paris, Rapport général*, 7 vols. (Paris: Imprimerie Nationale, 1932–1934), 2: 91.

3. Meeting notes of the Comité technique, January 14, 1930, January 30, 1930, and May 5, 1930. Bazin worked for Lyautey in Morocco for four years. Letter from Léon Bazin to Hubert Lyautey, December 25, 1929, Archives d'Outre-Mer, Aix-en-Provence (AOMA), Exposition coloniale internationale de Paris, 1931, carton 96; Olivier, *Rapport général* 2: 90–91.

4. The architects for these pavilions were Jean Walter (Publicité), Le Faguays and Six (Aviation), Georges Wybo (Croisière Noire), and Leroy and Cury (Bois Coloniaux).

5. Marcel Zahar, "L'Architecture [de l'Exposition coloniale]," *Renaissance de l'art* 14, no. 8 (1931): 228.

6. Marcel Temporal, "De la lettre de l'esprit de l'architecture dite 'moderne' à l'Exposition coloniale internationale de 1931," *L'Architecture d'aujourd'hui* 1 (June–July 1931): 149–151.

7. Albert Laprade, "Avant-promenade à travers l'Exposition coloniale," *L'Architecture* 54, no. 4 (1931): 119–122.

8. Zahar, "L'Architecture [de l'Exposition coloniale]," 227.

9. Guy de Madoc, "Coup d'oeil sur l'exposition coloniale," *Cité moderne* 11, (June 11, 1931): 7.

10. Jean Gallotti, "Traité de géographie de l'exposition coloniale d'après les plus récentes découvertes," *Vu* 4, no. 168 (1931): 778.

11. Ibid., 782.

12. Pierre Loti, *Le mariage de Loti. Rarahu* (Paris: Calmann Levy, 1880); Victor Ségalen, *Essai sur l'exotisme: Une esthétique du divers* ([Montpellier]: Fata Morgana, 1978).

13. Paul Morand, " Rien que la Terre à l'exposition coloniale," *Revue des deux mondes* 101 (July 15, 1931): 334–335.

14. Letter from Ginestou (commissioner of the French establishments in India section) to the governor of the French establishments in India, February 20, 1929, AOMA, Exposition coloniale internationale de Paris, 1931, carton 9.

15. Maurice Leenhardt, "La Nouvelle Calédonie," *Revue des deux mondes* 101 (September 15, 1931): 366.

16. Anonymous letter, April 29, 1929; correspondence between Marcel Olivier and the Minister of the Colonies, May, June, July, and August 1931, AOMA, Exposition coloniale internationale de Paris, 1931, carton 10. See also Herman Lebovics, *True France: The Wars over Cultural Identity, 1900–1945* (Ithaca, NY: Cornell University Press, 1992), 103, note 13.

17. Morand, 335.

18. Olivier, *Rapport général*, vol. 5, part 2: 1013–1014.

19. Géo Baysse, *En dansant la biguine. Souvenir de l'exposition coloniale 1931* (Senlis: Imprimerie réunies, 1931), 11, 23.

20. Ibid., 105.

21. Correspondence among Lyautey, Olivier, and commissioner of the Guadeloupe section, February 5, 1931, February 18, 1931, and May 28, 1931, AOMA, Exposition coloniale internationale de Paris, 1931, carton 8.

22. Pierre Courthion, "L'Architecture à l'exposition coloniale," *Art et décoration* 60 (July 1931): 41.

23. Morand, 335–336.

24. *Paul Tournon, architecte 1881–1964* ([Paris]: Dominique Vincent, [1976]), 114.

25. The commissariat building was originally constructed for the 1925 Decorative Arts Exposition as the Indochinese pavilion, AOMA, Exposition coloniale internationale de Paris, 1931, carton 135.

26. de Madoc, 7.

27. Gallotti, "Traité de géographie," 777.

28. Antony Goissaud, "Les Pavillons de l'Indo-Chine," *Construction moderne* 17, no. 5 (1931): 76.

29. Ibid., 70.

30. Ibid.

31. Letter from Guesde to Olivier, July 1931, AOMA, Exposition coloniale internationale de Paris, 1931, carton 9.

32. Morand, 338.

33. Germaine Olivier designed the French West African pavilions for the 1925 Decorative Arts Exposition and the 1937 Universal Exposition in Paris. Jacques-Georges Lambert designed the French Equatorial African pavilion for the 1937 exposition.

34. Susan Denyer, *African Traditional Architecture: An Historical and Geographical Perspective* (London: Heinemann and Africana Publishing Company, 1978), 169.

35. Pierre Mille, "À l'exposition coloniale: vue d'ensemble," *Revue des deux mondes* 101 (May 15, 1931): 267.

36. Denyer, 131; Olivier, *Rapport général*, 2: 104.

37. Courthion, 45.

38. Georges Hardy, "Le Maroc," *Revue des deux mondes*, 101 (August 1, 1931): 595.

39. Olivier, *Rapport général*, vol. 5, part 2: 181 and 175.

40. Jean Gallotti, "L'Afrique du Nord," *L'Art vivant* 7, no. 151 (1931): 394.

41. Olivier, *Rapport général*, vol. 5, part 2: 105–106. Victor Valensi wrote a treatise on the traditional Tunisian house, *L'Habitation tunisienne* (Paris: Charles Massin, 1928). See Serge Santelli, "Tunis La Blanche," in *Architectures françaises outre-mer*, Mauric Culot and Jean-Marie Thiveaud, Eds. (Liège: Mardaga, 1992), 77–103.

42. Gallotti, "Traité de géographie," 779.

43. See Wright; and David Prochaska, *Making Algeria French: Colonialism in Bône, 1870–1920* (Cambridge: Cambridge University Press, 1990).

44. Olivier, *Rapport général*, vol. 5, part 2: 30.

45. André Maurois, *"Sur le vif,"* *L'Exposition coloniale* (Paris: Degorce, 1931), 1.

46. Olivier, *Rapport général,* vol.5, part 2: 443–444. Boileau was an active member of the Parisian architectural community who built numerous schools and apartment buildings during the 1920s and 1930s. See Bertrand Lemoine and Philipe Rivoirard, *L'Architecture des années 30* (Lyon: Manufacture, 1987).

47. The Togo and Cameroon pavilions were preserved after the Exposition. They were sold to the construction firm Les Charpentiers de Paris, which gave them to the city of Paris for use as a Museum of Colonial Wood. They are currently used as a Buddhist center. "Achat des Pavillons du Togo-Cameroun aux charpentiers de Paris par le Commissariat général," 17 January 1932, AOMA, Exposition coloniale internationale de Paris, 1931, carton 144; Nadine Beauthéac and François-Xavier Bouchart, *L'Europe exotique* (Paris: Chêne, 1986), 189.

48. Charles D'Ydewalle, "Le Congo Belge," *Revue des deux mondes* 101 (1 October 1931): 617, 619.

49. Courthion, 44.

50. Denyer, 86–87.

51. André Gide, *Voyage au Congo* (Paris: Gallimard, 1927).

52. Cogniat, 327 and 330.

53. Henry Thétard, "Le Parc zoologique de l'Exposition coloniale," *L'Art vivant* 7, no. 151 (1931): 407. Hagenbeck advised the organizers on the enclosures and their construction, supplied animals to the zoo, and cared for them during the Exposition. AOMA, Exposition coloniale internationale de Paris, 1931, carton 112.

54. Gallotti, "L'Afrique du Nord," 402.

55. "Premier bilan de l'exposition coloniale," July 3, 1931 [Paris, 1931]. Reprinted in José Pierre, Ed. *Tracts surréalistes et Déclarations collectives* (Paris: Le terrain vague, 1980), 1: 198.

56. Antoine Cabaton, "Le Pavillon rebâti: les Indes néerlandaises," *Revue des deux mondes* 101 (September 15, 1931): 381.

57. Olivier, *Rapport général,* 7: 278–279.

58. Cogniat, 325.

59. Meeting notes, Comité central d'organisation des Beaux-Arts, March 12, 1931, AOMA, Exposition coloniale internationale de Paris, 1931, car-

ton 19. On colonial artistic societies, see Gustave Vuillemot, "La Villa Abd El Tif," in Emmanuel Bréon and Michèle Lefrançois, Eds. *Coloniales 1920–1940* (Boulogne-Billancourt: Museé Municipal de Boulonge-Billancourt, 1989), 45–51.

60.   Gallotti, "L'Afrique du Nord," 394.

61.   Morand, 343.

62.   "Participations étrangères à l'exposition coloniale, 1927–1931," Archives Nationales, Paris (ANP), F^{12} 11934.

63.   Olivier, *Rapport général*, 7: 121.

64.   Cogniat, 338.

65.   Courthion, 41.

66.   Morand, 340.

67.   Madoc, 8.

68.   Georges Charensol, "La Nuit coloniale," *L'Art vivant* 7, no. 151 (1931): 387.

69.   Jean Camp and André Corbier, *À Lyauteyville. Promenades sentimentales et humoresques à l'Exposition coloniale* (Paris: Société nationales d'éditions artistiques, 1931), 10.

Chapter 2

1.   Marcel Olivier, *Rapport général*, I: xi–xiii.

2.   For histories of the colonial sections at the universal expositions, see Zeynep Çelik, *Displaying the Orient: Architecture of Islam at Nineteenth-Century World's Fairs* (Berkeley, CA: University of California Press, 1992); Paul Greenhalgh, *Ephemeral Vistas: World Exhibitions, 1851–1939* (Manchester: Manchester University Press, 1988); and Sylviane Leprun, *Le Théâtre des colonies: scénographie, acteurs et discours de l'imaginaire dans les expositions, 1855–1937* (Paris: L'Harmattan, 1986).

3.   A. Autrand, "Mémoire de M. le Préfet de la Seine au Conseil Municipal, L'Exposition Coloniale Interalliée de Paris en 1925" (Paris: Imprimerie municipale, 11 mars 1921), Archives de Paris (AP), V.R. carton 265.

4.   Olivier, *Rapport général*, I: 17.

5.   Ibid.

6.   AOMA, Exposition coloniale internationale de Paris, 1931, carton 63.

7.   According to Messimy, senator and member of the Conseil supérieur of the Exposition, all their difficulties had their origin in the sharp

opposition met by Angoulvant in the Finance Committee of the senate. Without giving details of the opposition, he stated that "if the Commissioner General and the Adjunct Commissioners General do not resign their functions, it will be necessary to renounce any colonial exposition in France." Minutes of the Conseil supérieur meeting, July 8, 1927, AOMA, Exposition coloniale internationale de Paris, 1931, carton 160. Later that month, the Finance Committee passed legislation barring any member of the Senate or Chamber of Deputies from concurrently holding a position in the administration of the Colonial Exposition, thereby ousting Angoulvant, elected deputy from French India, and his two assistants, Outrey and Robaglia, who were also deputies. Minutes of the Conseil supérieur meeting, July 22, 1927, AOMA, Exposition coloniale internationale de Paris, 1931, carton 160.

8. Minutes of the Conseil supérieur meeting, July 22, 1927, AOMA, Exposition coloniale internationale de Paris, 1931, carton 160; Olivier, *Rapport général,* I: 74.

9. The state voted a special avenant in December of 1927 to this effect. "Avenant du 31 December 1927 à la Convention du 9 mai 1927," AP, Exposition coloniale internationale de Paris, carton 52, 106/50/1.

10. Léon Bérard, Sénateur, in Olivier, *Rapport général,* 4: 22.

11. William B. Cohen, *Rulers of Empire: The French Colonial Service in Africa* (Stanford, CA: Stanford University Press, 1971), 105–106; Erik Orsenna, *L'Exposition coloniale* (Paris: Seuil, 1988).

12. Raymond Betts, Tricouleur: *The French Overseas Empire* (London: Gordon and Cremonesi, 1978), 74.

13. Dominique Borne and Henri Dubief, *La Crise des années 30, 1929–1938* (Paris: Seuil, 1989), 63.

14. Olivier, *Rapport général,* I: xiii.

15. Louis Hubert Gonzalve Lyautey, "Inauguration de l'Exposition coloniale internationale (6 mai 1931)," in Olivier, *Rapport général,* 4: 376.

16. Olivier, *Rapport général,* I: xix.

17. André Gide, *Voyage au Congo;* and *Le Retour du Tchad* (Paris: Éditions de la nouvelle révue française, 1929); Albert Londres, *Terre d'ébène* (Paris: Albin Michel, 1929); Andrée Viollis, *Indochine SOS* (Paris: Gallimard, 1935); Viollis, *Tempête sur l'Afghanistan* (1929); Viollis, *L'Inde contre les*

Anglais (Paris: Éditions des Portiques, 1930); André Malraux, *La Voie royale* (Paris: Grasset [1930]). Malraux also wrote articles protesting the treatment of the Indochinese by French officials. Jacques Thobie et al., *Histoire de la France coloniale, 1914–1990* (Paris: Armand Colin, 1990), 207.

18. Claude Liauzu, *Aux origins des tiers-mondismes. Colonies et anticolonialisme en France entre 1919 et 1939* (Paris: L'Harmattan, 1986), 80–86.

19. Olivier, *Rapport général,* I: xviii.

20. Edmond du Vivier de Streel, *Les Enseignements généraux de L'exposition coloniale* (Paris: Musée Social, 1932), 5–6. Vivier de Streel was director of congresses held at the Colonial Exposition. On the involvement of Musée Social members in colonial policy and urbanism, see Gwendolyn Wright, *The Politics of Design in French Colonial Urbanism* (Chicago: University of Chicago Press, 1991), 21–30.

21. Lyautey, "Cérémonie de la pose de la première pierre du musée des colonies (5 novembre 1928)," in Olivier, *Rapport général,* 4: 364.

22. Morand, 334.

23. Fernand Sabatté, "Au pays des tours carrée et des minarets pointus," *L'Art* 3 (September–October, 1931): 83.

24. Jean Camp and André Corbier, *A Lyauteyville. Promenades sentimentales et humoresques à l'Exposition coloniale* (Paris: Société nationales d'éditions artistiques, 1931), 9–10.

25. French colonization's success, and the *bonne conscience* of French colonizers came out of positive benefits—education, sanitation, roads, etc. See Henri Brunschwig, *French Colonialism 1871–1914: Myth and Realities,* trans. William Glanville Brown (New York: Praeger, 1966), 167–182; Henri Grimal, *La Décolonisation de 1919 à nos jours* (1965; Brussels: Editions Complexe, 1985), 27–30; and Jacques Marseille, *L'Age d'or de la France coloniale* (Paris: Albin Michel, 1986), 5–6 on *la bonne conscience* and its connections with the *mission civilisatrice.*

26. Morand, 330.

27. Lyautey, "Cérémonie," in Olivier, *Rapport général,* 4: 367.

28. "Le Règlement général et la Classification générale," in Olivier, *Rapport général,* I: 219–285.

29. Olivier, *Rapport général,* vol. 5, part I: 51.

30. Ibid., 52.

31. Michel Foucault, *The Order of Things: An Archeology of the Human Sciences* (New York: Vintage Books, 1973), 132.

32. Susan Stewart, *On Longing* (Baltimore: Johns Hopkins University Press, 1984), 151–152.

33. Krzysztof Pomian, *Collectors and Curiosities: Paris and Venice, 1500–1800*, trans. Elizabeth Wiles-Portier (Cambridge: Polity Press, 1990), 9.

34. The team included Griaule, trained at the Ecole des langues orientales and the Institut d'ethnologie; Marcel Larget, carpenter and mechanic; Jean Mouchet, linguist; Michel Leiris, writer and secretary-archivist; Eric Lutten, in charge of management and technological investigations; André Schaeffner, musicologist; Deborah Lifchitz, Oriental linguist; and Gaston-Louis Roux, painter. [Paul Rivet], "Mission ethnographique et linguistique Dakar-Djibouti," *Bulletin du Musée d'ethnographie du trocadéro* I (January 1931): 11.

35. The most original fund-raising event for the Mission was a boxing match staged between African-American boxer Al Brown and a French fighter, and attended in force by Parisian society. Brown knew Georges-Henri Rivière, director of exhibits at the Musée d'ethnographie du Trocadéro, who convinced him to contribute his skills. Herman Lebovics, *True France: The Wars over Cultural Identity, 1900–1945* (Ithaca, NY: Cornell University Press, 1992), 153. Geneviève Calame-Griaule, "Marcel Griaule et la Mission Dakar-Djibouti," in *Coloniales 1920–1940*, Emmanuel Bréon and Michèle Lefrançois, Eds. (Boulogne-Billancourt, 1989), 103–104; James Clifford, *The Predicament of Culture: Twentieth-Century Ethnography, Literature, and Art* (Cambridge: Harvard University Press, 1988), 136.

36. "Mission ethnographique et linguistique Dakar-Djibouti," 11.

37. Calame-Griaule 104; Clifford, 137.

38. Marcel Griaule, "Mission Dakar-Djibouti (Journal-rapport général mai 1931–1932), *Bulletin de la société des africanistes* 2 (1932): 116.

39. Mauss, a follower of Emile Durkheim, was a prominent ethnographer in Paris during the 1920s and 1930s. In 1925 he founded the *Institut d'ethnologie* with Maurice Delafosse, Lucien Lévy-Bruhl, and Paul Rivet, all important figures in sociology and anthropology at the time. Mauss's most influential text is *The Gift*, published as "Essai sur le don" in 1923. See Marcel Mauss, *The Gift*, trans. Ian Cunnison (New York: Norton, 1972).

40. Perret, "La Perception de l'objet africain," in Bréon and Lefrançois, Eds., 111–112.

41. Marcel Mauss (with Michel Leiris and Marcel Griaule), *Instructions sommaires pour les collecteurs d'objets ethnographiques* (Paris: Musée d'ethnographie et Mission scientifique Dakar-Djibouti, Palais du Trocadéro, 1931), 5.

42. Ibid., 5–6.

43. Ibid., 6. Talal Asad, George Stocking, and a number of other historians and critics of anthropology delineated anthropology and ethnography's complicity with colonialism. Talal Asad, Ed. *Anthropology and the Colonial Encounter* (Atlantic Highlands, NJ: Humanities Press, 1973); Jean Copans, *Anthropologie et impérialisme* (Paris: Maspéro, 1973); George Stocking, Ed. *History of Anthropology.* Vol. 7, *Colonial Situtations: Essays on the Contextualization of Ethnographic Knowledge* (Madison: University of Wisconsin Press, 1991).

44. Mauss, *Instructions sommaires,* 7–8.

45. Clifford, 62–64.

46. Edward Said, *Orientalism* (New York: Vintage Books, 1978); Robert Goldwater, *Primitivism in Modern Art* (New York: Random House, 1938); Jean Laude, *La Peinture français (190–914) et "l'art nègre"* (Paris: Klincksieck, 1968); Clifford, 189–214.

47. René Maran, *Batouala, véritable roman nègre* (Paris: Albin Michel, 1921).

48. Claude MacKay, *Banjo* (Paris: Rieder, 1928); Pierre Mille, *Chez les fils de l'ombre et du soleil* (Paris: Firmin-Didot, 1931). On colonial literature, see Roland Lebel, *Histoire de la littérature coloniale en France* (Paris: Larose, 1931); Eugène Pujarniscle, *Philoxène ou de la littérature coloniale* (Paris: Firmin-Didot, 1931); Martine Astier Loutfi, *Littérature et colonialisme: L'expansion coloniale vue dans la littérature romanesque français, 1871–1914* (Paris: Mouton, 1971); and Léon Fanoudh-Siefer, *Le Mythe du nègre et de l'Afrique noire dans la littérature française de 1800 à la 2e Guerre Mondiale* (Dakar: Les Nouvelles Éditions Africaines, 1980).

49. *L'Atlantide,* by Jacques Feyder, 1921; *Yasmina,* by André Hugon in 1926 and filmed in Tunis; and *Le Bled* by Jean Renoir, made to celebrate the Algerian centenary in 1930. See Pierre Boulanger, *Le Cinéma colonial de "L'Atlantide" à "Lawrence d'Arabie"* (Paris: Seghers, 1975); Michèle Lagny, Marie-Caire Ropars, and Pierre Sorlin, *Générique des années 30* (Saint-

Denis: Presses Universitaires de Vincennes, 1986), 127–176; and Fa-timah Tobing Rony, *The Third Eye: Race, Cinema, and Ethnographic Spectacle* (Durham, NC: Duke University Press, 1996).

50. The Société des peintres orientalistes was founded by Gérôme in 1893, the Société coloniale des artistes français in 1907, and the Prix de la lit-térature coloniale in 1921.

51. Pomian, 20–30.

52. Simon, 6–7.

53. Mouslim Barbarim [Les Jeunes Marocains], *Tempête sur le Maroc* (Paris, 1931); Ferhat Abbas, *Le Jeune algérien* (Paris: Editions de la Jeune Parque, 1931).

54. Quoted in Thobie et al., 209.

55. Thobie, 61–78.

56. Terence Ranger, "The Invention of Tradition in Colonial Africa" in Eric Hobsbawm and Terence Ranger, Eds., *The Invention of Tradition* (Cambridge: Cambridge University Press, 1983), 212.

57. Nicholas Thomas, "Licensed Curiosity: Cook's Pacific Voyages," in *The Culture of Collecting*, John Elsner and Roger Cardinal, Eds. (Cambridge: Harvard University Press, 1994), 122.

58. Clifford, 228, 231.

59. Carol A. Breckenridge, "The Aesthetics and Politics of Colonial Collecting: India at World Fairs," *Comparative Studies in Society and History* 31, no. 2 (1989): 212.

60. AOMA, Exposition coloniale internationale de Paris, 1931, carton 21.

Chapter 3

1. Saumane, "L'Exposition coloniale internationale," *Race nègre* 4, no. 4 (1931): 1.

2. "Quelques Critiques sur l'Organisation de l'Exposition," [n.a., n.d.], AOMA, Exposition coloniale internationale de Paris, 1931, carton 19.

3. Reports on Bolshevism, AOMA, Agence France Outre-Mer, carton 908, dossier 2700.

4. Léon Blum, "L'Exposition coloniale—moins de Fêtes et de Discours, plus d'Intelligence Humaine!", *Populaire* 14 (May 1, 1931): 7.

5. On the Popular Front's reaffirmation of French colonial policy, see

Catherine Coquery-Vidrovitch, "La colonisation français 1931–1939," in Thobie, 259–263; and Liauzu, 92–96.

6. Coquery-Vidrovitch, 224; Catherine Hodeir and Michel Pierre, *L'Exposition coloniale* (Brussels: Éditions Complexe, 1991), 119–120.

7. "Lenin's Theses on the National and Colonial Questions Adopted by the Second Comintern Congress, July 27, 1920," in Louis L. Snyder, Ed., *The Imperialism Reader: Documents and Readings on Modern Expansionism* (Princeton, NJ: Van Nostrand, 1962), 548–549.

8. "The Program of the Communist International on the Colonial Struggle, September 1, 1928," in Snyder, 551–553.

9. Thobie et al., 190.

10. *L'Humanité*, May, June, August, and November 1931. Coquery-Vidrovitch, 224.

11.   Soleil soleil d'au-delà des mers tu angélises
     la barbe excrémentielle des gouverneurs
     Soleil de corail et d'ébène
     Soleil des esclaves numérotés
     Soleil de nuditésoleil d'opium soleil de flagellation
     Soleil du feu d'artifice en l'honneur de la prise de la Bastille
     au-dessus de Cayenne un quatorze juillet

     Il pleut il pleut à verse sur l'Exposition Coloniale

     Louis Aragon, "Mars à Vincennes," *L'Œuvre Poétique* (Paris: Livre Club Diderot, 1975), 5: 216.

12. The signatories were André Breton, Paul Eluard, Benjamin Péret, Georges Sadoul, Pierre Unik, André Thirion, René Crevel, Aragon, René Char, Maxime Alexandre, Yves Tanguy, and Georges Malkine. Breton et al., "Ne visitez pas l'Exposition coloniale," [Paris 1931], 1. Reprinted in José Pierre, Ed. *Tracts surréalistes et déclarations collectives* (Paris: Le Terrain vague, 1980), 1: 194–195.

13. Ibid., 2.

14. Ibid.

15. Ibid.

16. He also reported to José Pierre that, in August 1931, Henri Lefebvre wrote

him a letter describing the students as enthusiastic about the tract and professors less so. André Thirion, letter to José Pierre, 29 July 1976, quoted in Pierre, I: 453.

17. Signed by Yves Tanguy, Georges Sadoul, Aragon, André Breton, André Thirion, Maxime Alexandre, Paul Eluard, Pierre Unik, René Char, Benjamin Péret, René Crevel, Georges Malkine, and "twelve foreign comrades." Thirion, in a letter to José Pierre, indicated that this tract was inspired by Paul Eluard and edited by Eluard and Breton. Pierre, I: 453.

18. Yves Tanguy et al., "Premier bilan de l'exposition coloniale."

19. Ibid.

20. Ibid.

21. The Communist Party headquarters now stands on this site. André Thirion, *Revolutionaries Without Revolution*, trans. Joachim Neugroschel (New York: Macmillan, 1975), 289.

22. Henri Grimal, *La Décolonisation de 1919 à nos jours* (Brussels: Editions Complexe, 1985), 38–39.

23. Thirion, *Revolutionaries Without Revolution*, 289. According to police reports in Colonial Exposition files, the Ligue asked the organizers for permission to erect a stand and also sought photographs and documents on the oppression of natives in the colonies from colonial authorities. These requests were denied. Letter from the Ministère des Colonies to Lyautey, 5 March 1931. AOMA, Exposition coloniale internationale, carton 27.

24. "Campagne communiste contre l'Exposition coloniale," April 16, 1931, AOMA, Exposition coloniale internationale, carton 27.

25. Thirion mistakenly attributed the building to the Vesnin brothers, a mistake that Lebovics repeated. Thirion, *Revolutionaries Without Revolution*, 289; Lebovics, *True France*, 106. On the Soviet pavilion, see Jean-Louis Cohen, "The Misfortunes of the Image: Melnikov in Paris, 1925 (Architecture and Photography)," in *ArchitectuReproduction*, Beatriz Colomina, Ed. (New York: Princeton Architectural Press, 1988), 100–121.

26. Thirion, *Revolutionaries Without Revolution*, 289.

27. Marcel Cachin, "Une visite à l'Exposition anti-impérialiste," *L'Humanité* (5 novembre 1931): 1.

28. Hodeir and Pierre, 127.

29. Cachin, "Une visite à l'Exposition anti-impérialiste," 1.

30. Ibid.

31. Louis Aragon, "Une préface morcelée 5, l'An 31 et l'envers de ce temps," in *L'Œuvre Poétique* (Paris: Livre Club Didedrot, 1975), 5: 180.

32. Thirion, *Revolutionaries Without Revolution*, 290.

33. Ibid., 289; Aragon, "Une préface morcelée 5," 180.

34. Liauzu, 38.

35. Yves Tanguy et al. "Premier bilan de l'Exposition coloniale"

36. On *négrophilie*, see Jean Laude, *La Peinture française (1905–1914) et "l'Art nègre"* (Paris: Editions Klincksieck, 1968); and James Clifford, "1933, February: Negrophilia," in *A New History of French Literature*, Dennis Hollier, Ed. (Cambridge: Harvard University Press, 1989), 901–908.

37. Raymond Cogniat, "L'Exposition coloniale (Les Palais métropolitains, les colonies étrangères, les pays sous mandet)," *L'Architecture* 53, no. 9 (1931): 339.

38. Michel Leiris, "Civilization," *Documents* 1929, trans. Lydia Davis in *Sulfur* 15 (1986): 94.

39. Ibid., 93.

40. According to James Clifford, Lévy-Bruhl was widely read and his work "gave scholarly credence to a common image of black societies as 'mystical,' 'affective,' and 'prelogical'." James Clifford, "1933, February: Negrophilia," 901. Evan Maurer linked Lévy-Bruhl and the Surrealists, as evidenced in Jules Monnerot's *La Poésie moderne et le sacré* (1945), which emphasized the centrality of myth and dream to both primitivism and Surrealism. Evan Maurer, "Dada and Surrealism," in *"Primitivism" in 20th Century Art: Affinity of the Tribal and the Modern*, vol. I, William Rubin, Ed. (New York: Museum of Modern Art, 1984), 543.

41. Lucien Lévy-Bruhl, *Primitive Mythology: The Mythic World of the Australian and Papuan Natives*, trans. Brian Elliot (St. Lucia: University of Queensland Press, 1983), 32–38; Lévy-Bruhl, *Primitive Mentality*, trans. Lilian A. Clare (Boston: Beacon, 1966), 98.

42. See Alan Stoekl. "1937, March, The Avant-Garde Embraces Science," in *A New History of French Literature*, Hollier, Ed., 929–935.

43. See André Breton, *What Is Surrealism?*, trans. David Gascoyne (London: Faber and Faber, 1936), 50–64; and Robert Goldwater, *Primitivism in Modern Art* (1938; Cambridge: Harvard University Press, 1986), 216–224.

44. Louis Aragon, *Paris Peasant*, trans. Simon Watson Taylor (London: Jonathan Cape, 1971), 130.

45. Lucien Lévy-Bruhl, *Primitive Mythology*, 256.

46. James Clifford, "On Ethnographic Surrealism," in *The Predicament of Culture: Twentieth-Century Ethnography, Literature, and Art* (Cambridge: Harvard University Press, 1988), 136–37.

47. Louis Aragon, *Paris Peasant*, 27–28.

48. Ibid.

49. Ibid., 148.

50. "What a sight would the perplexing and envied labours of a European minister of State present to the eyes of a Caribbean! How many cruel deaths would not this indolent savage prefer to the horrors of such a life, which is seldom even sweetened by the pleasure of doing good!" Jean-Jacques Rousseau, "A Discourse on the Origin of Inequality," in *The Social Contract and Discourses*, trans. G.D.H. Cole (London: Dent, 1973), 115. Alessandra Ponte delineated the connection between nineteenth-century theories of the park and its role in civilizing the working class. Alessandra Ponte, "Le parc publique en Grand-Bretagne et aux Etats-Unis. Du 'genius loci' au 'genie de la civilisation,'" in *Histoire des jardins de la Renaissance à nos jours*, Monique Mosser and Georges Teyssot, Eds. (Paris: Flammarion, 1991), 369–382.

51. Aragon, *Paris Peasant*, 13–34.

52. René Passeron, *Phaidon Encyclopedia of Surrealism*, trans. John Griffiths (London: Phaidon, 1978), 259.

53. Clifford, "On Ethnographic Surrealism," 132.

54. Numerous works elaborated this critique of avant-garde appropriations of "primitive" art, particularly around William Rubin's ill-conceived "'Primitivism' in 20th Century Art" show at the Museum of Modern Art in 1984–1985. See Dore Ashton, "On An Epoch of Paradox: "Primitivism" at the Museum of Modern Art," *Arts Magazine* 59, no. 3 (1984), 76–79; Clifford, "Histories of the Tribal and the Modern," in *The Predicament of Culture*, 189–214; and Marianna Torgovnick, "William Rubin and the Dynamics of Primitivism," in *Gone Primitive: Savage Intellects, Modern Lives* (Chicago and London: Chicago University Press, 1990), 119–137.

55. André Breton, *L'Amour fou* (Paris: Gallimard, 1937), 40–57, quoted in

Rosalind E. Krauss, "No More Play," in *The Originality of the Avant-Garde and Other Modernist Myths* (Cambridge: MIT Press, 1985), 43.

56. Maurice Tranchant, *Le Tour du monde en un jour à l'Exposition coloniale* (Paris: Studio du Palmier Nain, 1931), 15.

57. Ibid., 20–21.

58. On touristic experience and "staged authenticity," see John Urry, *The Tourist Gaze: Leisure and Travel in Contemporary Societies* (London: Sage Publications, 1990); and Dean MacCannell, *The Tourist: A New Theory of the Leisure Class* (New York: Schocken Books, 1989).

59. Letter from Gratien Candace, Député, Chambre des Députés to Maréchal Lyautey, June 25, 1931; letter from [Lyautey] to Gratien Candace, July 1931, AOMA, Exposition coloniale internationale de Paris, 1931, carton 8.

60. AOMA, Exposition coloniale internationale de Paris, 1931, carton 9.

61. Burton Benedict, *The Anthropology of World's Fairs* (London and Berkeley: Scolar Press, 1983), 52.

62. Ibid., 43–46.

63. Ibid., 48.

64. Timothy Mitchell, *Colonising Egypt* (Cambridge: Cambridge University Press, 1988), 1.

65. Zeynep Çelik and Leila Kinney, "Ethnography and Exhibitionism at the *Expositions Universelles*," *Assemblage* 13 (1990): 34–59.

66. They numbered 476, including 26 Dahomeans, 21 Senegalese, 124 Malagasy, 140 Tunisians, and 165 Indochinese. Jules Charles-Roux, *Exposition universelle de 1900, Les Colonies françaises, Rapport général* (Paris: Imprimerie Nationale, 1902), 216.

67. Benedict, 51–52. See Robert Rydell, *All the World's a Fair: Visions of Empire at American International Expositions, 1876–1916* (Chicago: Chicago University Press, 1984); and Robert Rydell, *World of Fairs: The Century-of-Progress Expositions* (Chicago: University of Chicago Press, 1993).

68. Olivier, *Rapport générale,* I: xix.

69. The League for Defense of the Black Race was founded by Lamine Senghor, one of the few prominent black Communists in France. Leaders such as Nguyen The Truyen and Hadj Ali radicalized the anticolonial arms of the French Communist Party during the mid-1920s, calling for a more direct intervention on behalf of nationalist parties. Liauzu, 19, 130–131, 269–270.

70. Ibid., 80–86.

71. Ibid., 106.

72. Thobie, et al., 190; Liauzu, 21.

73. Saumane, "L'Exposition coloniale internationale," *Race nègre*, I, and "La Vérité sur les colonies," *Cri des nègres* I, no. 3 (October 1931): I; Philippe Dewitt, *Les movements nègres en France, 1919–1939* (Paris: L'Harmattan, 1985), 247–248, 283–294.

74. See Delord, "A l'Exposition coloniale, Le pavillon de la guadeloupe," *La Dépêche africaine* 4, no. 38 (July I, 1931): I; Dewitt, 247–248, 253, 255–259.

75. AOMA, Exposition coloniale internationale de Paris, 1931, carton 27; and AOMA, Fonds d'Outre-Mer (FOM), carton 908, dossier 2700. The CAI was the agency charged with surveillance of natives living in France. It was succeeded by the *Service de Liason entre les Originaires de Territoires d'Outre-Mer* (SLOTFOM). For more on CAI, SLOTFOM, and Indochinese protests at the 1931 Colonial Exposition, see Lebovics, *True France*, 102–110.

76. "Rapport confidential à M. le résident supérieur Guesde de Jean-Jacques Gautier, administrateur des services civil de l'Indochine," April 15, 1931, AOMA, FOM, carton 908, dossier 2700.

77. CAI report, May 9, 1931, AOMA, FOM, carton 908, dossier 2700.

78. "Note du Préfecture de Police, Service des Affaires Indigènes Nord-Africains, Protection et Surveillance des Indigènes Nord-Africains à M. le Commissaire Général," August 7, 1931, AOMA, Exposition coloniale internationale de Paris, 1931, carton 27.

79. Gaston Joseph, Directeur des Affaires Politique, CAI, "Annex à la note du 14 Avril 1931, Papillons edités par le Parti communiste français," AOMA, FOM, carton 908, dossier 2700.

80. [Tran Thien Tuong and Tran Van Kieh], quoted in "Campagne communiste contre l'Exposition coloniale," April 16, 1931, AOMA, Exposition coloniale internationale de Paris, 1931, carton 27.

81. CAI report, April 27, 1931, AOMA, FOM, carton 908, dossier 2700.

82. Letter from Bonamy, Gouverneur des Territoires sous Mandat, to Lyautey, September 3, 1931, AOMA, Exposition coloniale internationale de Paris, 1931, carton 27.

83. A facsimile of this pamphlet is reproduced in Liauzu, 239–244.

84. Report on "un Tract communiste," Poste du Gardinage, Exposition coloniale internationale, June 21, 1931, AOMA, Exposition coloniale internationale de Paris, 1931, carton 27.

85. Olivier, *Rapport générale,* I: xviii.

86. Ibid., I: xvii.

Chapter 4

1. Paul Morand, "Rien que la Terre à l'Exposition coloniale," *Revue des deux mondes* 101 (July 15, 1931): 334.

2. I use the definition of collage as "an assemblage of diverse fragments" rather than the stricter sense of "an artistic composition made of various materials (as paper, cloth, or wood) glued on a picture surface." According to Marjorie Perloff and James Clifford's theories, collage generates new meanings, new "possibilities of signification," through the juxtaposition of things taken from their contexts and "forced into jarring proximity." *Webster's New Collegiate Dictionary,* s.v. "collage;" Marjorie Perloff, "The Invention of Collage," in Collage, Jeanine Parisier Plottel, Ed. (New York: New York Literary Forum, 1983), 10; James Clifford, *The Predicament of Culture: Twentieth Century Ethnography, Literature and Art* (Cambridge: Harvard University Press, 1988), 146.

3. M. Simon, "En visitant l'Exposition coloniale," *Cité moderne* 12 (Summer 1931): 6.

4. Paul-Emile Cadilhac, "Une heure en Tunisie," *L'Illustration* 89, no. 4603 (special number, 1931): n.p.

5. Ibid.

6. The present *Périphérique* (ring road) around Paris sits on edge of the former zone. On the history of the fortifications and the zone, see Jean-Louis Cohen and André Lortie, *Des fortifs au Périf : Paris, les seuils de la ville* (Paris: Picard : Pavillon de l'Arsenal, 1991).

7. A. Autrand, "Mémoire de M. le Préfet de la Seine au Conseil Municipal, L'Exposition Coloniale Interalliée de Paris en 1925" (Paris: Imprimerie municipale, 11 mars 1921), AP, V.R. carton 265; Olivier, *Rapport général,* I: 35.

8. Olivier, *Rapport général,* I: 37; "L'Emplacement de l'Exposition," report of the Musée Social (n.a., n.d.), AOMA, Exposition coloniale internationale de Paris, 1931, carton 21.

9. Olivier, *Rapport général,* I: 46; "L'Emplacement de l'Exposition," 5.

10. Olivier, *Rapport général,* I: 50.

11. "Organisation de l'Exposition coloniale en 1927," *Bulletin municipal officiel* (Paris: Imprimerie municipale, December 31, 1923), 5626.

12. Olivier, *Rapport général,* I: 52; "Avenant à la Convention du 26 juillet 1921 entre M. le Préfet de la Seine, Hippolyte Juillard, et M. le Ministre des Colonies, Albert Sarrault," Paris, March 25, 1924, AOMA, Exposition coloniale internationale de Paris, 1931, carton 21.

13. *Bulletin municipal officiel* (December 31, 1923): 5626.

14. "L'Emplacement de l'Exposition," 2–4.

15. [Léon Jaussely], "Liste des Plans, Croquis et Etudes Exécutées par les Agences de Travaux et de l'Architecture," October 1926, AOMA, Exposition coloniale internationale de Paris, 1931, carton 63.

16. "Avenant à la Convention du 25 mars 1924," AP, Exposition coloniale internationale de Paris, 1931, 106/50/1, carton 52.

17. The "Avenant du 23 juillet 1929" and "Avenant du 11 juillet 1930," added the lawns beside bastions 4 and 5 and the triangular piece of land near avenue de Charenton, which became the Parc des Attractions; Lyautey to Préfet de la Seine, 25 June 1929; Ministre de la Guerre to Ministre des Colonies, 28 August 1929; and Direction des Travaux to Lyautey, 11 June 1930. AOMA, Exposition coloniale internationale de Paris, 1931, carton 21.

18. Edmond A. Delaire and Louis F. Roux, *Les Architectes élèves de l'Ecole des Beaux-Arts,* 2nd ed. (Paris: Librairie de la Construction Moderne, 1907), 414.

19. Marcel Zahar. "Bâtir! Informer!" *L'Art vivant* 7, no. 151 (1931): 384.

20. Raymond Cogniat, "L'Exposition coloniale (Les palais métropolitains, les colonies étrangères, les pays sous mandat)," *L'Architecture* 44, no. 9 (1931): 317–319.

21. Cadilhac, "Une heure en Tunisie."

22. Henri Prost, "*Rapport général,*" *L'Urbanisme aux colonies et dans les pays tropicaux,* Jean Royer, Ed. (La-Charité-sur-Loire: Delayance, 1932), I: 22.

23. Edmond du Vivier de Streel was director of the congresses at the 1931 Colonial Exposition. Edmond du Vivier de Streel, "Introduction," in Royer, I:11.

24. See Albert Laprade, *Lyautey urbaniste: souvenirs d'un témoin* (Paris: La Renaissance du Livre, 1947); Gwendolyn Wright, *The Politics of Design in French*

Colonial Urbanism (Chicago: Chicago University Press, 1991); and Zeynep Çelik, *Urban Forms and Colonial Confrontations: Algiers under French Rule* (Berkeley: University of California Press, 1997).

25. Janet Abu-Lughod, *Rabat: Urban Apartheid in Morocco* (Princeton, NJ: Princeton University Press, 1980).

26. See Mary Louise Pratt, *Imperial Eyes: Travel Writing and Transculturation* (London and New York: Routledge, 1992).

27. Anne McClintock, *Imperial Leather: Race, Gender and Sexuality in the Colonial Contest* (New York: Routledge, 1995), 40.

28. Michel Leiris, "The Sacred in Everyday Life," in Denis Hollier, Ed. *The College of Sociology* (Minneapolis: Minnesota University Press, 1988), 27. Leiris presented this theory to the Collège de Sociologie, a group founded by himself, Georges Bataille, and Roger Caillois to create a "sacred sociology" and to rediscover the experience of the sacred in modern society's secular rituals. Alan Stoekl, "1937, March, the Avant-Garde Embraces Science," in *A New History of French Literature*, Denis Hollier, Ed. (Cambridge: Harvard University Press, 1989), 929–935.

29. *Muirhead's Paris and Its Environs*, Findlay Muirhead, Ed. (London: Macmillan, 1921), 79.

30. Edward Jefford and John George Bartholomew, *Paris pour tous* (Paris: J.M. Dent et Fils, [1919]), 12–13.

31. Norma Evenson, *Paris: A Century of Change, 1878–1978* (New Haven, CT, and London: Yale University Press, 1979), 213–216.

32. *Muirhead's Paris and Its Environs*, 90.

33. Paul Leroy-Beaulieu, *La Question ouvrière au XIXe siècle* (1872), quoted in Evenson, 209–210.

34. See Tyler Stovall, *The Rise of the Paris Red Belt* (Berkeley: University of California Press, 1990).

35. ANP, Fonds Laprade, 475 AP/26.

36. Letter from Bourdaire to Lyautey, October 31, 1927, ANP, Fonds Lyautey, 475AP/208.

37. Ibid.

38. Bourdaire, "Note Complementaire au Sujet du Musée Colonial," letter to Lyautey, December 9, 1927. ANP, Fonds Lyautey, 475 AP/208. Lyautey directed the prefect of the Seine of research alternative sites for

the Museum of the Colonies. In a December 1927 memo, the prefect analyzed two sites in the center of Paris: the military bakehouse on Quai Debilly (now the site of the Palais Tokio) and the annexes of the Ecole Militaire. He stated that both would involve paying the city for the Vincennes land and replacing the existing facilities, neither of which options the Exposition could afford. "Note sur le recherche d'un emplacement pour la construction du Musée permanent des Colonies," Prefecture de la Seine, Extension de Paris, December 1927, ANP, Fonds Lyautey, 475 AP/208.

39. Léandre Vaillat, "Le Décor de la vie: L'Exposition Coloniale de 1931," *Temps* 71 (March 13, 1928): n.p.

40. "Allocution de M. le Marshall Lyautey," in *Exposition coloniale internationale de Paris, 1931. Son but, son organisation.* Allocutions prononcéés à l'occassion du 25e Anniversaire de la Féderation des Industriels et des Commerçants français, (Paris: Féderation des Industriels et des Commerçants français, 1928).

41. "Pour une avenue de la Victoire vers l'Est," *Vie* 18, no. 1 (1929): 2.

42. Marius-Ary Leblond, "L'Exposition coloniale dotera-t-elle Paris d'une avenue de la Victoire qui par Vincennes ira vers la Marne et Strasbourg reconquise?", *Vie* 18, no. 1 (1929): 2.

43. Lyautey quoted by Leblond, 4.

44. Lyautey to Wladimir d'Ormesson, 27 August 1928, quoted in André Le Révérend, *Lyautey* (Paris: Librairie Arthène Fayard, 1983), 447–448.

45. Jean-Jacques Brousson, "La Mort des 'Fortifs,'" *Vers un Paris nouveau?* (Paris: Les Beaux-Arts, [1932]), 91.

46. Guy le Halle, *Les Fortifications de Paris* (Le Coteau: Editions Horvath, 1986), 161–238.

47. *The Concise Oxford French Dictionary,* s.v. "zone."

48. Molly Nesbit, *Atget's Seven Albums* (New Haven, CT: Yale University Press, 1992); Colette, *L'ingenue libertine* (Paris: A. Michel, [1926]); Guillaume Apollinaire, "Zone," *Alcools* (Paris: Gallimard, 1928); Blaise Cendrars, *Aujourd'hui* (Paris: B. Grasset [1931]); Jean Ajalbert, *Dans Paris, la grand'ville* (Paris: G. Cres, 1916); Georges Charles Lecomte, *Raffaelli* (Paris: Rieder, 1927). The zone was also commemorated in such films as Lacombe's *La Zone* (1928), Marcel Carné's *Nogent, Eldorado du dimanche* (1930), Fritz Lang's, *Liliom* (1934), and René Char's, *Porte de Lilas,* and

former zonard Auguste Le Breton's novel, *Fortif's* (Paris: Hachette, 1982).

49. Leiris, "Sacred," 24.

50. Ibid.

51. Hollier, *The College of Sociology*, 400 n, 7.

52. Apollinaire, 15.

53. See Sally Price, *Primitive Art in Civilized Places* (Chicago: University of Chicago Press, 1989), 82–99; and Robert Goldwater, Primitivism in Modern Art (1938; Cambridge: Harvard University Press, 1986).

54. Madeleine Fernandez, *La Zone: Mythe et Réalité* ([Paris]: Ministère de la Culture, 1983), 9.

55. Eugène Buret, *De la misère des classes laborieuses en Angleterre et en France,* 2 vols. (Paris: Paulin, 1840); Louis Chevalier, *Laboring and Dangerous Classes,* trans. Frank Jellinek (New York: Howard Fertig, 1973).

56. Alexandre Privat d'Anglemont, *Paris anecdote* (1854; Paris: Editions de Paris, 1984), 173–174, 181.

57. André Warnod, *Les Fortifs, Promenades sur les anciennes fortifications et la zone* (Paris: Editions de l'Epi, 1926), n.p.

58. The Rif War started in what had been Spanish Morocco and spread to French Morocco under the leadership of Abd el-Krim who aspired to be the leader of a Rif nation in northern Morocco. Pierre Montagnon, *La France coloniale, La gloire de l'empire* (Paris: Pygmalion, 1988), 435–442.

59. Warnod.

60. Ibid.

61. Fernandez, 16, 2.

62. Ibid., 28.

63. Bernard Marrey, "Adolphe Thiers' Fortified Wall," in Paris: *La Ville et ses Projets, A City in the Making,* Jean-Louis Cohen and Bruno Fortier, Eds. (Paris: Editions Babylone; Pavillon de l'Arsenal, 1988), 206.

64. Fernandez, 31. Jean-Louis Cohen and André indicated that more than 12,132 constructions were built by the zoniers, including 932 industrial or commercial edifices and 295 investment properties. Cohen and Lortie, 67.

65. Cohen and Lortie, 225–230; Marrey, 184; Fernandez, 37–38.

66. The city attempted to find an alternative site throughout 1927, 1928, and 1929, even attempting to use part of the site of the future Cité Universitaire. On the fortified ring, only the zonier plots on the territory

annexed from Boulogne, Montrouge, and Gentilly were expropriated under the 1919 law. As officials engaged in the search noted, however, "because of the grave difficulties to which the first expropriations have given rise and the pressing claims that the zoniers have formed on this subject, the city of Paris has had for many years to suspend all expropriation procedure on the zonier territories. The city has not, otherwise, been able to amicably acquire a single piece of ground sufficient for even a playground." Préfet de la Seine to Sous-Secrétaire, May 4, 1929, AP, Exposition coloniale internationale, 106/50/1, carton 52.

67. Directeur d'Exploitation technique to Commissaire Général, 9 February 1928, AOMA, Exposition coloniale internationale de Paris, 1931, carton 102.

68. Louis Aragon, *Paris Peasant*, trans. Simon Watson Taylor (London: Jonathan Cape, 1971), 148.

69. *Muirhead's Paris and Its Environs*, 87.

70. Ibid.; René Héron de Villefosse, *Prés et bois parisiens* (Paris: Editions des Portiques, 1934), 235–237. For more on the Château de Vincennes, see Alain Erlande-Brandenburg and Bertrand Jestaz, *Le Château de Vincennes* (Paris: Picard, [1989]).

71. *Mémoires du baron Haussmann*, 1: 210, quoted in Thomas von Joest, "Paris vert, Paris d'Haussmann?"; *Histoire des jardins de la Renaissance à nos jours*, Monique Mosser and Georges Teyssot, Eds. (Paris: Flammarion, 1991), 388.

72. *Du faubourg Saint-Antoine au bois de Vincennes. Promenade historique dans le 12e arrondissement* (Paris: Les Musées de la Ville de Paris, 1983), 59.

73. *Muirhead's Paris and Its Environs*, 88–89.

74. Olivier, *Rapport général*, 2: 37.

75. John Dixon Hunt, *Gardens and the Picturesque: Studies in the History of Landscape Architecture* (Cambridge: MIT Press, 1992), 272.

76. Le Corbusier, *Des canons, des munitions? merci! Des logic … SVP* (Paris: Editions de l'Architecture d'aujourd'hui, 1937), 52.

77. Léandre Vaillat, "Le Décor de la vie: Tour d'horizon parisien," *Temps* 71 (August 22, 1931): n.p.

78. Vaillat, "Le Décor de la vie."

79. Albert Laprade, "L'Exposition et la cité moderne," *Cité moderne* 11 (June 1931): 910.

80. Ibid. On Sellier's career as an urban reformer, see Paul Rabinow *French Modern: Norms and Forms of the Social Environment* (Cambridge: MIT Press, 1989), 260–267.

81. Albert Laprade, "L'Art et l'Exposition coloniale," unpublished manuscript, 15 January 1931, ANP, Fonds Laprade, 475 AP/26.

82. Rabinow, 332.

83. Cogniat, 317–319.

84. Marjorie Perloff, *The Futurist Moment: Avant-Garde, Avant Guerre, and the Language of Rupture* (Chicago: University of Chicago Press, 1986), 52.

85. Clifford, 146.

Chapter 5

1. Marcel Zahar, "L'Architecture [de l'Exposition Coloniale]," *Renaissance de l'Art* 14, no. 8 (1931): 223.

2. See Zeynep Çelik, *Displaying the Orient: Architecture of Islam at Nineteenth-Century World's Fairs,* Berkeley: University of California Press, 1992); and Paul Greenhalgh, *Ephemeral Vistas: World Exhibitions, 1851–1939* (Manchester: Manchester University Press, 1988).

3. William B. Cohen, *The French Encounter with Africans: White Response to Blacks, 1530–1880* (Bloomington: Indiana University Press, 1980), 212, 218.

4. George Stocking, "Colonial Situations," in *History of Anthropology.* vol. 7, *Colonial Situtations: Essays on the Contextualization of Ethnographic Knowledge* (Madison: University of Wisconsin Press, 1991), 4. See also Jean Copans, *Aus origins de l'anthropologie française* (Paris: Place, 1994); and Talal Asad, Ed., *Anthropology and the Colonial Encounter* (Atlantic Highlands, NJ: Humanities Press, 1973).

5. Marcel Olivier, "Avant-Propos," *Le Livre d'or de l'Exposition coloniale internationale de Paris, 1931* (Paris: Librairie ancienne Honoré Champion, 1931), 11.

6. Zahar, "L'Architecture [de l'Exposition coloniale]," 223.

7. Anne Buttimer, *Society and Milieu in the French Geographic Tradition* (Chicago: Rand McNally, 1971), 44.

8. Quoted in Buttimer, 62. Brunhes wrote one of the most comprehensive applications of Vidal's theories in his regionalist study, *La Géographie humaine* (Paris: Féliz Alcan, 1925).

9. Paul Vidal de la Blache, *Principles of Human Geography,* trans. Millicent Todd Bingham (New York: Henry Holt, 1926), 163.

10. Vidal, 323.

11. Vidal, 183, 186, 255, 272.

12. Vidal, 334.

13. Robert J.C. Young, *Colonial Desire: Hybridity in Theory, Culture, and Race* (London: Routledge, 1995), 99.

14. Alice Conklin, *A Mission to Civilize: The Republican Idea of Empire in France and West Africa, 1895–1930* (Palo Alto, CA: Stanford University Press, 1997), 16.

15. Raymond Betts, *Assimilation and Association in French Colonial Theory, 1890–1914* (New York: Columbia University Press, 1961), 8.

16. Arthur Girault, *Principes de colonisation et de législation coloniale,* 5th ed. (Paris: Recueil Sirey, 1927), 106.

17. Algeria was not completely "pacified" until many years after 1830. Abd-el-Kader, the Algerian caliph, was captured and exiled in 1847, and civilian rule was not established until 1879. Raymond Betts, *Tricouleur: The French Overseas Empire* (London and New York: Gordon and Cremonesi, 1978), 58.

18. David Prochaska, *Making Algeria French: Colonialism in Bône, 1870–1920* (Cambridge: Cambridge University Press, 1990), 85. See also Zeynep Çelik, *Urban Forms and Colonial Confrontations: Algiers under French Rule* (Berkeley: University of California Press, 1997).

19. In Algiers, "wide new streets and formal *places* were soon cut through the Medina; barracks and a spacious Place d'Armes on the city's northern periphery indicated the strong military presence which formed the backbone of French urbanism there." Gwendolyn Wright, *The Politics of Design in French Colonial Urbanism* (Chicago: University of Chicago Press, 1991), 78. Jacques Thobie noted that indigenous education was a highly contested subject in Algeria and other colonies, with most *colons* opposed to schooling natives in the French language since they might then learn subversive ideas or give them the tools for dominating the French. They preferred to leave indigenous education to missionaries, to tailor instruction to vocational subjects such as practical agricultural techniques, or to learn local languages. Jacques Thobie et al., *Histoire de la France coloniale, 191–990* (Paris: Armand Colin, 1990), 33–35.

20. Linda L. Clark, *Social Darwinism in France* (Birmingham: University of Alabama Press, 1984), 51–67; Betts, *Assimilation and Association,* 24.

21. Thobie et al., 25–37.

22. Betts, *Assimilation and Association,* 35. See Jules Harmand, *Domination et colonisation* (Paris: Flammarion, 1910); Paul Leroy-Beaulieu, *De la colonisation chez les peuples modernes* (Paris: Guillaumin et Cie, 1874).

23. Clark, 54–55.

24. Alfred Fouillée, "Le Caractère des races et l'avenir de la race blanche," *Revue des deux mondes* 124 (July 1, 1894): 89, 91.

25. Ibid., 92.

26. Fouillée, "Caractère," 93 and 97. See Michael Adas, *Machines as the Measure of Men: Science, Technology, and Ideologies of Western Dominance* (Ithaca, NY: Cornell University Press, 1989) on the importance given to mechanical and scientific technology in social Darwinist hierarchies.

27. Alfred Fouillée, *Education from a National Standpoint,* trans. W.J. Greenstreet (New York: Appleton, 1892), 25.

28. Fouillée, "Caractère," 106.

29. Albert Sarraut, *La Mise en valeur des colonies françaises* (Paris: Payot, 1923), 104. Albert Sarraut was former governor-general of Indochina and a powerful radical politician. He served as minister of the colonies from January 1920 to March 1924. His theories of colonial development and *politique indigène* were widely read; they include *La Mise en valeur des colonies francaises,* and *Grandeur et servitude coloniales* (Paris: Sagittaire, 1931). Christopher M. Andrew and A.S. Kanya-Forstner, *France Overseas: The Great War and the Climax of French Imperial Expansion* (London: Thames and Hudson, 1981), 210–211.

30. Sarraut, *Mise en valeur,* 118.

31. Papillault, 53.

32. On the segregation of indigenous and French cities in Morocco, see Janet Abu-Lughod, *Rabat: Urban Apartheid in Morocco* (Princeton, NJ: Princeton University Press, 1980).

33. See Henri Descamps, *L'Architecture moderne au Maroc* (Paris: Librairie de la Construction Moderne, 1930); Léandre Vaillat, *Le Visage français du Maroc* (Paris: Horizons de France, 1931); Mission scientifique du Maroc, *Villes et tribus du Maroc,* 11 vols. (Paris: E. Leroux, 1915–1932); Joseph de la Nézière, *Les Monuments mauresques du Maroc* (Paris: A. Lévy, 1922); Henri

Terrasse and Jean Hainaut, *Les Art décoratifs au Maroc* (Paris: Henri Laurens, 1925); Georges Marçais, *Manuel d'art musulman* (Paris: A. Picard, 1926–1927); Robert Montagne, *Villages et kasbas berbères: tableau de la vie sociale des Berbères . . .* (Paris: Felix Alcan, 1930).

34. The most thorough study of French architectural regionalism is Jean-Claude Vigato's unpublished doctoral dissertation, "Le Régionalisme dans le Débat architectural" (Université de Bretagne Occidentale, Brest, 1990).

35. Romy Golan, *Modernity and Nostalgia: Art and Politics in France Between the Wars* (New Haven, CT, and London: Yale University Press, 1995), 7.

36. Léandre Vaillat, "Le Régionalisme de l'Architecture," in *La Cité renaissante* (Paris: Librairie Larousse, 1918), 45; and "La Tendance régionale à l'Exposition des arts décoratifs," *L'Illustration* 92, no. 4303 (1925): 187.

37. Vaillat, "Le Regionalisme de l'architecture," 49.

38. "Ideologically, the nationalism of the last 15 years of the nineteenth century combined social Darwinism, racism and anti-positivism, and reflected the intellectual changes of the turn of the century." Zeev Sternhell, "The Political Culture of Nationalism," in *Nationhood and Nationalism in France: From Boulangism to the Great War*, Robert Tombs, Ed. (New York and London: HarperCollins, 1991), 26–27.

39. Maurice Barrès, "La Terre et les Morts," in *Scènes et doctrines du nationalisme* (Paris: Plon, 1902) quoted in Raoul Girardet, *Le Nationalisme français, 1871–1914* (Paris: Armand Colin, 1966), 187. One of the founders of twentieth-century regionalism, Jean Charles-Brun, gave Barrès an important place as a source of regionalist nationalism, according to Vigato. Vigato, "Le Régionalisme dans le Débat architectural," 37.

40. François Jean-Desthieux, *L'Évolution régionaliste. Du Félibrige au Fédéralisme* (Paris: Bossard, 1918), 30–31. See Girardet, 195–205.

41. Paul Rabinow, *French Modern: Norms and Forms of the Social Environment* (Cambridge: MIT Press, 1989), 108–110; Alfred Cobban, *A History of Modern France. Vol. 3, France of the Republics, 1871–1962* (Hammondsworth: Penguin, 1965) 40.

42. Rabinow, 200. See Vaillat, *La Cité renaissante,* 43–52.

43. Léandre Vaillat, "La Tendance nationale à l'Exposition des Arts décoratifs," *L'Illustration* 92, no. 4307 (1925): 273.

44. Vaillat, "La Tendance régionale," 187.

45. In 1923 Charles Letrosne published one of the primers for French regionalist architecture, with a preface by Vaillat: *Murs et toits pour les pays de chez-nous* (Paris: Niestlé, 1923). The three volumes of *Murs et toits* illustrated civic and commercial building types and houses in styles appropriate to each region, such as a city hall for Flanders, a Breton school, a post office in the Meuse, and a Basque worker's house, among others.

46. Robert de la Sizeranne, "La Renaissance des arts indigènes," *Revue des deux mondes* 101 (August 1, 1931): 575–577.

47. Vaillat, "La Tendance régionale," 188.

48. Marcel Olivier, "Les Origines et les buts de l'Exposition coloniale," *Revue des deux mondes* 101 (May 1, 1931): 53.

49. Zahar, "L'Architecture [de l'Exposition coloniale]," 223.

50. See Jean-Louis Cohen and Monique Eleb, "L'esperienza urbana di Casablanca (1912–1940)," *Casabella* 61 no. 593 (1992): 30–41, 67–70; Sylviane Leprun and Alain Sinou, *Espaces coloniaux en Afrique noire* (Paris: Laboratoire Architecture et Anthropologie [Université de Paris 6], 1984); and "Hybrid Architecture," special issue of *Lotus International* 26 (1980).

51. Jacques Marseille, *L'Age d'or de la France coloniale* (Paris: Albin Michel, 1986), 15.

52. Raymond Cogniat, "L'Exposition coloniale (Les Palais métropolitains, les colonies étrangères, les pays sous mandat)," *L'Architecture* 44, no. 9 (1931): 339.

53. Albert Sarraut, "L'Exposition coloniale," *L'Art vivant* 7, no.151 (1931): 373.

54. Annie Coombs, "Inventing the 'Postcolonial': Hybridity and Constituency in Contemporary Culture," *New Formations* 18 (Winter 1992): 39.

55. Homi K. Bhabha, "Signs Taken for Wonders: Questions of Ambivalence and Authority under a Tree Outside Delhi, May 1817," in *"Race," Writing, and Difference*, Henry Louis Gates Jr., Ed. (Chicago: University of Chicago Press, 1986), 176.

56. Ibid.

57. Webster's New Collegiate Dictionary, s.v. "hybrid."

58. Young, 26.

59. Ella Shohat and Robert Stam, *Unthinking Eurocentrism: Multiculturalism and the Media* (London and New York: Routledge, 1994), 42.

60. Fouillée, "Caractère," 96

61. Benedict Anderson, *Imagined Communities: Reflections on the Origin and Spread of Nationalism* (London and New York: Verso, 1991), 184–185.

62. Young, 94–95.

63. Georges Papillault, Report on the anthropological exhibition at the Musée des Colonies, in Olivier, *Rapport général*, vol. 5, part I: 52–53. Dr. Papillault was a professor at the Ecole d'anthropologie, held a degree in medicine, and wrote an investigatory questionnaire for colonial officials and tourists. He was in charge of the section on the physical anthropology of the colonized indigenous races. Herman Lebovics, *True France: The Wars over Cultural Diversity, 1900–1945* (Ithaca, NY, and London: Cornell University Press, 1992), 99–100.

64. Bhabha, "Signs," 170.

65. Franz Fanon, *The Wretched of the Earth*, trans. Constance Farrington (New York: Grove, 1963), 38–39.

66. Fanon, 39.

67. Bhabha, "Signs," 171.

68. Pierre Courthion, "L'Architecture à l'Exposition coloniale," *Art et décoration* 60 (July 1931): 37–38.

69. Zahar, "L'Architecture [de l'Exposition coloniale]," 223.

70. Pierre Mille, "A l'Exposition coloniale: vue d'ensemble," *Revue des deux mondes* 101 (May 15, 1931): 269. Emphasis added.

71. Zahar, "L'Architecture [de l'Exposition coloniale]," 223.

72. Ibid.

73. Cogniat, 319.

74. Ibid., 330.

75. In 1934 Nivelt won a scholarship to the Villa Abd El Tif in Algiers where he received room and board and a studio for painting. He also painted decorative panels for the French West African pavilion at the 1931 Colonial Exposition. Gustave Vuillemot, "La Villa Abd El Tif," and Emmanuel Bréon, "Les Peintres de la Plus Grande France," in *Coloniales 1920–1940*, Emmanuel Bréon and Michèle Lefrançois, Eds. (Boulogne-Billancourt: Musée Municipal de Boulogne-Billancourt, 1989), 27 and 51.

76. Letter from the commissioner of Guadeloupe to the governor general of the Exposition [Olivier], February 5, 1931; letter from Olivier to the

commissioner of Guadeloupe, February 18, 1931; memorandum from Lyautey, May 28, 1931, AOMA, Exposition coloniale internationale de Paris, 1931, carton 8.

77. Albert Laprade, "Avant-promenade à travers l'Exposition coloniale," *L'Architecture* 54, no. 4 (1931): 116.

Chapter 6

1. Pierre Courthion, "L'Architecture à l'exposition coloniale," *Art et décoration* 60 (July 1931): 37–38.

2. Robert J. OC. Young, *Colonial Desire: Hybridity in Theory, Culture, and Race* (London: Routledge, 1995), 95. See Mary Cowling, *The Artist as Anthropologist: The Representation of Type and Character in Victorian Art* (Cambridge: Cambridge University Press, 1989).

3. Anne Buttimer, *Society and Milieu in the French Geographic Tradition* (Chicago: Rand McNally, 1971), 68.

4. Emile Bayard, *L'Art de reconnaitre les styles coloniaux de la France* (Paris: Garnier Frères, 1931), 4, 9.

5. "The most merciful form of what I ventured to call 'eugenics' would consist in watching for indications of superior strains or races, and in so favouring them that their progeny shall outnumber and gradually replace that of the old [low] one." Francis Galton, *Inquiries into Human Faculty and Its Development* (London: Dent, 1911), 199–200.

6. Ibid., 10.

7. Ibid., 4.

8. Ibid., 7.

9. Allan Sekula, "The Body and the Archive," in *The Contest of Meaning: Critical Histories of Photography*, Richard Bolton, Ed. (Cambridge: MIT Press, 1989), 372.

10. Pierre Guesde, "L'Indochine à l'Exposition de Vincennes," *Dépêche coloniale et maritime* (November 7, 1928): 1.

11. Jean Gallotti, "Traité de géographie de l'exposition coloniale d'après les plus récentes découvertes," *Vu* 168 (June 3, 1931): 778.

12. Courthion, 45.

13. Bayard, 147–148.

14. Marcel Zahar, "L'Architecture [de l'Exposition coloniale]," *Renaissance de l'art* 14, no. 8 (1931): 223.

15. The Malagasy consist of eighteen different tribes, who have differing ethnic characteristics and occupy separate areas of Madagascar. The Betsileo live in central Madagascar, around the city of Fianarantsoa. The Mahafaly live in the desert of southwestern Madagascar. The Bara are nomads who live in the highlands of southern Madagascar. Arthur Stratton, *The Great Red Island* (New York: Charles Scribner, 1964), 84–85.

16. Ludovic Naudeau, "Madagascar," *L'Illustration* 89, no. 4155 (1922): 395.

17. Zahar, "L'Architecture [de l'Exposition coloniale]," 223.

18. Gustave Henri Julien, "Madagascar," in *L'Habitation indigène dans les possessions françaises* (Paris: Société d'Éditions Géographiques, Maritimes et Coloniales, 1931), 71.

19. Stratton, 334; Michel Thiout, *Madagascar et l'âme malgache* (Paris: Horizons de France, 1961), 93, 95.

20. Stratton, 186.

21. Julien, 62.

22. Stratton, 186.

23. Julien, 63.

24. "Madagascar," in "L'Effort colonial dans le Monde," *Sud-Ouest économique* 2, no. 213 (special edition, August 1931): 794

25. Julien, 44–71.

26. See Duc de Nemours, *Madagascar et ses richesses* (Paris: Editions Pierre Roger, 1930); Jean d'Esme, *L'Ile rouge* (Paris: Plon, 1928); *L'Essor de Madagascar* (Paris: La Dépêche Coloniale, 1931); André Dandouau, *Géographie de Madagascar* (Paris: Larose, 1922); and Jules Gaston Delélée-Desloges, *Madagascar et dépendances* (Paris: Société d'Editions Géographiques, Maritimes et Coloniales, 1931).

27. Delélée-Desloges, 6.

28. Eugène Delacroix, *Voyage au Maroc,* 1832 (Paris: Terquem, 1913); Pierre Loti, *Au Maroc* (1890; Paris: Calman-Lévy, 1927); Luitz-Morat and Alfred Vercourt, *Le Sang d'Allah* (1922); Pierre Boulanger, *Le Cinéma colonial: de "l'Atlantide" à "Lawrence d'Arabie"* (Paris: Seghers, 1975), 43–45.

29. Under Lyautey, Georges Hardy was director of the Institute of Advanced Moroccan Studies and of public education in Morocco and later head of the Ecole coloniale in Paris. Georges Hardy, *L'Ame marocaine d'après la littérature française* (Paris: Larose, 1926); *Histoire de la colonisation française*

(Paris, Larose, 1928). On Morocco in French literature, see Roland Lebel, *Histoire de la Littérature coloniale en France* (Paris: Larose, 1931); *Les Voyageurs français du Maroc: l'exotisme marocain dans la littérature de voyage* (Paris: Larose, 1936).

30. Zahar, "L'Architecture [de l'Exposition coloniale]," 226.

31. Pierre Mille, "A L'exposition coloniale: Vue d'ensemble," *Revue des deux mondes* 101 (May 15, 1931): 267.

32. Zeynep Çelik, *Displaying the Orient: Architecture at Nineteenth-Century World's Fairs* (Berkeley: University of California Press, 1992), 61, 124, 135.

33. Naudeau, "L'Exposition coloniale de Marseille," 371.

34. François Béguin, *Arabisances: Décor architectural et tracé urbain en Afrique du Nord 1830–1950* (Paris: Dunod, 1983), 1.

35. Laprade arrived in Morocco in 1915, a wounded soldier given special duty. He worked for Henri Prost, Lyautey's director of architecture and urbanism, until 1920 when he returned to France. Auguste Cadet and Edmond Brion completed the New Medina after Laprade left Morocco. André Le Révérend, *Lyautey Écrivain, 1854–1934* (Paris: Ophrys, 1976), 351, note 115; Jean-Louis Cohen, "Casablanca, banco di prova per l'urbanistica dell'ampliamento (1912–1930)," *Casabella* 56, no. 593 (1992): 37.

36. Jean Gallotti, *Le Jardin et la maison arabes au Maroc*, 2 vols. (Paris: Albert Levy, 1924). Jean Gallotti was an inspector for the Bureau of Fine Arts and Historique Monuments in Morocco. Gwendolyn Wright, *The Politics of Design in French Colonial Urbanism* (Chicago: University of Chicago Press, 1991), 110.

37. Gallotti, "Traité de géographie de l'Exposition coloniale, 779–780.

38. Bayard, 206.

39. On the myth of Indochina, which was itself a French invention created out of many separate nations, see Panivong Norindr, *Phantasmatic Indochina: French Colonial Ideology in Architecture, Film, and Literature* (Durham, NC: Duke University Press, 1996).

40. Pierre Loti, *Un Pèlerin d'Angkor* (Paris: Calmann-Lévy, 1912), 154–155.

41. Paul Vidal de la Blache, *Principles of Human Geography*, trans. Millicent Todd Bingham (New York: Henry Holt, 1926), 334.

42. George Cœdès, *Ankgor: An Introduction*, trans. Emily Floyd Gardiner (Hong Kong and London: Oxford University Press, 1963), 11–12; Henri

Marchal, *Guide archéologique aux temples d'Angkor* (Paris: Les Editions G. Van Oest, 1928), I; Bruno Dagens, Angkor: *La forêt de pierre* (Paris: Gallimard, 1989), 26–27; Claude Jacques, *Angkor* (Paris: Bordas, 1990), 164.

43. Loti, *Angkor*, 3, I, 9.

44. Henri Dufour, an architect, and Charles Carpeaux, a photographer and son of the sculptor, prepared a monograph on the Bayon, one of the largest monuments at Angkor. In addition to clearing the complex of vegetation, they reconstructed parts of the temple and thoroughly documented it in photographs and drawings. Their work was published as *Le Bayon d'Angkor Thom (Bas-Reliefs)*, 2 vols. (Paris, 1910–1914) with archeological descriptions of the monument by Jean Commaille and George Cœdès.

45. Loti, *Angkor*, 57–59.

46. This *Commission d'exploration du Mékong*, consisting of naval officers Delaporte, Ernest Doudart de Lagrée, and Francis Garnier; diplomat Louis de Carné; botanist Clovis Thorel; geologist Eugène Joubert, and photographer Gsell, set out to document the "limits of ancient Cambodia according to the collected traditions and according to the position of the principal ruins." After Louis Delaporte's own expeditions to Indochina in 1873–1874 and 1890–1891, he was director of the Musée indochinois du Trocadéro from 1880 to his death in 1925. He published two major works on Cambodia: *Voyage au Cambodge, l'architecture khmère* (Paris: Delagrave, 1880); and *Les Monuments du Cambodge*, 4 vols. (Paris: Commission Archéologique de l'Indochine, 1914–1924). Marchal, 32; Dagens, 48–49, 58, 64; René Dumont, "Angkor Vat à l'exposition coloniale internationale de 1931," in *Le Moulage. Actes du Colloque internationale*, I–2 avril 1987 (Paris: La Documentation française, 1988), I22.

47. Doudart's first architectural and sculptural molds were displayed at Saigon in 1866, then exhibited in 1867 at the Exposition Universelle, and finally transferred to the Exposition permanente des colonies. Dagens, 60.

48. Francis Garnier, *Voyage d'exploration en Indo-Chine effectué pendant les années 1866, 1867 et 1868 par une commission présidée par M. le capitaine de frégate Doudart de Lagrée* . . . (Paris: Hachette, 1873).

49. Mouhot was commissioned by the Royal Geographical Society in London

to document the botany of Indochina. Henri Mouhot, *Voyage dans les royaumes de Siam, de Cambodge, de Laos* (Paris: Hachette, 1868).

50. Dagens, 64; Nadine Beauthéac and François-Xavier Bouchart, *L'Europe Exotique* (Paris: Chêne, 1986), 47.

51. The Cochinchina pavilion reconstructed a temple like the Annamite temples studied by its architect Foulhoux, director of public works in Cochinchina. Designed by architect Auguste Henri Vildieu, the Annam-Tonkin pavilion reproduced the porch of the Quan-Yen pagoda. Beauthéac, 44.

52. Ibid., 44, 47.

53. E. Lainé, *Le Livre d'or de l'exposition coloniale nationale de Marseille 1906* ([Marseilles]: Lainé, [1906]), 18.

54. Suryavarman II, who ruled from 1113–1145, built Angkor Wat as his mausoleum and principal temple. Jayavarman VII, who ruled from 1181 until about 1220, constructed the Angkor Thom complex, of which the Bayon, dedicated to Buddha rather than Vishu or Siva, is part. Joan Lebold Cohen and Bela Kalman, *Angkor: Monuments of the God-Kings* (New York: Abrams, 1975), 229.

55. Guesde, "L'Indochine à l'Exposition de Vincennes," 1.

56. Ibid.

57. *Le Petit Robert: Dictionnaire*, s.v. "reconstitution."

58. Bayard, 220–221.

59. Zahar, "L'Architecture [de l'Exposition coloniale]," 224.

60. Pierre Guesde, "Note relative aux moulages du Temple d'Angkor," Commissariat du Gouvernement général de l'Indochine, Exposition coloniale internationale de Paris, February 13, 1931, AOMA, Exposition coloniale internationale de Paris, 1931, carton 27.

61. Pierre Guesde, "Note relative aux moulages du Temple d'Angkor;" Victor Goloubew, "Procès-Verbal de Reception," June 26, 1930 (receipt of molds from Cambodia); Georges Groslier, "Liste des Moulages envoyés à Monsieur le Commissaire de l'Indochine à l'Exposition de Paris," March 5, 1930; letter from Victor Goloubew to Pierre Guesde, February 13, 1931, AOMA, Exposition coloniale internationale de Paris, 1931, carton 27.

62. Guesde, "Note relative aux moulages du Temple d'Angkor."

63. Ibid.

64. There is no evidence that Charles and Gabriel Blanche themselves made any such archeological discoveries, although they apparently went to Angkor to observe the temple firsthand. "La Section indochinoise à l'Exposition colonial internationale de 1931," AOMA, Exposition coloniale internationale de Paris, 1931, carton 9.

65. Zahar, "Batir! Informer!", *L'Art vivant* 7, no. 151 (1931): 384.

66. *L'Afrique noire française* included French West Africa, Equatorial French Africa, and Togo and Cameroon, territories under French mandate. Louis Gallouedec, Fernand Maurette, and J. Martin, *Géographie. Cours supérieure 1ère année* (Paris: Hachette, 1938), 20.

67. Olivier, *Rapport général*, vol. 5, part 2: 277.

68. Georges Hardy, *L'Art nègre: l'Art animiste des Noirs d'Afrique* (Paris: Laurens, 1927), 1–3, 9.

69. The final layout of the exhibits in the main hall was different from that shown in figure 3.64.

70. Louis Valent, "L'Afrique occidentale française à Vincennes," *Le Livre d'or de l'Exposition coloniale internationale de Paris*, 1931 (Paris: Honoré Champion, 1931), 83.

71. In construction, the mosque and main pavilion were made with two walls on a steel framework (for the large pavilions) or wood frame (for the smaller pavilions), to create the appearance of very thick walls. Exterior facades were made of ceramic lath and a mortar of lime and cement designed to imitate the appearance of the thick, crude plaster coating called laterite. Antony Goissaud, "Le Palais de l'Afrique occidentale française," *Construction moderne* 46, no. 43 (1931): 685.

72. A document produced by the French West African commission describes the diorama artists as "artists of value, *boursiers* [scholarship recipients] to French West Africa," indicating that these artists received stipends from the colonial administration to travel to the colony and produce works based on their firsthand observations. "Notes sur le Palais de l'Afrique Occidentale à l'Exposition coloniale internationale de Paris de 1931," AOMA, Exposition coloniale internationale de Paris, 1931, carton 8.

73. Sarrabezolles was a Prix de Rome winner. On the careers of Anna Quinquaud and Carlos Sarrabezolles, see Michèle Lefrançois, "La sculpture coloniale: une leçon des choses?", in *Coloniales 1920–1940*, Emmanuel Bréon and Michèle Lefrançois, Eds. (Boulogne-Billancourt: Musée Mu-

nicipal de Boulogne-Billancourt, 1989), 29–43. See also Lefrançois, "Art et aventure au féminin," *Coloniales 1920–1940,* 53–65.

74. Goissaud, 678, 682, 685.

75. Georges Angoulvant, "L'Afrique occidentale française," *Revue des deux mondes* 101 (August 15, 1931): 838.

76. Valent, 83.

77. Olivier, *Rapport général,* vol. 5, part 2: 280. The Exposition administrators issued press releases describing in detail the architecture, decoration, and exhibits of various pavilions, including details about the provenance of architectural styles in which the pavilions were designed. Many contemporary accounts literally copied these press releases without modification. For example, the one for the West African section referred to the *tata* as "autrefois résidence des rois noirs, aujourd'hui demeure des grands chefs" [formerly residence of the black kings, today dwelling for the great chiefs], AOMA, Exposition coloniale internationale de Paris, 1931, carton 8. This exact wording was used in articles by Louis Valent, Antony Goissaud, Georges Angoulvant, and in texts in the *Rapport général.* The official account of the Exposition's architecture was thus disseminated by the press, which received substantial subsidies from the Exposition to write favorable articles based on press releases and other materials produced by the organizers. Most descriptions of the colonial pavilions drew directly on these sources.

78. André Maurois, *"Sur le vif," L'exposition coloniale* (Paris: Degorce, 1931), 8.

79. Olivier, *Rapport général,* vol. 5, part 2: 279.

80. Letter from Camille Guy, Gouverneur des Colonies, Commissaire du Gouvernement Général de l'Afrique occidentale française, to the Commissaire général de l'Exposition coloniale internationale de Paris [Lyautey], April 5, 1927, AOMA, Exposition coloniale internationale de Paris, 1931, carton 8.

81. Zahar, "L'Architecture [de l'Exposition coloniale]," 225

82. Gallotti, "Traité de géographie de l'Exposition coloniale," 778.

83. Goissaud, 686.

84. Documents examined at the Archives d'Outre-Mer in Aix-en-Provence, the Archives Nationales, and Archives d'Architecture du XXe Siècle in Paris contained no records of Olivier and Lambert's design process or explicit references to sources that they might have used to design the

French West Africa section. References cited here were in part drawn from two exemplary works on West African architecture: Labelle Prussin, *Hatumere: Islamic Design in West Africa* (Berkeley: University of California Press, 1986); and Pierre Maas and Geert Mommersteeg, *Djenné: Chef-d-œuvre architectural* (Bamako: Institut des Sciences Humaines; Eindhoven: Université de Technologie, 1992).

85. For histories of European colonization in West Africa, see Catherine Coquery, *La Découverte de l'Afrique* (Paris: Juillard, 1965); A.S. [Alexander Sydney] Kanya-Forstner, *The Conquest of Western Sudan: A Study in French Military Imperialism* (London: Cambridge University Press, 1969); Pierre Gourou, L'Afrique (Paris: Librairie Hachette, 1970); Patrick Manning, *Francophone sub-Saharan Africa, 1880–1985* (London: Cambridge University Press, 1988); and Thobie 1990, op. cit.

86. Jean Laude speculates that fetish worship objects could not be purchased because of their sacred worth and that other objects were too "bizarre" in appearance to appeal to European explorers. Only a few pieces from this period survive in European collections, for example, in the Weydmann Collection in Ulm and the Kunstkammer in Dresden. Jean Laude, *The Arts of Black Africa*, trans. Jean Decock (Berkeley: University of California Press, 1971), 4–5.

87. Prussin, 9; Laude, *The Arts of Black Africa*, 10.

88. Sally Price, *Primitive Art in Civilized Places* (Chicago: University of Chicago Press, 1989), 37; Laude, *The Arts of Black Africa*, 10.

89. Saint-Louis was founded by the Compagnie Normande in 1659, the date often given for the establishment of what became the colony of French West Africa. Xavier Yacono, *Histoire de la colonisation française* (Paris: Presses Universitaires de France, 1969), 41.

90. Léon Abensour and René Thévenin, *A.O.F.–A.E.F. La France noire* (Paris: Société parisienne d'Edition, [1931]), 160; Prussin, 11.

91. For a general survey of West Africa in French literature, see Roland Lebel, *L'Afrique occidentale dans la littérature française depuis 1870* (Paris: Larose, 1925).

92. Prussin, 13.

93. See Sylviane Leprun, *Le Théâtre des colonies: Scénographie, acteurs et discours de l'imaginaire dans les expositions, 1855–1937* (Paris: L'Harmattan, 1986), 108–129 152–170.

94. Yvonne Brunhammer, Ed. *Le Livre des expositions universelles, 1851–1989* (Paris: Union Centrale des Arts Décoratifs, 1983), 36–37.

95. Leprun, 112.

96. Charles Garnier and Auguste Amman, *L'Habitation humaine* (Paris: Hachette, 1892), 872. These huts were modeled after buildings in the Ségou region; Leprun, 112.

97. Ibid., 115.

98. Felix Dubois, *Tombouctou la mystérieuse . . . Illustré de nobreuses gravures uniquement executées d'après les photographies de l'auteur et de M.J. Drilhon* (Paris: Flammarion, 1897).

99. Leprun, 118.

100. Beauthéac, 186–189.

101. Leprun, 108.

102. "L'Afrique occidentale française," in *Exposition nationale coloniale de Marseille décrite par ses auteurs* (Marseilles: Commissariat général de l'exposition, 1922), 100.

103. "L'Afrique occidentale française," in *Rapport général*, vol. 5, part 2: 278.

104. André Gide, *Voyage au Congo* (Paris: Gallimard, 1927).

105. Albert Londres, *Terre d'ébène (La Traite des Noirs)* (Paris: Albin Michel, 1929).

106. "Considérations générales sur l'esthétique de l'exposition coloniale," *Rapport général*, vol. 5, part I: 390.

107. Edward Said, Orientalism (New York: Vintage Books, 1978), 206–208.

Chapter 7

1. Albert Guérard, *L'avenir de Paris* (Paris: Payot, 1929), 88, quoted in Anthony Sutcliffe, *Paris: An Architectural History* (New Haven, CT.: Yale University Press, 1993), 145.

2. Albert Sarrault, "L'Exposition coloniale," *L'Art vivant* 7, no.151 (1931): 373.

3. Olivier, *Rapport général*, vol. 5, part I: 10.

4. On the museum's history after the Colonial Exposition, see Sylvie Cornilliet-Watelet, "Le Musée des Colonies et le Musée de la France d'Outre-Mer (1931–1960)," in *Coloniales 1920–1940*, Emmanuel Bréon and Michèle Lefrançois, Eds. (Boulogne-Billancourt: Musée Municipal de Boulogne-Billancourt, 1989), 83–94.

5. Olivier, *Rapport général*, vol. 5, part I: 23.

6. Ibid., 1: 14, 2: 65.

7. Ibid., 2: 65.

8. ["L'Exposition coloniale"], *L'Architecte* (September 1931): 73–80.

9. Jaussely won the competition for a city plan for Barcelona in 1903, and in 1919, he, Roger-Henri Expert, Gaston Redon, and Louis Sellier won the competition for a plan for greater Paris, the *Plan d'extension de Paris*. Jean-Louis Cohen, "De la Ville à la Région: L'Extension de Paris au XXe Siècle," in *Paris: La Ville et Ses Projets/A City in the Making*, Jean-Louis Cohen and Bruno Fortier, Eds. (Paris: Editions Babylone and Pavillon de l'Arsenal, 1988), 214.

10. Jaussely created schemes for the site on the Champs-de-Mars in 1921, alternative sites at the Ecole Militaire, Bois de Boulogne in 1926, and for the Bois de Vincennes site in 1924. In 1927 he became too ill to fulfill his duties as Architect en Chef for the Exposition, and Albert Tournaire was appointed to the post. AOMA, Exposition coloniale internationale, 1931, carton 63.

11. [Albert Laprade,] "Note pour Monsieur le Maréchal Lyautey Relative au Musée Permanent, Vincennes," [n.d.], ANP, Fonds Lyautey, 403AP/12.

12. Léandre Vaillat, "Le Décor de la vie: L'exposition coloniale de 1931," *Temps* 71 (March 13, 1931): n.p.

13. In Michel Foucault's terms this was the shift from the classical episteme, which relied on representation and the corporal actuality of the king's body to that established on nonrepresentational, "human" institutions. "In a society like that of the seventeenth century, the King's body wasn't a metaphor, but a political reality. Its physical presence was necessary for the functioning of the monarchy." Michel Foucault, *Power/Knowledge: Selected Interviews and Other Writings, 1972–1977* (New York: Pantheon Books, 1980), 55. See also Foucault, *The Order of Things: An Archeology of the Human Sciences* (New York: Vintage, 1970), 303–318.

14. Robert Tombs, "Introduction," in *Nationhood and Nationalism in France: From Boulangism to the Great War, 1889–1918* (London and New York: Harper Collins Academic, 1991), xi.

15. Yves Lequin, Ed. *Histoire des Français XIXe–XXe siècles*, 2 vols. (Paris: Armand Colin, 1984), 1: 91.

16. See Pierre Nora's monumental anthology on French national culture, *Les Lieux de Mémoire* (Paris: Gallimard, 1984).

17. Ernest Renan, "What is a nation?" (11 March 1882), trans. Martin

Thom, in *Nation and Narration*, Homi Bhabha, Ed. (London and New York: Routledge, 1990), 20.

18. Renan, 13–19.

19. Paul Greenhalgh, *Ephemeral Vistas: World Exhibitions, 1851–1939* (Manchester: Manchester University Press, 1988), 118.

20. Eugen Weber, *Peasants into Frenchmen: The Modernization of Rural France, 1870–1914* (Stanford, CA: Stanford University Press), 112.

21. Carol Duncan, "The Art Museum as Ritual," *Art Bulletin* 77, no. 1 (1995): 12.

22. Paul Leroy-Beaulieu, *De la colonisation chez les peuples modernes* (Paris, 1874), quoted in Raoul Girardet, *Le Nationalisme français, 1871–1914* (Paris: Armand Colin, 1966), 86.

23. "La politique coloniale est fille de la politique industrielle." Ferry also tied colonization to the need for naval provisioning bases outside the Mediterranean to compete with the English and German navies. Jules Ferry, *Le Tonkin et la Mère-Patrie* (1890), quoted in Girardet, 102, 106–107.

24. Laprade was appointed Jaussely's assistant after Jaussely became too ill to continue as Architecte en Chef.

25. [Laprade].

26. Albert Laprade, "Notes for M. Yvanoe Rambosson of the *Revue de l'art ancien et moderne*," January 15, 1931, ANP, Fonds Laprade, 403AP/26.

27. Albert Laprade, "Description du Musée," [n.d.]. ANP, Fonds Laprade, 403AP/26.

28. Ibid.

29. Albert Laprade, "Mementos," [n.d.], ANP, Fonds Laprade, 403AP/26.

30. Laprade, "Note."

31. Laprade, "Mementos."

32. Laprade, "Note." Laprade here refers to Le Corbusier's *Esprit nouveau* journal and his theory of a new architecture based on standardization and a machine aesthetic. Romy Golan elucidates Le Corbusier's shift from the machine aesthetic of his *Esprit nouveau* period to the organicism and primitivism of his work in the 1930s. Romy Golan, *Modernity and Nostalgia: Art and Politics in France Between the Wars* (New Haven, CT, and London: Yale University Press, 1995), 100–101, 110–114.

33. Golan, ix.

34. Franco Borsi, *The Monumental Era: European Architecture and Design, 1929–1939*, trans. Pamela Marwood (New York: Rizzoli, 1987), 52–93.

35. Bertrand Lemoine and Philippe Rivoirard, *L'Architecture des années 30* (Lyon: La Manufacture, 1987); Jean-Claude Vigato, "Notes sur la question stylistique. France, 1900–1940," *Cahiers de la recherche architecturale* 15–17 (May 1985): 126–131.

36. This group included Roux-Spitz himself, Georges Chédanne, Auguste Perret, Henri Sauvage, Rob. Mallet-Stevens, Jean Ginsberg, Bruno Elk-ouken, and Pierre Patout. Jean-Claude Delorme incorporated Le Corbusier and Willem-Marinus Dudok in his account of the Paris School. See Michel Roux-Spitz, "Entre le régionalisme et le machinisme," *L'Architecture française* 28 (1943). Jean-Claude Delorme and Philippe Chair, *L'ecole de Paris. 10 Architects et leurs immeubles, 1905–1937* (Paris: Moniteur, 1981), 79; Sutcliffe, 153.

37. Quoted in Borsi, 139.

38. Marcel Zahar, "L'Architecture [de l'Exposition coloniale]," *Renaissance de l'art* 14, no. 8 (1931): 227.

39. Jean-Paul Bouillon, *Art Deco 1903–1940* (New York: Rizzoli, 1989), 215. See Nancy Troy, *Modernism and the Decorative Arts in France* (New Haven, CT: Yale University Press, 1991) for an account of these groups.

40. Zahar, 226–227.

41. Gallotti wrote *Le Jardin et la maison arabes au Maroc,* a survey of Moroccan houses and gardens illustrated with drawings by Albert Laprade and photographs by Lucien Vogel, 2 vols. (Paris: Albert Levy, 1924).

42. Jean Gallotti, "Le Palais permanent des Colonies," *L'Illustration* 89, no. 4603, (1931): n.p.

43. Ibid.

44. For the most comprehensive accounts of these fashions in architecture, see Nadine Beauthéac and François-Xavier Bouchart, *L'Europe exotique* (Paris: Chêne, 1986); and Patrick Connor, *Oriental Architecture in the West* (London: Thames and Hudson, 1979).

45. Emile Bayard, *L'Art de reconnaître les style coloniaux de la France* (Paris: Garnier Frères, 1931), 2.

46. Ibid., 3.

47. Donald Drew Egbert, *The Beaux-Arts Tradition in French Architecture* (Princeton, NJ: Princeton University Press, 1980), 192–196.

48. Numerous commissions for decorative programs in public buildings in the colonies were given to French artists. For lists of artists, scholarships,

and commissions, see Emmanuel Bréon, "Les Peintres de la plus grande France," 13–27 and Gustave Vuillemot, "La Villa Abd El Tif," 45–51, in Bréon and Lefrançois.

49. According to Leroy-Beaulieu, colonization "is the expansive force of a people, its reproductive strength, its dilation and multiplication across space; it is the submission of the universe, or a vast part [of it], to its customs, its ideas, and its laws." Paul Leroy-Beaulieu, *De la colonisation chez les peuples modernes,* cited in Girardet, 86.

50. Wright, 67.

51. The *Mosquée* of Fréjus was constructed after the First World War for Senegalese troops stationed in the region. Beauthéac, 193.

52. Nancy George, "La Mosquée de Paris," *L'Illustration,* no. 4315, (1925): 520.

53. [Laprade], "Note."

54. Gallotti, "Le Palais permanent des Colonies," n.p.

55. One critic found this statue regrettably placed since it hampered circulation into the museum, especially during ceremonies and parties, and was sculpted in a *pompier* or old-fashioned manner. Antony Goissaud, "Le Musée permanent des Colonies," *Construction moderne* 47 (January 31, 1931): 284. After the Exposition closed, the statue was moved to the head of Avenue Daumesnil at Porte Dorée.

56. Original choices for sculptor of the bas-relief were either Antoine Bourdelle (who sculpted the bas-reliefs for the Théâtre des Champs-Elysées) or Paul Landowski, established artists who worked in colonial styles. Both were too busy to take on the commission, so Janniot and Henri Bouchard were proposed to the committee charged with selecting the sculptor. "Note of December 4, 1928," AOMA, Exposition coloniale internationale, 1931, carton 129.

57. Gabriel Forestier, Charles Barberis and thirty nameless assistants assisted Janniot on the museum's vast bas-relief. Armand Dayot, "Voyage à travers nos colonies," *L'Art et les Artistes* 25, no. 117 (1931): 269, 274; Goissaud, 279.

58. Dayot, 261.

59. "Le Musée permanent des Colonies, à Paris," *L'Architecte* 9, no. 10, (1931): 87.

60. "Promenade à travers l'Exposition. Le Musée permanent des Colonies," *Miroir du monde* 2, no. 63 (1931): 587.

61. The UAM was founded by Francis Jourdain, Rob Mallet-Stevens, and Pierre Chareau in 1929; Bouillon, 215.

62. Bruno Foucart, "Art on Board Normandie," *Normandie: Queen of the Seas* (New York: Vendome, 1985), 54–56.

63. Golan, 106.

64. Ibid., 116.

65. The style of Ducos de la Haille's frescoes recalls that of Puvis de Chavannes as well as the republican imagery of nineteenth-century *pompier* painters. He also belonged to the school of classicizing modern painters of which Jean Dupas was one of the most prominent. Dupas's decorative panel "Les Perruches" was the focal point of Ruhlmann's interior for the Hôtel du Collectionneur at the 1925 exposition. Bouillon, 168–169; Victor Arwas, *Art Deco* (New York: Abrams, 1992), 185–218.

66. I am grateful to my colleague Conrad Rudolf for providing me with this reference.

67. Goissaud, 575.

68. Golan, 108.

69. "Le Musée permanent des colonies," *Miroir du monde 2*, no. 63 (May 16, 1931: 587.

70. Ibid.

71. Gallotti, "Le Palais permanent des Colonies," n.p.

72. Sylvie Cornilliet-Watelet, "Le Musée des Colonies et le Musée de la France d'Outre-mer (1931–1960)," in Bréon and Lefrançois, 85–86. The display of indigenous arts was organized by Jean Gallotti, who held the title of Inspecteur des Beaux-Arts in Morocco. Olivier, *Rapport général*, 5/–4.

73. Ibid., 51.

74. Ibid., 52.

75. Ibid., 57.

76. Ibid., 60.

77. Michel Foucault, *The Order of Things*, xv.

78. Duncan, 12–13.

79. Carol A. Breckenridge, "The Aesthetics and Politics of Colonial Collecting: India at World Fairs," *Comparative Studies in Society and History* 31, no. 2, (1989): 212.

80. Albert Laprade, "Note memento au sujet de l'aménagement intérieur," ANP, Fonds Laprade, 403AP/26.

81. This painting is reproduced in the *Guide* to the Musée des arts africains et océaniens. The caption identifies the men, but not the woman in the image. *Guide: Musée national des arts africains et océaniens* (Paris: Editions de la Réunion des musées nationaux, 1987), 14.

82. Sally Price, "Anonymity and Timelessness," *Primitive Art in Civilized Places* (Chicago: University of Chicago Press, 1989), 56–67.

83. See Mark Wigley, *The Architecture of Deconstruction: Derrida's Haunt* (Cambridge: MIT Press, 1993); and Jennifer Bloomer, "Abodes of Theory and Flesh: Tabbles of Bower," *Assemblage* 17, (1992): 6–29 for recent investigations of the relation among structure and ornament, architecture, and the "minor" arts.

84. Jacques Derrida, *The Truth in Painting*, trans. Geoff Bennington and Ian McLeod (Chicago: University of Chicago Press, 1987), 37–82.

Conclusion

1. Paul Morand, "Rien que la Terre à l'Exposition coloniale," *Revue des deux mondes* 101 (July 15, 1931): 334.

2. Ibid.

3. "Récapitulation des Opérations, Tableaux des Dépenses et Recettes," in Olivier, *Rapport général*, 4: 591–603.

4. Jean Camp and André Corbier, *À Lyauteyville. Promenades sentimentales et humoresques à l'Exposition coloniale* (Paris: Société nationales d'éditions artistiques, 1931), 9–10.

5. Marshal Lyautey, "Discours, Banquet de Clôture de l'Exposition coloniale internationale (14 novembre 1931)," in Olivier, *Rapport général*, 4: 521–523.

6. Walter Benjamin, "Theses on the Philosophy of History," in *Illuminations*, trans. Harry Zohn (New York: Schocken Books, 1969), 256.

7. Marcel Mauss, *Instructions sommaires pour les collecteurs d'objets ethnographiques* (Paris: Musée d'ethnographie et mission scientifique Dakar-Djibouti, Palais du Trocadéro, 1931), 7.

8. Marcel Griaule, "Mission Dakar-Djibouti (journal-rapport général mai 1931–1932), *Bulletin de la société des africanistes* 2 (1932): 116; Elizabeth A. Williams, "Art and Artifact at the Trocadéro: *Ars Americana* and the Primitivist Revolution," in *Objects and Others: Essays on Museums and*

Material Culture, George W. Stocking, Jr., Ed. (Madison: University of Wisconsin Press, 1985), 146–166.

9. James Clifford, "On Ethnographic Surrealism," *The Predicament of Culture: Twentieth Century Ethnography, Literature and Art* (Cambridge: Harvard University Press, 1988), 132.

10. M. Simon, "En visitant l'Exposition coloniale," *Cité moderne* 12 (Summer 1931): 6.

11. Jean Baudrillard, *Simulations,* trans. Paul Foss, Paul Patton, and Philip Beitchman (New York: Semiotext(e), 1983), 5.

12. Marcel Zahar, "Batir! Informer!" *L'Art vivant* 7, no. 151 (1931): 384.

13. Michel Leiris, "Jazz," interview conducted and translated by Michael Haggerty, *Sulfur* 15 (1986): 99–100.

14. Homi K. Bhabha, "Signs Taken for Wonders: Questions of Ambivalence and Authority under a Tree Outside Delhi, May 1817," in *"Race," Writing, and Difference,* Henry Louis Gates, Jr., Ed. (Chicago: University of Chicago Press, 1986), 176.

15. Marcel Griaule, "Un coup de fusil," *Documents* 2, no. 1 (1930): 46. Translated as "Gunshot" by Dominic Faccini, *October* 60 (Spring 1992).

16. Michel Leiris, "In the Musée de l'Homme," trans. James Clifford, *Sulfur* 15 (1986): 111.

17. Judith Butler, *Bodies That Matter: On the Discursive Limits of "Sex"* (New York and London: Routledge, 1993), 124, 133.

18. Kumkum Sangari, "The Politics of the Possible," in *The Post-Colonial Studies Reader,* Bill Ashcroft, et al., Eds. (London and New York: Routledge, 1995), 147.

Index